EU Conflict Prevention and Crisis Management

Conflict prevention and crisis management has become a key activity for the EU since the creation of the Common Security and Defence Policy in 1999. The rapid growth of this policy area, as well as the number of missions deployed beyond the EU's border raise important questions about the nature of the EU's international role and its contribution to international security.

The contributions to *EU Conflict Prevention and Crisis Management* analyze European conflict prevention and crisis management in terms of the EU's evolving global role, its institutions and its policies. The volume analyzes the EU's position in relation to the US, the UN and other regional security organizations, and applies three different institutionalist perspectives – historical, rational choice and sociological institutionalism – to explain the increasing institutionalization of EU crisis management. It also critically analyzes the application of EU policies in West Africa, Afghanistan and the Caucasus. Providing a comprehensive analysis of EU crisis management, the volume explores what role EU conflict prevention and crisis management plays in a European and a global context.

Offering a comprehensive and original contribution to the literature on EU foreign and security policy, this volume will be of interest to students and scholars of European politics, international relations and security studies.

Eva Gross is Senior Research Fellow for European Foreign and Security Policy at the Institute for European Studies, Free University Brussels.

Ana E. Juncos is Lecturer in European Politics in the School of Sociology, Politics and International Studies at the University of Bristol.

Routledge/UACES Contemporary European Studies

Edited by Federica Bicchi, *London School of Economics and Political Science*, Tanja Börzel, *Free University of Berlin*, and Roger Scully, *University of Wales, Aberystwyth*, on behalf of the *University Association for Contemporary European Studies*.

The primary objective of the new Contemporary European Studies series is to provide a research outlet for scholars of European Studies from all disciplines. The series publishes important scholarly works and aims to forge for itself an international reputation.

EU Conflict Prevention and Crisis Management

Roles, institutions and policies

**Edited by Eva Gross and
Ana E. Juncos**

Routledge
Taylor & Francis Group
LONDON AND NEW YORK

First published 2011 by Routledge
2 Park Square, Milton Park, Abingdon, Oxfordshire OX14 4RN

Simultaneously published in the USA and Canada
by Routledge
711 Third Avenue, New York, NY 10017

First issued in paperback 2014

Routledge is an imprint of the Taylor & Francis Group, an informa business

© 2011 Eva Gross and Ana E. Juncos for selection and editorial matter;
individual contributors, their contribution.

Typeset in Times New Roman by Swales & Willis Ltd, Exeter, Devon

British Library Cataloguing in Publication Data
A catalogue record for this book is available from the British Library

Library of Congress Cataloging in Publication Data
p. cm. — (Routledge / UACES contemporary European studies ; 17)
1. Conflict management—European Union countries. 2. Crisis management—
European Union countries. 3. European Union countries—Foreign relations.
4. European Union countries—Military policy. 5. National security—
European Union countries I. Gross, Eva. II. Juncos, Ana E.
JZ6368.E93 2011
341.50941—dc22
2010031266

ISBN 13: 978-0-415-57235-4 (hbk)
ISBN 13: 978-1-138-82989-3 (pbk)

Contents

Notes on contributors

Giselle Bosse joined the Politics Department in Maastricht in 2007 and has been Assistant Professor since 2008. She holds an MA degree from the College of Europe (Natolin) in Warsaw, Poland and a PhD from the University of Aberystwyth, UK. Her research focuses on the European Neighbourhood Policy (ENP) and the Eastern Partnership (EaP). She focuses in particular on the impact and legitimacy of the EU's efforts to promote its political values and practices in the Eastern neighbourhood, as well as the effectiveness of the European Neighbourhood and Partnership Instrument (ENPI). Recent publications include 'Challenges for EU Governance through Neighbourhood Policy and Eastern Partnership: The Values/Security Nexus in EU–Belarus Relations', *Contemporary Politics*, 2009, and 'Changing Belarus? The Limits of EU Governance in Eastern Europe and the Promise of Partnership', *Cooperation and Conflict*, 2009, with E. Korosteleva.

Marie V. Gibert is a Postdoctoral Research Fellow in the Department of International Relations at the University of the Witwatersrand, Johannesburg, South Africa. She holds a PhD from the School of Oriental and African Studies (SOAS), University of London. Her research focuses on multilateral cooperation between Europe and West Africa in the field of security and has led her to carry out field research in a number of capital cities in West Africa and Europe. Recent publications include 'The Linkage between Security, Governance and Development: The European Union in Africa', *Journal of Development Studies*, Vol. 45(5), 2009, with Niagalé Bagayoko; and 'The Securitisation of the EU's Development Agenda in Africa: Insights from Guinea-Bissau', *Perspectives on European Politics and Society*, Vol. 10(4), 2009.

Eva Gross is Senior Research Fellow for European Foreign and Security Policy at the Institute for European Studies, Vrije Universiteit Brussel. She has a PhD from the London School of Economics and has held visiting appointments at the Center for Transatlantic Relations, Johns Hopkins University-SAIS in Washington, DC (2010); the EU Institute for Security Studies (2008) and CERI-Sciences Po (2005), both in Paris; and at the Centre for European Policy Studies in Brussels (2006). In 2005/06 she was a fellow of the European Foreign and Security Policy Studies Program. Recent publications include *The Europeanization of National Foreign Policy: Continuity and Change in European Crisis*

Management, Palgrave, 2009; *Security Sector Reform in Afghanistan: The EU's Contribution*, Occasional Paper, EU Institute for Security Studies, 2009; and *EU and the Comprehensive Approach*, DIIS Report 2008:13, Danish Institute for International Studies.

Ana E. Juncos is Lecturer in European Politics in the School of Sociology, Politics and International Studies at the University of Bristol. Previously, she was a Postdoctoral Research Fellow at the University of Bath, working on a project on the 'EU's Global Role', in cooperation with the Federal Trust and funded by the James Madison Trust. She holds a PhD in Politics, International Relations and European Studies from Loughborough University. Her research interests include EU foreign and security policy in Bosnia, the Europeanisation of the Western Balkans and security sector reform. In other projects, she has explored international socialisation and learning processes within EU institutions, with particular reference to European foreign policy. She has published articles in *Journal of Common Market Studies*, *Journal of European Integration*, *European Foreign Affairs Review* and *European Integration online Papers*.

Nadia Klein is a research associate at the Jean Monnet Chair for Political Science at the University of Cologne. Her research interests include the European foreign and security policy, the EU and multilateralism and institutionalist approaches to the EU. She studied in Paris and Cologne and holds a PhD in Political Science. Her PhD thesis focused on the civil-military crisis management of the EU, particularly towards the Western Balkans. From 2006 to 2007, she was a member of the UACES research group 'European Conflict Prevention and Crisis Management Policies'. From 2006 to 2008, she was a fellow of the joint research and training programme 'European Foreign and Security Policy Studies' (Compagnia di San Paolo; Riksbankens Jubileumsfond; Volkswagen-Stiftung). She is the author of *European Agents Out of Control? Delegation and Agency in the Civil-Military Crisis Management of the European Union 1999–2008* (Nomos, 2010).

Xymena Kurowska is Assistant Professor at the Central European University in Budapest. She completed her PhD at the European University Institute, Florence in 2008 with a thesis *The Politics Behind a Policy: Framing European Security and Defence Policy*. Within her post-doctoral research financed within the European Foreign and Security Policy Studies programme, she conducted fieldwork in Ukraine in connection with EU's border management projects. Her recent publications include: 'The Role of ESDP Operations' in: Michael Merlingen and Rasa Ostrauskaite (eds) *European Security and Defence Policy: An Implementation Perspective*, Routledge, 2008; 'EU Border Assistance Mission to Ukraine and Moldova – Beyond Border Monitoring?' (with Benjamin Tallis) in *European Foreign Affairs Review*, 14(1) (2009); and the co-edited special issue (with Patryk Pawlak) of *Perspectives on European Politics and Society*, 10(4) (2009): 'The Politics of European Security Politics. Actors, Dynamics and Contentious Outcomes'.

Petar Petrov is Assistant Professor in IR and EU External Relations in the Political Science Department at the Maastricht University. He holds a Master's Degree in Political Science from Sofia University St Kliment Ohridski, Bulgaria, an M/Res. in EU Politics and Public Policy and a PhD in EU Politics from the University of Manchester, UK. His research is in the field of EU crisis management in the Western Balkans, governance of the ESDP/CFSP and the development of EU military capabilities. Currently he is researching the inter-institutional dynamics and the political role of the EU in Kosovo in the context of the Rule of Law Mission (EULEX) Kosovo.

Thomas Seitz is Assistant Professor of International Studies at the University of Wyoming. He is leading an ongoing project on Crisis Management and Human Security in the University's Institute of Global Studies. He has published articles on nation building processes in European and Southeast Asian contexts, and is currently writing a book on the development of nation building programs in US foreign policy. He received his PhD from Cambridge and his MA from the University of Kent at Canterbury.

Emma J. Stewart studied at the University of Edinburgh and the University of Exeter, and was awarded her PhD from Loughborough University in 2005. She is the author of *The European Union and Conflict Prevention: Policy Evolution and Outcome* (Münster: Lit Verlag/Kiel Peace Research Series, 2005) and has published in *European Foreign Affairs Review* and *Contemporary Security Policy*. She recently undertook postdoctoral work on the South Caucasus under the European Foreign and Security Policy Studies Programme at the University of Bath and has also worked for the London-based Federal Trust.

Acknowledgments

The present volume is the result of a collaborative effort in the framework of the University Association for Contemporary European Studies (UACES)-funded Student Forum Specialist Group on European Union Conflict Prevention and Crisis Management (EUCPCM). EUCPCM was a transnational research network composed of a group of emerging EU foreign policy scholars based in the UK and other European universities. The chapters in this book were originally presented at workshops organized at the London School of Economics, Loughborough University, the Institute d'Etudes Politiques, Paris and at a final two-day conference held in Brussels. These events provided a friendly and constructive atmosphere where EUCPCM members could present work in progress and receive quality feedback from other colleagues, senior scholars and experts from the field. Our thanks go to all those who participated in these workshops and conferences and who were instrumental in making EUCPCM, as well as the individual events, a success. We owe the biggest thanks, however, to the contributors of this volume for their patience during the editing process and always responding promptly to what we hope were constructive comments.

We would also like to thank Sebastien Loisel for his substantive contribution to the founding (and initial funding) of EUCPCM; Stephan Davidshofer for his support in the organization of the Paris workshop; and Dr Mathias Jopp of the Institut fuer Europaeische Politik (IEP) in Berlin for co-organizing the Brussels conference.

Finally, we thank the Compagnia di San Paolo (Italy) for their financial support of the workshop series, and the VolkswagenStiftung (Germany) for their generous support of the final conference in Brussels. We would also like to express our gratitude to the European Foreign and Security Policy Studies Programme, a joint research and training programme of the Compagnia di San Paolo, the Riksbankens Jubileumsfond and the VolkswagenStiftung, which supported the larger research projects on which the majority of these chapters are based – and which provided an intellectual background for additional discussions on EU foreign and security policy that inform the individual chapters of this book.

Finally, we are grateful to the editors of the Routledge/UACES Contemporary European Studies Series, the two anonymous reviewers who provided invaluable comments on an earlier draft of this volume, and to the Routledge editorial team for their able guidance in putting together this volume.

Eva Gross and Ana E. Juncos

1 Introduction

Eva Gross and Ana E. Juncos

From ambition to reality

Since the launch of the first police mission in Bosnia and Herzegovina in 2003, European Union (EU) crisis missions have been deployed with increasing frequency and geographical scope. The launch of an EU Monitoring Mission to Georgia in response to the crisis in August 2008 and the antipiracy operation EU NAVFOR (Operation Atalanta) off the Somali coast represent the latest manifestations of the EU's growing role in international security. At the same time, conflict prevention, a key component in EU foreign policy (Smith 2003), has increasingly been streamlined with other policy areas, including development policies. This gives the EU a wide range of political, economic and military instruments to undertake conflict prevention and crisis management policies beyond its borders. Clearly, efforts to realize the EU's ambition to turn itself into a security provider both for its own citizens, but also in pursuit of its foreign policy goals are bearing fruit.

Perhaps because of the speed of developments over the past seven years, which have included the launch of 27 civilian and military missions across the globe (see Table 1.1; Council of the European Union 2010), coupled with impressive institutional developments in Brussels, a comprehensive scholarly analysis of these developments as well as their implications for EU foreign and security policy has not been forthcoming. This volume and its contributions seek to fill this gap by combining theoretically informed analyses of recent policy developments with empirical evidence from a range of geographical but also functional areas of EU conflict prevention and crisis management policies. Importantly, this book goes beyond existing studies on aspects of this subject that have tended to analyze the role of the EU in conflict resolution (see Coppieters 2004; Tocci 2007), that have concentrated exclusively on military crisis management (Blockmans 2008) or that have focussed on the analysis of the Common Security and Defence Policy (CSDP) proper (Howorth 2007a; Merlingen and Ostraskaite 2008). Instead, contributors to this volume seek to offer a comprehensive view of the genesis and recent development of EU conflict prevention and crisis management policies, as well as aspects of its implementation in a number of geographical and functional settings.

Table 1.1 EU civilian and military crisis management operations, 1991–2010

Name	Location	Nature	Type	Duration
ECMM/EUMM	Western Balkans	Civilian	Monitoring	1991–2007
EUPM	Bosnia	Civilian	Police	Since 2003
Concordia	FYROM	Military	Military	2003
Artemis	RD Congo	Military	Military	2003
EUPOL Proxima	FYROM	Civilian	Police	2004–2005
EUJUS Themis	Georgia	Civilian	Rule of law	2004–2005
EUFOR Althea	Bosnia	Military	Military	Since 2004
EUPOL Kinshasa	RD Congo	Civilian	Police	2005–2007
EUSEC	RD Congo	Civil-Military	Security sector reform	Since 2005
EUJUST LEX	Iraq/Brussels	Civilian	Rule of law	Since 2005
Support to AMIS	Sudan	Civil-Military	Assistance	2005–2006
AMM	Aceh/Indonesia	Civilian	Monitoring	2005–2006
EUBAM Rafah	Palestinian Territories	Civilian	Border	Since 2005
EUBAM	Ukraine-Moldova	Civilian	Border	Since 2005
EUPOL COPPS	Palestinian Territories	Civilian	Police	Since 2006
EUPAT	FYROM	Civilian	Police	2006
EUPT	Kosovo	Civilian	Planning	2006–2008
EUFOR	RD Congo	Military	Military	2006
EUPOL	RD Congo	Civilian	Police	Since 2007
EUPOL	Afghanistan	Civilian	Police	Since 2007
EUFOR	Tchad/RCA	Military	Military	2008–2009
EU SSR	Guinea-Bissau	Civil-Military	Security sector reform	Since 2008
EULEX	Kosovo	Civilian	Rule of law	Since 2008
EUMM	Georgia	Civilian	Monitoring	Since 2008
EUNAVCO	Somalia	Military	Assistance	2008
EUNAVFOR	Somalia	Military	Military	Since 2008
EUTM	Somalia	Civilian	Training	In preparation

Source: Council of the EU (2010), *Overview of the missions and operations of the European Union*, February 2010, online, available at: http://www.consilium.europa.eu/showPage.aspx?id =268&lang=EN (accessed 5 March 2010).

Adopting a broad view of conflict prevention and crisis management holds several advantages. The wide range of topics covered in this book reflects the fact that the EU has gradually taken on policy functions that go some way beyond the EU's initial foreign policy preoccupation with successful crisis management in the Balkans and the launch of CSDP operations in sub-Saharan Africa. Over the past years, EU missions have increasingly focussed on aspects of rule of law and security sector reform throughout Europe's neighbourhood and beyond, including Afghanistan, and the EU has increased its linkages with other international institutions in the pursuit of 'effective multilateralism'. At the same time, and as a result of these developments, the EU has taken on security roles previously reserved for NATO, the UN, and the Organization for Security and Co-operation in Europe (OSCE). This raises questions about the nature of the EU's interactions with other actors in international security. The increasing conceptual link between economic development and security in the broader context of state failure as a strategic security threat begs the question of how well the EU is able to integrate these two policy areas (Youngs 2007). The coherence of policy instruments located in the first and the second pillar as well as member states' foreign policies has revealed itself as a key challenge in crisis management. At a broader, geostrategic level, these developments raise questions not just over the meaning of the changing nature of the EU's security architecture for the EU and its member states but also for the EU's changing strategic role on the world stage. Contributions on these diverse but essentially interlinked aspects of conflict prevention and crisis management thus offer not just a comprehensive analysis but also an opportunity to compare conclusions as to the successes, failures and likely future trajectories of EU conflict prevention and crisis management activities.

The EU's involvement in conflict prevention and crisis management: a brief historical overview

The rapid development of EU foreign policy in recent years belies the long gestation period and the cumbersome start of efforts to assert the EU's place on the world stage. Conflict prevention has been one of the key policy aims of the European Union since its creation – after all, the creation of the EU itself constituted a peace project, designed to make war in Europe unthinkable – and was also one of the assumptions behind enlarging the EU to include the countries of Central and Eastern Europe and later also the Balkans. With respect to foreign policy, throughout the Cold War, member states used the framework of European Political Cooperation (EPC) to reduce tensions and to propose solutions to conflicts in Afghanistan or the Middle East (see Smith 2003), although these policy efforts were hampered by the loose intergovernmental framework of EPC. It was not until the end of the Cold War that efforts to increase foreign policy cooperation bore fruit. A rapidly shifting security environment gave rise to increased foreign policy cooperation through first the creation of the Common Foreign and Security Policy (CFSP) and later the CSDP (see Howorth 2007a).

Since the end of the Cold War, conflict prevention has become part of the EU's foreign policy identity. The 2001 Gothenburg European Council set out a 'Programme for the Prevention of Violent Conflicts' that would consist of setting political priorities for preventive actions; improvement of the EU's early-warning, action and policy coherence; enhancement of its instruments for long- and short-term prevention; and building effective partnerships for prevention (see Cameron 2007). Today, conflict prevention is still at the heart of EU foreign policy, with the Lisbon Treaty mentioning the prevention of conflict as one of the Union's external action objectives (Art. 21.2). Conflict prevention is usually understood in EU documents as a long term process aimed at structural change, 'addressing the root-causes of conflict' (European Council 2001: 1). Implicitly, the broad remit of measures falling under the label of 'conflict prevention' suggests that policy tools used to achieve these aims are located both in the first and second pillar, and consist of political and economic tools.[1]

The history of the concept of 'crisis management', on the other hand, is more recent as it was only formally introduced in the EU jargon by the Cologne Declaration (1999) (Missiroli 2001: 4). European crisis management policies moved to the forefront of EU foreign policy activities with Javier Solana's successful mediation efforts in the crisis in the Former Yugoslav Republic of Macedonia (FYROM) in 2001 and the EU's gradual take-over of the security functions in the Balkans from NATO and the UN by means of CSDP missions. Operational priorities have since evolved beyond the early narrow geographic focus on the Balkans and sub-Saharan Africa to include a focus on effective multilateralism and coordination with other institutional actors such as the UN, NATO and the OSCE; improving the coherence of policy instruments located in the first and second pillar; and in recalibrating the relationship between NATO and the EU, including growing transatlantic pressures for the EU taking on a greater role in civilian crisis management in pursuit of more equitable transatlantic burden-sharing.

Meeting the capacity requirements needed for carrying out an increasing number of crisis missions has carried its own challenges, both with respect to meeting civilian as well as military headline goals – the Helsinki Headline Goal 2010 calls for member states 'to be able by 2010 to respond with rapid and decisive action applying a fully coherent approach to the whole spectrum of crisis management operations covered by the Treaty on the European Union', whereas the 2008 Headline Goal includes the development of integrated civilian crisis management packages, the ability to conduct concurrent civilian missions; and coherence of CSDP actions with longer-term Community programmes (Council of the European Union 2004b). Nevertheless, capability shortfalls in military and civilian crisis operations continue to plague crisis missions, as well as the need for building up a cadre of personnel for tasks relating to the reform of police forces, justice systems, and border police.

Given the fast institutional and operational developments, the state of play with respect to the geographical range of the EU's crisis missions and with respect to CSDP's operational priorities has changed rapidly, with conflict prevention and crisis management and long- and short-term approaches increasingly treated jointly. The increasing complexities of EU foreign policy activity thus raise questions not just about a changing European security architecture where the EU rather than NATO or the OSCE is assuming increasing security functions, but more broadly about the nature of the EU's global role as well as the success of its policies in theatre.

Increasing EU activity in both conflict prevention and crisis management does not mean, however, that the EU resembles a monolithic actor; rather, semantic differences and bureaucratic politics among Commission departments and between Council and Commission – if not outright turf wars – highlight the fact that coherence between policy instruments presents a significant challenge. Unsurprisingly, therefore, in Euro-jargon the terms conflict prevention and crisis management are still surrounded by a great deal of terminological confusion. In the Commission's parlance (see European Commission 2001a), conflict prevention refers to both long-term and short-term measures; it covers the stages before and after the break out of a conflict. In this view, conflict prevention refers to promoting stability and peace-building measures, as well as quickly preventing conflicts that are on the verge of outbreak or to prevent the escalation of current conflicts, including post-conflict stabilization. In sum, only one phase of the conflict cycle escapes from the Commission's definition of conflict prevention: the management of an open crisis (war). From the Council's point of view, crisis management not only includes peace-making and peace-keeping, but also other state-building, confidence-building and monitoring activities taking place in the post-conflict stabilization phase, such as police missions, monitoring missions and border assistance missions. Thus, the possibility of overlaps between Commission and Council's instruments is a real one in the post-conflict stabilization stage.

Moreover, although the distinction between conflict prevention and crisis management sketched in the different documents adopted by EU institutions between 1999 and 2001 might seem analytically useful (European Commission 2001a; European Council 1999b and 2001), developments in practice have meant that this distinction has become gradually blurred. First, traditional crisis management instruments such as the use of armed force play an important role in the prevention of violent conflicts. As noted by the Goteborg European Council, 'the development of the European Security and Defence Policy (ESDP) has, since the outset, also been intended to strengthen the EU's capacity for action in the crucial field of conflict prevention' (European Council 2001).[2] As the EU develops its military and civilian crisis management capabilities, the credibility of the EU increases and, thus, its ability to mediate in and prevent conflicts, particularly in its neighbourhood. Second, traditional Community instruments such as humanitarian aid are often required during the short term phase of crisis management. Third, institutional turfs have also played a role in this conceptual confusion, with the Council Secretariat trying to increase the scope of 'crisis management' including some activities that had traditionally been carried out by the Commission (e.g. institution-building, assistance to border activities, etc.). The Commission has also attempted to expand its areas of competencies in crisis management, if not as a conscious strategy, then as a reaction to the Council's threatening moves (see Schroeder 2007).

Despite the lack of agreed or coherent definitions, what seems clear is that the EU is in a unique position to make a significant contribution to conflict prevention and crisis management due to the broad range of instruments at its disposal. This together with the increase in the geographical scope of the EU's conflict prevention and crisis management policies, with more and more CSDP operations being deployed 'out of area', raises important questions about (1) how the EU's engagement in conflict prevention and crisis management shapes the EU's international role; (2) the impact of institutional developments on EU foreign policy; and (3) the effectiveness and coherence of these policies on the ground. The chapters in this volume seek to address the aforementioned questions.

Conflict prevention and crisis management: Conceptual and theoretical issues

This section provides a brief insight into the conceptual and theoretical context in which work on the EU's foreign relations to date has been grounded so as to set the stage for the individual contributions to this book.

There is a wide literature on this topic in international relations, conflict studies and peace research (Ackermann 2003; Carment and Schnabel 2003; Nye, 2009; Ramsbotham *et al.* 2005). In European studies, growing interest in conflict prevention and crisis management has developed alongside institutional and policy development at the EU level (Barbé and Johansson 2001; Blockmans 2008; Kronenberger and Wouters 2004; Smith 2003; Stewart 2006). Although there is some terminological confusion surrounding these two terms, this volume distinguishes between conflict prevention and crisis management. The former is understood here as 'those factors or actions which prevent *armed* conflicts or mass violence from breaking out' (Ramsbotham *et al.* 2005: 107, emphasis in the original). Conflict prevention includes a wide-ranging set of instruments, from economic assistance and humanitarian aid to mediation. Crisis management, on the other hand, usually refers to those short-term measures facilitating 'the settlement and containment of violent conflict' (Ramsbotham *et al.* 2005: 107), which might include *inter alia* peace-enforcement, peace-keeping and post-conflict stabilization (cf. Missiroli 2001: 8). Interestingly, the concept of crisis management has been less frequently used in the literature. Instead conflict management has been the preferred term (Butler 2009).

The contributors to this volume had some freedom as to how they would use these concepts in their work. Thus, contributions in this book range from those that adopt a minimalist approach, which focuses on the military dimension of crisis management (see Chapter 4 by Petrov and Chapter 6 by Juncos) to a maximalist one, looking at conflict prevention, inclusive of crisis management (see Chapter 3 by Stewart). Klein (Chapter 5) examines both the civilian and military components of crisis management. Kurowska and Seitz (Chapter 2) also concentrate on crisis management policies, but their understanding of crisis management not only includes traditional military and civilian instruments, but also increasingly other instruments linked to the development of the external dimension of Justice and Home Affairs. They also discuss EU crisis management against the backdrop of broader EU state-building strategies. Gross (Chapter 8) also adopts a broad view on EU policy activities in Afghanistan to include civilian crisis management instruments in the context of a simultaneous focus on conflict management and institution-building. Gibert and Bosse (Chapters 7 and 9) mainly examine current EU conflict prevention policies, but they also refer to the EU's potential role in crisis management in West Africa and South Caucasus, respectively.

As for the theoretical debates, the study of EU foreign policy and more recently EU conflict prevention and crisis management has been said to suffer from under-theorizing, or an overly excessive focus on empirical analysis. This is despite the fact that the question of how to conceptualize EU foreign policy as well as the input of its member states has preoccupied academics and led to some interesting output on the nature of EU foreign policy, the EU's international presence, and the applicability of various theoretical frameworks that go beyond intergovernmental analysis and include constructivist approaches as well as those rooted in foreign policy analysis (see Tonra 2003). Specifically, an important body of literature has attempted to describe and analyse the nature of the EU in world politics (Galtung 1973; Allen and Smith 1990; Hill 1990, 1993; Piening 1997; Bretherton and Vogler 2006; Ginsberg 2001); whereas other work has introduced concepts with which to capture the substance of the EU's external activities, including that of 'presence' (Allen and Smith 1990), 'actorness' (Sjostedt 1977), 'impact' (Ginsberg 2001) and 'structural foreign policy' (Keukeleire 2003).

The contributions to this volume suggest three particularly useful – and inherently compatible – conceptual approaches for the analysis of EU conflict prevention and crisis management policies: a focus on the EU's international role, institutionalist approaches, and policy analysis. Analyses focussing on roles (see Chapters 2 and 3 in this volume) attempt to better capture the complex nature of EU external action by focussing on the interactions between capabilities, self-perceptions and expectations. Institutionalist approaches, which some of the contributors to this volume adopt (see Chapters 4–6), have become particularly relevant to the analysis of EU conflict prevention and crisis management policies. Given the fast progression of the institutionalization of foreign policy instruments in CFSP and CSDP and the resulting feedback onto member states' foreign policies, institutionalist interpretations can help shed light on the development but also implementation practice of CSDP. However, and despite increasing institutionalization, the role of member states remains an important factor especially when it comes to contested geographical and policy areas where the EU is bound to be afforded a smaller space for operating or decision-making, as contributions on the EU's policy in Western Africa, Afghanistan and Georgia demonstrate (Chapters 7–9). The interplay between member state and EU-level foreign policy thus remains an important factor in the assessment of the making, but also the implementation of EU foreign policy activities. By drawing on these different theoretical approaches, and by drawing on empirical evidence from several case studies, this volume aims to make an important and a comprehensive contribution to the study of the EU as an international actor.

Roles, institutions and policies: Introducing the contributions to this volume

The contributions to this volume have been structured around three main themes which, we argue, are key to understanding the main dynamics in the development of EU conflict prevention and crisis management: roles, institutions and policies. The first part of the book (Chapters 2–3) investigates what roles EU conflict prevention and crisis management policies play in a European and a global context, as well as what impact these policies have had on the EU's self-perception and other actors' expectations. Contributions to the second part of the book (Chapters

4–6) take a theoretical approach in the analysis of the institutional development and the impact of EU institutions on the formulation and implementation of these policies. They do so from three different institutionalist perspectives: historical, rational choice and sociological institutionalism. Finally, the last part of the book (Chapters 7–9) discuss three examples of EU policies in different regions: Chapter 7 analyzes EU development policy in West Africa; Chapter 8 provides an analysis of EU crisis management policy in Afghanistan, and Chapter 9 examines the EU's response to the conflict in Georgia in the framework of the European Neighbour-hood Policy (ENP). Beyond the institutional development of conflict prevention and crisis management instruments as well as their implementation in theatre, chapters pose the broader question as to the changing nature of the EU as a global actor.

One could certainly argue that these three themes (roles, institutions and poli-cies) run throughout all the chapters to a lesser or greater extent as they all raise important questions about what kind of role the EU plays in international affairs; deal with the role of different institutions in EU conflict prevention and crisis management; and look at different policies and instruments in various geographi-cal scenarios. However, the organization of the book around these three themes is designed to facilitate cross-comparison among the chapters within each section, without introducing an overly rigid framework for analysis.

Part I: Roles

Chapters 2 and 3 not only set the scene for other chapters to come, but also address key questions about the EU's international role. They take the nature of the EU's international identity as a starting point for deliberation. Historically, analysts have described the EU as a 'civilian power' (Duchêne 1972), 'superpower' (Galtung 1973), 'superstate' (Hill 2002) or 'normative power' (Manners 2002). Despite the lively and important debates surrounding the continued applicability of these con-cepts to the EU today (Smith 2000; Whitman 1998), these concepts seem insuf-ficient to grasp the shifting nature of the EU's influence in world politics and the complexity of the relationship between the self-perceptions of the EU and the expectations of other actors. Moreover, paying attention to the mutual interactions between agency and structure seems especially important given that EU foreign policy institutions continue to be in flux. In this respect, the concept of 'role' has increasingly been used in the literature as a heuristic tool to grasp the complexity and uniqueness of the EU as an actor in different external policies (see Aggestam 2004a; Elgström and Smith 2006).

The concept of role, understood here as a pattern of expected or appropriate behaviour determined both by an actor's self-image and the role expectations of other actors (see Aggestam 2004a, 2006; Chapter 2 of this volume) can be use-ful to scrutinize the development and impact of EU conflict prevention and crisis management policies in a European and global context. This concept highlights the interactional dimension of the EU's international character, a product of inter-nal processes (institutional and identity factors) and external expectations, as well as structural determinants. The value of the first two chapters lies in their attempt to disentangle how these two dimensions (one's self-image and others' expectations) interact with each other, shaping and constructing the EU's international role. This interactive perspective allows us to understand the complexity of the changing roles of the EU, as well as the impact that the recent development of its security capabilities has had on these interactions. Importantly, while role-taking always takes place in a particular context which shapes the range of options available, there is always some room for agents to forge a particular strategy or role from a scope of scenarios possible in a given setting.

The two chapters seek to investigate the impact of the development of EU crisis management capabilities on the Union's roles and self-perceptions. With a growing focus on military rather than merely civilian instruments, but also the increasing interactions with other international actors, one needs to explore the images and expectations that other international actors develop in relation to the European Union. Kurowska and Seitz take a global approach and look at the interactions between the EU and its 'significant others', the UN and the US. By adopting a role approach their contribution seeks to grasp the changing dynamics among these actors and their international role assignments. Of particular interest in this context is the EU-US division of labour, namely in the field of statebuilding, which the authors aptly explore in the chapter. Kurowska and Seitz conclude that the shifting dynamics within the EU-UN-US triad have given rise to a distinct pattern of expectations towards the EU, even if this arrangement has not yet solidified into a new security order as traditionally conceived in International Relations. Recognition of the EU's role in international crisis management by the UN has led to a mutual beneficial relationship between the UN and the EU. This recognition, however, has been more difficult to obtain vis-à-vis the US.

Stewart, for her part, discusses this issue in a European context, focusing on the key European security actors: the EU, the OSCE and NATO, and the co-ordination arrangements between these organizations. As this chapter shows, it is hard to find evidence of 'strategic design' in the development of the EU's conflict prevention and crisis management policies since the EU's role in the European security architecture has mostly developed as a result of incremental policies (see also Chapter 4 by Petrov). The idiosyncrasy of this historical development has led to inconsistencies with other international organizations. Stewart concludes that while the EU has successfully transformed itself into a comprehensive security actor, its role as a conflict prevention actor has not reached full potential. Furthermore, if the EU wants to ensure stability and security in its neighbourhood, it has to work harder to coordinate its activities with other actors in the pan-European area.

These two chapters raise at least two other pertinent issues: the role of the EU in promoting effective multilateralism; and the way in which the development of EU crisis management has affected the traditional self-image of the EU as a civilian power. On the former, Xymena Kurowska and Thomas Seitz argue that in the case of EU-UN relations, effective multilateralism has played a legitimizing role for CSDP, while the EU has been able to maintain some flexibility and forge a distinct role for itself. When it comes to EU-US relations however, the EU has not been able to play such a leading role, but instead has acted as an agent containing US unilateralist tendencies. The development of EU crisis management and its impact on the EU's civilian power is discussed by Emma Stewart. According to Stewart, by taking on military crisis management the EU might have undermined its established image of a civilian power that until then had been epitomized by the European Commission activities in the field of conflict prevention. Without greater efforts to find synergy between its civilian and military instruments, she argues, the EU's legitimacy as a security actor may be questioned.

Part II: Institutions

For many observers, European foreign policy has often been concerned with process rather than substance, and with the development of its institutional capabilities rather than with its external impact. Broadly speaking, the development of EU conflict prevention and crisis management has largely been an inward-looking process. Chapters 4–6 corroborate this view: institutions matter and we ought to focus on them if we are to understand the functioning of these policies. In a dense institutionalized context, it makes sense to examine the role of institutions and institutional factors in shaping these policies. However, as these chapters will show, a focus on institutions also allows for a better understanding of the impact of these policies, something that has so far been under-researched.

A preliminary question here refers to the definition of institutions as generally there is no agreement on the concept of institution in scholarly analyses. While some analysis of institutions has confined the meaning of institutions to formal bureaucratic organizations, other approaches have included in the definition of this term habits, customs or culture (Lowndes 2002: 103). The chapters take on different perspectives. While Nadia Klein adopts a narrower definition of institutions in Chapter 5, looking at the role of several EU bureaucratic bodies involved in crisis management (specifically the Council Secretariat and the Commission); Petar Petrov and Ana Juncos (Chapters 4 and 6, respectively) take on a broader meaning of institutions understood as 'the formal rules, compliance procedures, and standard operating procedures that structure the relationship between individuals in various units of the polity and economy' (Hall quoted in Peters 2005: 74). Building on this definition, and adding to the traditional meaning of institutions as formal organizations, institutions are conceptualized in these two contributions as including bureaucratic organizations, formal rules and informal practices.

Although all these three contributions draw on institutionalist theory, each of them adopts a different approach: historical (Chapter 4), rational choice (Chapter 5) and sociological institutionalism (Chapter 6). As a consequence, each chapter unveils different institutional dynamics and ascribes different causal weight to institutions. While for rationalist approaches, institutions only affect actors' behaviour, constraining or empowering certain strategies (Keohane *et al.* 1993; Moravcsik 1993); for sociological approaches, institutions also have deep effects on actors' interests and identities. For instance, for March and Olsen, institutionalization would lead to the emergence of 'codes of meaning, ways of reasoning, and accounts in the context of acting on them' (1998: 948). For its part historical institutionalism analyses 'the effects of institutions over time, in particular the way in which a given set of institutions, once established, can influence or constrain the behaviour of the actors who established them' (Pollack 2004: 139).

Chapter 4 by Petar Petrov discusses the institutional projects, ideas and processes that shaped and influenced the formal establishment of governance arrangements for conflict prevention and crisis management operations in the framework of CSDP. Adopting a historical perspective, this chapter shows that the timing and the design of the governance arrangements in this area were influenced by a particular 'path dependency' logic as well as several critical moments and critical junctures. Taking into account the strengths and weaknesses of the historical institutionalist approach to analyzing institutional change and development over time, the analysis reveals a dynamic picture of an incremental, slow, but also contested path to institutionalization.

Drawing on insights from rational choice institutionalism, the principal-agent model, and bureaucratic politics, Nadia Klein's chapter looks at what impact, if any, EU institutional actors have on the development of the Union's civil-military crisis management and its implementation. Klein conceives EU crisis management in terms of the interplay between member state principals and their institutional agents, namely the Council Secretariat and the European Commission. This chapter analyses several factors, including the actual delegation of competences, the control mechanisms established by the member states and possible overlaps of competences. In particular, both the dynamics of principal-agent relationships ('vertical control') and of agent-agent relationships ('horizontal control') are taken into account. The chapter concludes that, while both the Commission and the Council Secretariat have successfully exploited principal's monitoring and sanctioning costs to pursue autonomous preferences in EU crisis management, institutional turf battles still prevent them from fully exploiting their formal and informal competences.

Ana Juncos relies on a sociological institutionalist perspective, with an emphasis on the way institutions have shaped the design and performance of military crisis management operations, and in particular, EUFOR Althea in Bosnia. This contribution identifies factors such as institutional isomorphism, organizational routines and socialization processes that can help explain the policy process and policy substance of EU crisis management. Institutional isomorphism, for instance, explains why the EU has modelled its missions on those of other organizations – particularly NATO's operations – not because of the perceived effectiveness of those models, but in order to improve legitimacy, as a result of uncertainty or external pressures. This perspective also illustrates the often ineffective side of institutions since they might develop in a different way than was intended by their original designers, escaping from their control and producing unintended consequences. Finally, this analysis also highlights the impact of the institutional environment within which EU crisis management is embedded on actors' preferences through processes of socialization.

Despite the noticeable discrepancies between these different approaches, they are not mutually exclusive, and fruitful discussions can materialize from their application to conflict prevention and crisis management. Essentially, the three chapters and viewpoints offer explanations of different parts of CSDP: institutional processes that shaped the decision to create CSDP (Petrov); the influence of institutional actors on the development of the policy (Klein); and the day-to-day practice and implementation of CSDP (Juncos).

Part III: Policies

The final part of this book (Chapters 7–9) examines the wide range of EU policies covered by the label 'conflict prevention and crisis management'. Significantly, contributions in this section go beyond merely analysing second pillar crisis management policies, but offer a comprehensive analysis of long- and short-term conflict prevention and crisis management policies undertaken in various theatres and policy domains.

These chapters provide a fuller understanding of how the Union uses different policy instruments in different geographical scenarios. While Chapter 7 by Marie Gibert explores the European Union conflict prevention policies in West Africa, focusing on developmental and diplomatic activities, i.e. 'soft policies'; Eva Gross analyses EU engagement – including the deployment of an EU police mission – in an ongoing conflict setting in Afghanistan in Chapter 8. In Chapter 9, Giselle Bosse analyses the EU's response to the conflict in Georgia against the backdrop of the EU's long-term structural engagement in the Southern Caucasus through the European Neighbourhood Policy (ENP), a policy that combines diplomatic efforts in the mediation of the crisis, financial assistance for economic recovery and the deployment of an EU Monitoring Mission to oversee the ceasefire.

These contributions illustrate the extensive toolbox of instruments that the EU is capable of deploying in any specific situation, but also some of the flaws in the EU's policy formulation and implementation that have prevented it from using these instruments in an effective manner. They also raise significant questions regarding the effectiveness and coherence of these instruments.

Gibert's chapter shows that, in spite of the official rhetoric, the EU lacks the means and tools necessary to conduct an effective preventive diplomacy: EC delegations are technical aid agencies rather than embassies, member-states retain the bulk of Europe's diplomatic activity in Africa and the unclear division of labour between EU institutions further impedes a diplomaticization/politicization of the EU's role in Africa. Her chapter focuses on the gap (and the reasons for it) that lies between the European discourse in favour of a multilateral and diplomatic EU and the reality of what remains a developmental policy. Gibert argues that the emphasis on a technocratic rather than a political approach has diminished the EU's impact in the region. Eva Gross also draws attention to issues of coherence in EU crisis management, namely the coordination between the office of the EU Special Representative (EUSR), the EC delegation and the CSDP police mission in Afghanistan. She also analyzes the cooperation between the EU and the US in

Security Sector Reform (SSR). While 'Europeanizing' member state efforts offers the advantage of streamlining separate national efforts and of making the EU's presence in Afghanistan more visible, a deteriorating security situation coupled with shortfalls in resources, police reform in Afghanistan has been, and remains, a substantial challenge. In her chapter, Bosse argues the Union's policy towards the Southern Caucasus has, by and large, been of an *ad hoc* nature and characterized by half-hearted attempts to engage with the lingering frozen conflicts. Although the ENP has identified conflict resolution as a key priority, this chapter highlights the limitations of this policy to effectively 'add value' to the coherence of the Union's conflict resolution efforts in the Georgian breakaway republics of Abkhazia and South Ossetia in light of member state reluctance to review the EU's position towards Russia.

These three chapters also raise questions about the nature of the EU as an international actor. Rather than diplomacy, for Marie Gibert, the EU policy in West Africa can be better conceptualized as a 'transformational development policy', where 'Africa's insecurity and instability are thought to be best solved through a set of technical state reforms'. This term is not only more appropriate, but it also underlines the many similarities between the EU and other international actors' external relations like the US. While it questions the Union's claim to an original foreign policy, the EU's attempts at 'transformational diplomacy' in absence of an overtly political engagement also limit its foreign policy reach. Based on her analysis of the EU's contribution to establishing the rule of law in Afghanistan, Eva Gross concludes that, although the EU makes a valuable contribution, this contribution has come to be framed in terms of transatlantic burden sharing. US frustration with European military contributions to NATO mirror the lack of confidence in the EU to equip its police mission, EUPOL Afghanistan, with sufficient resources to carry out its task. Given the overall US military and political lead, the EU plays a secondary role. Despite significant resources extended in Afghanistan, the fragmentation of the EU's presence in Afghanistan coupled with member states transatlantic orientation when formulating policy on Afghanistan has meant that the EU has not been able to set strategic priorities in Afghanistan – for itself or the international community as a whole. Finally, Bosses' chapter concludes that although the EU's intervention in the 2008 crisis in Georgia displays much of the characteristics of the 'old' *ad hoc* EU approach based on member state governments' political will, the Union's response to the crisis also clearly reflects a growing sense of awareness among member states that, collectively, they must take greater care of and responsibility for the stability of the European security order. While member states' reactions to the war in Georgia, therefore, point towards a degree of congruence and what Bosse terms 'vertical consistency', this does not mean that there is institutional consistency between the ENP and the EU's conflict prevention and crisis management policies. While policy documents of the ENP and the Eastern Partnership (EaP) continue to pay lip service to the EU's conflict prevention objectives, these do not figure prominently either in the discourse or in EaP programmes. The conclusions of the three chapters on the EU's performance in a variety of geographical settings, and in pursuit of a number of different policy goals, hint at the need for a broader consideration of the EU's global role, which is explored in the last section of the book.

Conclusion

Taken together, the chapters in this book provide a timely assessment of the state of play of the EU's capacity to undertake and implement conflict prevention and crisis management policies in a variety of settings; the emergence of the EU as a global and perhaps also strategic actor; and the EU's position vis-à-vis its global partners. As such, they provide an excellent starting point for further exploration as they raise important analytical questions that ought to inform further research on the EU's institutional development as well as policy implementation in a changing security environment. As a new era for EU crisis management and conflict prevention opens with the implementation of the Lisbon Treaty, the analysis but also the stock-taking of EU activities in conflict prevention and crisis management to date are especially timely and pertinent.

Note

1 The Gothenburg Programme mentions the following long-term instruments: development co-operation, trade, arms control, human rights, environment policies and political dialogue. According to this document, '[s]tructures and capabilities for civil and military crisis management, developed within the framework of the ESDP, will also contribute to the capabilities of the EU to prevent conflicts' (European Council 2001: 3). This also illustrates the degree of terminological confusion in the EU's discourse.
2 With the ratification of the Lisbon Treaty in 2010 the European Security and Defense Policy (ESDP) was renamed as the Common Security and Defense Policy (CSDP). Although research for this book was completed before the entry into force of the Lisbon Treaty, this book adopts the new name throughout – with the exception of references to official documents that pre-date Lisbon.

Part I
Roles

2 The EU's role in international crisis management

Innovative model or emulated script?

Xymena Kurowska and Thomas Seitz

The last decade has seen the emergence and consolidation of Common Security and Defence Policy (CSDP) together with its wide range of crisis management tools. The EU has thus shifted towards an active international role in crisis management. Crucially however, the success of CSDP has relied to a great extent on the expansion of its civilian aspect, initially encompassing police reform and rule of law with the inclusion over time of security sector reform. This has driven the development of the policy despite a more controversial, and initially hardly expanded, military dimension and provided sufficient impetus while the military and civilian-military projects were far from operational (Kurowska 2008). Simultaneously, we have witnessed a robust externalization of the EU's Justice and Home Affairs (JHA) wherein border management issues and readmission agreements constitute an important way of shaping systemic reform in the EU's neighbourhood. These represent an instance of EU's statebuilding practices with statebuilding understood as the externally-assisted construction and reconstruction of the institutional infrastructure. Highly invasive forms of external regulation, they are regarded as a legitimate way of assisting disadvantaged communities if they are sought or requested. With the example of the EU, we see however that policies of statebuilding have become an important crisis management, or better put crisis prevention, strategy.

Different forms of non-military intervention aimed at moulding the outside environment in the pursuit of one's own security are hardly a novelty in international politics. Yet the EU's civil-military crisis management and external dimension of JHA acquire their own if contentious contours vis-à-vis the EU's rebranding on the global stage. The phenomenon seems to render moot the question whether the rise of ESDP demolishes the civilian character of the EU. What we witness instead is an accommodation of EU's purported strengths (e.g. development assistance, promotion of good governance and security sector reform) in the context of what Anderson and Seitz term the new global insecurity environment (NGIE) (2009). Surely, the EU is hardly the sole actor in this conundrum. Its role has emerged in tight interaction with other players. In the chapter, we use the heuristic perspective of the EU-US-UN dynamics to draw out this shifting interdependence of expectations and roles. We outline a pattern of role assignments that has emerged and consider the strategies of statebuilding demonstrated by EU and US to examine whether they represent different approaches to shaping 'the other' and thus an attempt to protect 'the self'.

We start with an outline of the role approach and its analytical purchase for grasping the politics of the international crisis management of today. We then go on to the analysis of different meanings of multilateralism which are significant for the understanding of the international role assignments as they correspond to visions of justifiable international cooperation. Substantively, we then look into statebuilding as a crisis management strategy of an increasing importance and differentiate it from the US label of nation-building. The EU's approach is thus juxtaposed with a historical background of the US case. This is to discuss in the conclusion whether the EU and US models are indeed radically different in their strategies of statebuilding, and if the latter inevitably smacks of 'imperialism'. In this context, we consider whether the EU's conduct represents an innovative model, or it rather borrows from the US historical experience, even if not deliberately, or to the same effect. As we argue, the existing differentiation, based to a large extent on the international perception of EU and US, should be played upon towards a more effective cooperation and division of labour.

Role approach to the EU internationality

International politics is inherently a theatre of contention, a daily struggle over meaning permeated by strategic interaction undertaken by actors in pursuit of particular agendas. Here role performance proceeds through intense image management where commitments declared are extensively framed to be followed. However, the image of meticulously designed and religiously implemented strategies is misleading for understanding the rules of the game underpinning international politics at any given time. So might be the notion that the international role of a post-Westphalian actor depends on how it conceptualizes itself (Larsen 2002: 286) and that for the postmodern state, as for the individual, identity is a matter of choice (Cooper 2003: 173). These fail to capture the social nature of role formation. Roles refer in this context to patterns of expected or appropriate behaviour and are determined both by an actor's own conceptions and the role prescriptions of others (Holsti 1970: 238–39). A role of an internationally present actor thus involves a claim on the international system, recognition thereof by other international actors, and a conception of an identity (Le Prestre 1997: 5–6). While 'the sharing of expectations on which role identities depend is facilitated by the fact that many roles are institutionalized in social structures that pre-date particular interactions' (Wendt 1999: 227), the roles an actor engages in are an effect of learning and socialization in interactive negotiation processes where self-conceptions are confronted with expectations (Aggestam 2004b). Expectations thus emerge in the process of interaction and in the dense web of meanings that each of the partners assigns to its own and others' position in international security. Accordingly, the establishment of roles is only possible within the engagement with other actors. While role assignments are not inherently malleable since their very existence induces a degree of orderly arrangement, they are hardly constant.

This process has multiple sources and, rather than being a result of a structural distribution of power, it takes shapes through the interplay of overlapping and cross-fertilising (self-)expectations, thereby allowing for considerable scope of 'role-playing' and room for manoeuvre. The shifting meanings of multilateralism and the differentiated perception of the EU and US in international crisis management illustrate the point.

Whereas the current 'distribution of expectations' in the EU-US-UN triangle has deep historico-ideational roots, the consolidation of the EU crisis management projects, conspicuously through ESDP and more quietly via the external dimension of JHA, sets new parameters for role-taking by the partners to the relationship. One may ask whether a specific cluster of role assignments amounts to a new international/security order. Depending on the definition of an international order adopted, i.e. whether we are after its thick version or remain satisfied with any indicators of quasi-orderly arrangement, the answer varies significantly. Similarly, the conceptualization hinges on whether the state-centeredness is a nucleus of the approach, or whether transnational and domestic dimensions are factored in. The proposition of the EU-US-UN functionally differentiated triad as a useful take on the problem deviates from the state-centred view. After Buzan and Little (2000: 87), we argue that it is functional units' differentiation, i.e. the specialization within a system, that is key to understanding change in international systems. Here the differentiation is expressed by the role assignment that becomes stabilized through contextual recurrent patterns of interaction that give rise to practices regulating the code of conduct in international politics. This further indicates the possibility of many such arrangements simultaneously unfolding, overlapping and permeating each other.

The analysis of the EU's crisis management initiatives and their recognition (including condescension towards it) is instructive for understanding one such instance. The initial US suspicion towards CSDP has evolved towards a pragmatic recognition of its value. The UN has embraced the development of EU crisis management capacities and advocated for its more extensive employment. The development of CSDP remains the venture point of the analysis but it should be seen against the broader EU's statebuilding repertoire. This reflects a more contextual picture of CSDP where a security and defence policy is mobilized to influence the systemic reform in the neighbourhood via civilian projects rather than expeditionary statebuilding of a military nature.

Performers – the EU and its significant others

Arguably, the EU is unique in a number of aspects: in its constitutive features and the character of its goals and values; in the configuration of political instruments used; and in its peculiar institutional construction (Elgström and Smith 2006: 2). Still, and as the neorealist argument has it (Hyde-Price 2006: 222),[1] similar to traditional great powers, the EU's objectives are framed as milieu goals which aim to shape the environment in which the actor operates (Hyde-Price 2006). Less sympathetic critics of the EU's assertiveness maintain that this ambition of shaping the neighbourhood reveals a policy of nascent neo-colonialism, even if vigorously denied (Chandler 2006). The enhanced focus on effective multilateralism with the aim to transfer the European miracle to the rest of the world would here be a current version of Europe's new 'mission civilisatrice' (Kagan 2004: 61). This would fit hand in glove with a traditional utopianism of projecting an EU as an ideal model (Nicolaïdis and Howse 2002), seeing the EU as a 'force for good' in international relations (Pace 2008) and CSDP as a mission for humanity (Merlingen and Ostrauskaite 2006).

In order to generate a more rigorous insight, rather than embracing the structural argument to counter the claim of the EU's uniqueness, we conceive of the EU's role within interaction with its significant others. Here the European Security Strategy (ESS) shows that the EU's rebranding does not unfold in isolation. Approached as the EU's international mission statement and the reflection of its self-perception, it was conceived as a response to the US international politics of George W. Bush administration.[2] The substance of the ESS thus unravels the mediation of the EU's image in relation to its significant others. Within the contours of the EU-US-UN relationship, the EU finds itself between a 'thin' global organization – with diluted influence and fraught with charges of inefficiency – and traditional modern state, with international preponderance and high degree of traditionally conceived efficiency. The character of each participant's agenda setting and the part played therein of the doctrine of multilateralism is instructive for drawing out these features.

The UN pursues an open security agenda, focussing on particular salient issues and with minimal degree of strategic agenda development. The established practice of swallowing the most devastating blows to its reputation has made the UN less susceptible to reputational concerns than is the case with other political entities. The UN can somehow afford to fail, which is a highly useful quality in the world of crisis management and humanitarian intervention. The experience of failure has not, however, been acknowledged to the extent of emasculation. With attempts at reform occurring regularly, the organization remains at the heart of maintaining global security and a useful reservoir of international legitimacy. The EU agenda is more streamlined which allows for deliberate investigation of opportunities for asserting the interests of the polity. The framing of the agenda, heavily focused on the ethical dimension and traditionally connected with the urge to civilize international politics, involves the moral obligation to respond to the conscious-shocking situations if the EU credibility is to be upheld. The US fares much better in the messianic respect, however. Rather than implicitly hinting at its superiority, the US, as a modern state with clearly formulated objectives, is not shy about its perceived supremacy. Whereas the UN can somehow afford to fail out of habit, the US can afford to fail thanks to its status as a superpower. An evocative quote concerning the US's performance in Iraq is illustrative:

America will remain the world's most powerful country regardless of how Iraq turns out and how much US foreign policy is blamed for it. The US will continue to enjoy a benign international context in which it faces no great

power rival, as it did throughout the Cold War and as great powers have traditionally done throughout history.

(Haass 2006)

Failure affordability does not appear so generous in the EU case. Perpetually
charged with ineffectiveness and inability to deliver on its promise to contribute to
international security, the EU's role creation via CSDP acquires an air of urgency
as it functions under considerable pressure to perform. This, rather than smothering
the policy, has proven a momentous factor behind its creation and consolidation,
with the recurring pronounced responsibility for the developments in the Balkans.
The argument of the necessity for quick response amidst an international crisis has
proven instrumental in making the policy a reality in international politics.[3]

Multilateralism and its meanings

The aspiration to multilateralism and the demand to build partnership has always
been at the core of the ESDP endorsement. If we regard multilateralism as an
organizational form, which links contextual practices and focuses predominantly
on pragmatic usefulness (Kratochwil 2006: 140), we can look at the intricacies of
the EU-US-UN triad through the lenses of one of the ESS's strategic objectives,
i.e. 'the promotion of an international order based on effective multilateralism'.
As expressed by one of ESDP ideational shapers:

> Multilateralism and the rule of law have an intrinsic value [. . .] Multilateral-
> ism – for which the EU stands and which is in some way inherent in its con-
> struction – is more than a refuge of the weak. It embodies at the global level
> the ideas of democracy and community that all civilized states stand for on
> the domestic level.

(Cooper 2003: 164, 168)

The quote further indicates how multilateralism's core revolves around the claim
to superior legitimacy as it is currently conceived in international relations. It
involves seeking the UN Security Council authorization for any operation carried out by a regional organization. While this perhaps exceeds the requirement
of the UN Charter, which requires obtaining consent only for forceful action, it
reflects the current conceptions of the role of the UN. Here, effective multilateralism demands meaningful and consistent communication with the UN throughout
the course of the operation as a reflection of Article 54.[4]

  The UN puts forward an elaborate understanding of what the role of the EU
could be with regard to its newly developed capabilities and ambitions (Annan
2005). The report by the UN Secretary-General delineates the EU's possible contribution to the UN-conceived understanding of security system. First, the EU, as
a regional organization, can help the UN in peacekeeping where the UN capacity
is stretched, in particular due to the preference to supply capabilities to *ad hoc*
ventures. Second, *qua* watchdog, the EU could work for spreading the adherence

to international norms. Third, the EU could adopt significant functions in implementation by leading by example and thereby solidifying some codified practices. Along these lines, the UN welcomes the EU as an intimate ally with converging interests in terms of advancing multilateral international relations. While in need of substantial support, the UN promises a tangible reward in return. Joining forces with the UN on upholding global values effortlessly brings rhetorical legitimacy. It conveys an impression of integrity and goodness, which may be implicitly played out in the interaction with the 'mighty' significant other (US). Yet, appearances aside, it is rather the EU that sets the agenda and defines the terms of the relationship which is demonstrated through the divide between what the UN wants and what the EU is willing to offer. Seemingly, the UN can be taken advantage of to seize global opportunities and thereby broaden and provide the EU agenda with an aura of righteous legitimacy. The UN further conjures up a slant of weakness, which may be brought into play in order to highlight the EU unique approach. 'We are not the UN!' was a mantra adopted by the EU Police Mission (EUPM) planning team to Bosnia and Herzegovina prior to the mission's launch (Orsini 2006: 9). It illustrates the EU's desire to differentiate itself from the UN on the ground as well as to find its own niche in the international policing/rule of law 'market'.

While Brussels has invariably supported the UN as a champion of effective multilateralism, CSDP has given it (potentially) even more powerful means than those available to the UN to promote values shared by both institutions. Illustratively in this respect, CSDP provides 'oxygen for the United Nations' (House of Lords Minutes of Evidence 2004: 7). The EU upholds the principle of the primacy of the Security Council in the maintenance of international peace and security, and it commits to contributing to the objectives of the UN in crisis management in accordance with the UN Charter.[5] Despite this acknowledgment, while the UN plays the role of a legitimizing body for CSDP, its consent may not always be indispensable (Tardy 2005: 49–51). The examples of CSDP operations launched without a UNSC resolution are numerous, both in Europe, such as the EU police Mission in Bosnia and Herzegovina, Concordia and Proxima in Macedonia, and beyond, for example with Themis (Georgia), EUJUST Lex (Iraq) and EUPOL Kinshasa (Congo). Whereas the EU recognizes the primacy of the UN, it does not want to be bound too strongly to it by means of an explicit mandate for each of its operations (Chinkin 2004: 1). There emerges a telling dualism where the recognition of primacy has to be reconciled with the EU's drive to set its own principles of cooperation (Novosseloff 2004: 7–8). The imbalance between the two is well captured through the UN insistence on institutionalising the cooperation and the EU recoiling from this. As Tardy illustrates, the UN has advocated an institutionalized partnership with the EU which would not be confined to the subcontracting model and *ad hoc* assistance, but committed the EU to direct contribution to the UN operations (2005: 67). While confirming the necessity of this cooperation, the EU favours its flexible, case-by-case variation, where its political autonomy would prevail and with no guarantee that the UN needs will ever be met (Tardy 2005: 67–68). In effect, through CSDP, the EU has become a major saviour of the

UN's reputation and an endorser of its declaratory politics, while at the same time forging a distinct profile for itself.

The relationship with the UN seems a reverse to the modalities of the EU-US relationship. A distinct appeal of the UN is their unswerving recognition of the EU's role in international crisis management. This differs significantly from the EU's position vis-à-vis the US or its protégé NATO, where the EU is compelled to strive to assert its standing. Quite apart from President's Obama recognition that 'on certain critical issues, America has acted unilaterally, without regard for the interests of others' (Obama 2009), Washington's fundamental approach to multilateralism has yet to shift significantly from the position it assumed in the Cold War. The US continues to presume that it should play the leading role in multilateral security institutions and assumes that it remains uniquely qualified to do so. This unquestioned assumption was originally a product of American exceptionalism and a view developed among elites throughout the early twentieth century of America's unique role in world affairs (Chotard 1997). The catalyst that hardened these presumptions of American leadership into the foundation stone of foreign policy was the onset of the Cold War, and the perceived high-stakes competition between the two superpowers emerging from the Second World War. Internal documents and memoranda of this period make repeated references to the magnitude of the threats embodied in that competition, as well as to America's lot as the *only* actor on earth capable of saving the world from domination by the competing superpower and its 'fanatical faith', communism.[6] Arguably, Washington's continuing assumption for itself of *the* leading role in security matters reflects a role conception shaped by the insecurity environment of the early Cold War and the relative positions of Europe and the UN within that environment. Largely unquestioned, this assumption continues to undermine effective multilateral security efforts long after the Cold War has given way to a markedly different insecurity environment.

Paradoxically, the EU's positioning as an agent amicably containing the US's vigorous unilateralism added particular legitimacy to the EU's action. It enhanced its image as a good-natured crisis manager, sending the signal of a non-confrontational posture and the desire to make the world a better place in an agreeable fashion. The rhetoric of the EU's uniqueness in the triangle re-emerges continuously in efforts at positioning and differentiating itself. The most fundamental message in this process is the implicit historical superiority disguised under rhetoric of equality. This finds its expression on the ground of the missions where the EU's approach, however ineffective and admittedly flawed with numerous imperfections, is framed to fare better as it embodies the 'European' solution. It remains to be seen whether the new US administration, leaning towards the necessity to forge some kind of progressive multilateralism, should redraw this picture.

The EU-US division of labour

The evolution of the American attitude towards CSDP has been an important factor in the development of the policy. Initially concerned with the potential of

CSDP to undermine NATO (Giegerich *et al.* 2006: 388),[7] the US has evolved into an important backer of the enterprise. Previous attempts by the EU to design its own security were approved provided they involved defence capabilities development within the European pillar of NATO, and that they aimed at transatlantic burden sharing. Now, despite the abandonment of the NATO option in favour of autonomous policy, the US sees ESDP as instrumental in cases when its status as the sole superpower and its correlated international image prevent it from effective crisis management. The EU is thus welcome as a deputy, preaching the same values but doing so in a less confrontational manner, which makes its involvement in certain regions more acceptable.

To be sure, the shift in the US approach has been an incremental and contested development. The context of launching Althea in 2004 in Bosnia and Herzegovina, a UN-mandated and NATO-supported first CSDP operation, illustrates the US's wavering position. The possibility of the EU taking over in Bosnia and Herzegovina was first suggested at the European Heads of State Summit in Copenhagen in December 2002, following the conclusion of negotiations on the 'Berlin-plus' agreement. Initial reactions to the proposal were mixed. The UK and France strongly advocated the move, while the US expressed concern over the EU's ability to take over the Bosnia operation successfully. Following extensive negotiations, NATO foreign ministers announced in December 2003 that the transition to a new EU-led mission within the framework of 'Berlin-plus' would nevertheless be undertaken. Apparently, the decision to conclude SFOR and accept the possibility of the EU takeover had been made with reticence. The International Institute for Strategic Studies concluded that 'even though the US military, severely overstretched, was eager to palm-off one of its many commitments, the Istanbul agreement on actually doing so was more than a minor achievement'(Ward 2004). More than a desire for burden-sharing, this arrangement reflects the realization that the American international posture has tied the US hands in many areas. A possible way of squaring this circle is to rely on an ally that is ideologically close and increasingly capable of particular (unthreatening) security actions. Illustratively, an honest broker image of the EU emerged in the case of EUBAM Rafah in autumn 2005, where it was the US side, and Condoleezza Rice personally, that negotiated EU involvement in the monitoring of the Israeli-Palestinian border. The question was first discussed with the EU Special Representative for this region, who subsequently reported the issue to the Political and Security Committee.[8] Reporting on the US image in the region, *European Voice* concluded in September 2006 that:

> Because of Iraq, Guantanamo and Abu Ghraib, the feeling is that the US has been discredited in the Middle East to such a degree that it is unable to act decisively [. . .] Many now question whether high-profile US engagement is still desirable or even possible [. . .] While the US has its hands tied, actors in the region are increasing turning to the EU. After years of favouring US involvement, Israel has [. . .] showed a willingness to see the EU play a greater role.
>
> (Beatty 2006)

The US now sees the EU as fit to become involved in a number of areas where the US's own engagement would prove an irritant but the EU's seemingly neutral approach is acceptable for the third party and politically secure for the US. This instrumental recognition of EU capabilities has given rise to a shift in role assignments and it paints an interesting picture of the transatlantic link in the EU-US-UN triad. The high-flying rhetoric on the EU's role coming from the Solana office could hardly acknowledge a somewhat secondary part to play.[9] Still, CSDP performers are happy to seize and skilfully build upon the distinctive scope of possibility that has emerged with respect to both the US and the UN (Kurowska 2008, 2009).

Statebuilding as a crisis management strategy: Different approaches, different roles?

Externally-assisted state-building is often defined as the construction of legitimate and effective governmental institutions in the state-recipient. It may however also seen as aiming to shape the governance system of the neighbours according to the model embraced by a particular entity in order to create a favourable environment for the latter. As such, statebuilding may be construed as an elaborate and long-term strategy geared toward preventing, and in some instances managing crises in the neighbourhood. Both EU and US are engaged in such projections but it remains an empirical question how the approaches adopted by these two differ considering their historical grounding and actual practice in today's politics.[10] We discuss it in brief to consider the potential for fruitful EU-US cooperation in crisis management that the differentiated, or perceived as such, approaches give rise to.

US policy in recent years represents a return to, or perhaps, a rediscovery of earlier approaches developed during the Cold War. Regrettably, the lessons of overseas internal security efforts instituted during the 1950s and 1960s[11] have been omitted from recent scholarship and analyses of US state/nation-building approaches.[12] As mentioned earlier, the Obama administration came into office in the face of almost unprecedented expectations – at home and abroad – for *change*, including expectations of a fundamental change in his approach to foreign policy. In large part, his presidency was greeted with worldwide enthusiasm because he signalled a break with the policies of his predecessor, George W. Bush. Bush and his most egregious policies in effect became symbolic of US foreign policy as a whole, and with the accession of Barack Obama, any change was presumed to be for the better.

In fact, one could observe significant changes in policy in the second Bush administration. Having reached the limits of their earlier, overtly military approach in Afghanistan and Iraq, the Bush administration began to talk of security in terms of not only defence, but also 'democracy and development' (Rice 2008; Gates 2009). In the final years of the Bush Presidency, the link between security and development abroad and security of the US itself had been rediscovered and returned to the fore of US foreign policy. This represents a change of tack, back onto a course pursued by Cold War presidents up to Richard Nixon.

This earlier policy was itself shaped by the international environment of the time. Washington had by then assumed for itself its leading role as the sole force standing between the free world and communist domination. In the context of the aforementioned high-stakes competition between the 'free world' and 'communist bloc', the emergence of newly independent states in less developed areas of the world posed an enormous security challenge. Informed by what Robert Packenham later called 'poverty theses' (1973), American leaders were convinced that economic and political instability in these areas – and the radicalization it could cause – played into the hands of the competing superpower. In their analysis, these leaders perceived a link between American security and the internal security of these new states. Accordingly, policy makers formulated programmes to stabilize these new states internally, rendering them resistant to 'subversion' and, ultimately, domination by and 'loss' to the opposing camp.

These efforts began modestly as police reform programmes. Such programmes were intended to reform local paramilitaries by instilling American-style police ethics as well as tactics, or as one planning document put it, 'to replace the culture of the submachine gun with that of the handgun' (White House Office, 1955). Other objectives included developing police forces as institutions separate from the military in recipient countries, and helping to create in each country an independent judiciary to help control the security forces. However, analyses of the situation on the ground in recipient countries caused these programmes to broaden into ambitious, multi-agency state/nation-building efforts, ranging from Defence Department projects to train local security forces to the State Department's efforts to improve relations between dissident ethnic groups and central governments in recipient states.

The economic assistance needed to support these efforts was also motivated and shaped by the actions of the competing superpower. Washington had shown little real inclination toward providing economic assistance to developing areas until the USSR instituted such programmes in the mid-1950s. The Soviets' economic aid to new states focused US policy makers' attention upon the need for development assistance as a *security* instrument. Tellingly, the Eisenhower administration's aid programmes for 1957 represented something of a turning point. In that year, for the first time since the outbreak of the Korean conflict, the administration's aid funding requests contained more for programmes of an ostensibly development nature than for military hardware (Rostow 1985: 86–87; Kaufman 1982: 135).

With the accession of the Kennedy administration, US striving for prestige in the developing areas reached its peak. During the Kennedy-Johnson years, state/nation-building approaches coalesced around modernization theory. The mostly young men making up the senior members of Kennedy's team saw theirs as a time of 'revolutionary change', especially in developing areas, which the decolonization process was reshaping in ways 'at least as significant as the breakdown of the Concert of Europe. They also felt that their communist competitors were trying to evict the US from its 'rightful place' in 'the vanguard of the revolution of rising expectations' (Schoenbaum 1988: 264–65). Their response to this challenge was the United States Overseas Internal Defence Program (USOIDP),[13] the overall policy framework that operationalized modernization theory in nation-building and counterinsurgency policy. The USOIDP was broader and more ambitious than earlier efforts, and like earlier efforts, was implemented in dozens of developing countries. The programme featured efforts to reform security institutions while simultaneously relying on local militaries as 'modernizing elites' tasked with carrying reforms forward. It also relied on local militaries as well as US military units to conduct 'civic action' duties, involving infrastructure development and social projects. USOIDP also sought to identify and develop local human resources that could drive further development. The programme supported institution building, from various levels of government to intellectual groups.

In the early years, these programmes were largely uninformed by theory, other than presumptions that development was largely a matter of economic growth and that growth was largely a matter of attracting private sector investment. Even after modernization theory became the backbone of these approaches, there was little questioning of the universal applicability of US approaches, norms or institutions. When questions arose regarding models against which local institutions would be judged, those benchmark models would be Western, if not American. There was little debate over whether there existed a sufficient degree of shared ethos between the US and elites in recipient countries regarding the best approaches to governance and development.[14] This was true even when those elites, upon which the US was relying to implement change, had a considerable stake in keeping things as they were. More recent internal security programmes in Afghanistan, Iraq and elsewhere suggest this same lack of reflection. Even when the forms, trappings and rituals reflect local culture, the essential nature and ethos of institutions seems firmly rooted in the Western and especially American experience. Finally, thorny questions regarding the relationship between order and development continue to plague policymaking.

On the growing mythology that sees the EU as a key transferable model for all future reconstruction efforts (Williams 2007: 549), the EU has been endorsing its self-image as a 'force for good' (Pace 2008). The Brussels policy-makers have been busy continuously validating and reproducing this representation, and the academic constructions of the EU as a normative or transformative power and thus necessarily benign, have reinforced this image (Pace 2008). This may play to the advantage of the EU as a crisis manager and statebuilder: the reputation of an honest broker is a crucial ingredient in the process. Yet, it dangerously hinders a more sustained discussion about the EU's statebuilding practice. First, the EU remains committed to the taken-for-granted legitimacy and responsibility to project its model of good governance. Second, in spite of relative openness to criticism about implementation, there has developed an assumption that the EU does indeed possess the most adequate package of capacities in civilian and military crisis management, the right mix of tools that makes it a major player in this realm. In this context and despite declared cooperation with UN, EU actors present themselves as insufficiently versed in a wider debate on peace- and statebuilding. Third, these have stifled the EU's engagement with the local politics while amplifying the tendency to overestimate the accomplishment of the EU's projection. The mantra of local ownership is repeatedly compromised, although at times as a result of implicit pact between the EU actors and the local elites.[15] Strangely enough, this depiction seems to emulate the kind of hubris demonstrated in the US practice. It is all the more paradoxical as the EU's framing rests on an attempt to differentiate its image from that of the US. Is there therefore but little innovation in the EU's approach to crisis management?

This might be too hasty a conclusion. Despite the self-aggrandisement that the EU is prone to, there are indeed some features inherent in its system that may make it a viable and sustainable crisis manger of different than US qualities. The intrinsic multinational diversity of the EU and the necessity of multilevel continuous negotiation in its system of governance make it potentially more likely to forging solutions based on difference and compromise rather than imposing a template. The EU-level policy discourse endorses the notion of the EU 'best practice' and the implementation documents are subsequently framed in terms of 'bringing the stockholders' governance in line' with the latter. The officers on the ground however readily recognize the futility of such an approach. Obviously, no such thing as the EU-wide best practice in any policy area exists. Conceptual confusion and ensuing inefficiency are frequently blamed for the EU's underperformance. Yet this common absence of ready-made solutions on the part of the EU may encourage designing bottom-up benchmarking schemes that rely on the knowledge and experience of field officers co-located in national institutions and exposed to their daily functioning. This by no means denotes a radical shift away from imposing templates. The proposition rather is that the 'exercise in Europeaness' that they undergo while working in EU environments and the 'lived experience' of difference may translate onto corresponding relationships with non-EU actors, creating opportunities for local ownership that amount to more than a pretence.

Conclusion

In the chapter, we relied on the EU-US-UN heuristic perspective to illustrate the shift in the international role assignment in the realm of crisis management. A distinct appeal of the UN is their unswerving recognition of the EU's consolidating role in international crisis management. The resort to the UN legitimising capacity is mutually beneficial. The EU obtains a mandate for action, an ally in championing the effective multilateralism, and simultaneously provides the UN oxygen for acting, becoming the latter's reputational saviour. This differs significantly from the EU position vis-à-vis the US or its protégé NATO, where the EU has been compelled to strive to assert its standing. Yet the shift towards a greater recognition of the EU's role has been facilitated by the notoriety that the US earned under the George W. Bush administration. The US is barely able to act unilaterally so it looks to the EU where its direct and evident participation would merely exacerbate tensions. The EU's image is meanwhile acceptable and thus capable of influencing the situation in the direction favoured by the US. It ultimately denotes a pragmatic recognition of the EU's role for crisis management where US involvement is not welcome. This role relies on the acknowledgment of ideological affinity between the two and the diffusion of shared ideals, even if in evidently dissimilar ways. While this should not be construed as an entirely harmonious marriage, it reveals a relationship reading from common script. Further still, it allows the EU to play out its strengths in crisis management and carve out a sustainable international security role.

Referring to the (ultimately) effective combination of European and American efforts in stabilising Bosnia, Andrew Williams declared: '[t]he blend of American hard power and European soft power that made that happen in the former Yugoslavia needs no explanation here, but it cannot be underestimated as a source not only of effectiveness but also of widely accepted legitimacy' (2007: 548–49). And yet, such US-EU 'symbiosis' has been difficult to recreate. As described earlier, challenges comprising the NGIE have brought the EU's emerging foreign policy strengths and crisis management capabilities to centre stage, while US security planners, having confronted the limits of largely 'kinetic' operations, have of late been moving in a similar direction.

As the challenges of the NGIE exceed the capability of either the US or the EU, cooperation is essential. The question that remains is, how best to establish an effective division of labour? The issue is in all cases bound to be sensitive among the peoples in regions where interventions take place and no less so among the peoples of Europe and the US. On one hand, successful EU missions in Macedonia and in Bosnia and Herzegovina have shown labour can be divided in terms of workload or in terms of the type of mission and the capabilities required. However, there is already a vague and unpopular notion that too often in international crises the US 'cooks the meal', leaving Europe to 'do the dishes'. On one hand, Europeans bristle at the seemingly open-ended commitments and unglamorous nature of the job, while Americans balk at bearing the brunt of combat casualties in initial security efforts. Similarly, we have argued that foreign policy behaviour by the US, particularly during (but not limited to) the George W. Bush years, has severely impacted the image and thus the effectiveness of the US as a crisis manager in the Middle East and other areas. In these contexts, local perceptions and sensitivities allow the EU to involve itself more effectively, safely and legitimately than the Americans. However, this ultimately represents a geographic division of labour, requiring great care to avoid evoking an apparent renaissance of imperialism in the style of the late nineteenth century.

Perhaps the most difficult question is whether state-building in the cause of crisis management is itself a form of imperialism. Whether undertaken by the US or the EU, these programmes tend to involve the reform or even establishment of institutions considered integral to 'good governance'. Both US and EU programmes strive to transfer or develop 'best practices' through training and mentoring. Whether a key, overt element of the overall security effort, as in George W. Bush's goal of transferring democracy to the Middle East, or something to be consciously guarded against, as often seems the case with the EU, these programmes seem bound to transfer – if not impose – elements of the donor's ethos and political culture. Are these state-building projects by their very nature imperialism? Williams states that such efforts are driven by a 'norm of reconstruction':

'if it is imposed it is imperialist but if it is welcomed then it is no more imperialist than Kantian thinkers and practitioners want it to be' (2007: 551). If state-building will prove effective in addressing or preventing the threats that emanate from 'weak, failed or failing states' (Gates 2009), then the stakes in such efforts can be very high. At the same time, the world cannot allow Iraq or Afghanistan to be the paradigm for crisis management through state-building.

The European Union in particular must be cautious to avoid fanning the anti-imperialist sentiments that still smoulder in many former colonial areas. In part, this is because much of the world has come to expect the worst from the US while expecting the EU to be a non-confrontational honest broker in its crisis management approach. Should high-profile actions by the EU, or anyone representing the EU, tarnish this polished image, those actions would undermine the development of the EU as a global actor as well as its own internal identity-building project (Anderson 2008; Seitz and Anderson 2008). Much of the power driving both of these comes from perceived differences between the EU and the US. This would be truly unfortunate, for perhaps nothing so much as the rise of the EU as a prominent and effective international actor could cause the US to rethink its own Cold War-era role conception and make way for a truly multilateral approach to security and crisis management.

Notes

1 Kurowska would like to thank the editors for this reminder.
2 For an analysis along these lines, see e.g. Bereskoetter 2005.
3 For an analysis of the policy's entrepreneurs, see Kurowska 2009.
4 For the requirements of effective multilateralism as currently set by the UN, see Guéhenno 2005.
5 See e.g. Council of the European Union 2003c.
6 For a classic example and clear articulation of this rationale, see US Department of State (1950).
7 The American insistence on the three Ds (no decoupling of European security from that of America's; no duplication of effort and capabilities; and no discrimination against the allies who are not the EU members) marked the US approach at the ESDP conception (see Albright 1998), although they feature less in the current debate.
8 Interviews in the office of the EC representative to the Political and Security Committee, 25 November 2005.
9 Javier Solana has addressed the transatlantic relationship numerous times, pointing in particular to partnership of choice wherein both parties possess dissimilar yet complementary assets (Solana 2003), or insisting that no single country can tackle today's problems on its own (Council of the European Union 2003d).
10 For the sake of clarity in terminology, it is important to add that some American policy analysis confuses statebuilding and nation-building (e.g. Dobbins *et al.* 2003) and predominantly uses the latter term. We see these as very distinct although connected concepts: the efforts towards moulding the outside environment go hand in glove with self-fashioning and external recognition. This contributes to the consolidation of the internal project, although not necessarily along the 'nationhood' lines, of which the EU is a very good example.
11 The broadest, most ambitious programs of this era were the NSC 1290-*d* program, initiated in December of 1954 and re-designated the Overseas Internal Security Program in

1957, and the United States Overseas Internal Defence Program, adopted with NSAM 182 in 1962.

12 James Dobbins and his collaborators, for example, in their book *America's Role in Nation Building from Germany to Iraq* (Dobbins *et al.* 2003) jumps from post-war Germany and Japan to Somalia in the 1990s.

13 The USOIDP was accepted by the President as policy in National Security Action Memorandum 182 in August of 1962.

14 Even when officers in the field raised such issues. See OCB Report pursuant to NSC Action 1290-d, 23 November 1955.

15 For an example of one such instance in the conception and implementation of European Union Assistance Mission to Ukraine and Moldova, see Kurowska and Tallis 2009.

3 European Union conflict prevention and the European security architecture

Emma J. Stewart

Introduction

The European Union's role in the post-Cold War era has expanded from a minor international actor to a key player in pan-European security. Conflict prevention – a policy designed to avert, or to mitigate, the destruction caused by violent conflict – is an external relations objective adopted by the EU that has accelerated this development. Conflict prevention (inclusive of crisis management)[1] has become the driving force behind the Common Security and Defence Policy (CSDP), and features prominently in the 2003 European Security Strategy and in the European Neighbourhood Policy. EU development aid contributes to the promotion of democracy and stability, and EU civilian and military missions have been acting to prevent and manage conflict across Europe and the world.

Yet this transformation has not taken place in a vacuum: the EU has expanded its external remit alongside other European security organizations that have also had to adapt to post-Cold War challenges. The self-perception of the EU as a stability projector in the post-Cold War era was instrumental in the adoption of conflict prevention as a key policy objective. Moreover, the EU's role was shaped and guided by the actions and expectations of other European security actors, such as the North Atlantic Treaty Organization (NATO) and the Organization for Security and Cooperation in Europe (OSCE), as well as the expectations of Europe's citizens in the aftermath of the Balkan wars. The expansion of the EU's international role is reflected in the EU's development of a conflict prevention capacity: in the early 1990s, conflict prevention was a vague notion located in the development sphere, but by the early 2000s, it was a fleshed-out policy that served to unify the EU's dual ambitions in civilian and military crisis management.

This chapter seeks to address two key questions relating to the EU's role in the European security architecture. First, what does the development of EU conflict prevention tell us about the changing role of the EU? It is argued that the EU's international role has shifted away from its civilian origins towards that of a hybrid civil-military organization, with conflict prevention as the primary external policy that serves to unify the civilian and military spheres. This process, however, has been problematic, and it is debatable how successful the EU has been in combining its civilian and military competences. Second, how has the EU's role shaped, and been shaped by, other European security organizations? All European organizations faced the challenges of survival and adaptation in the post-Cold war era. Conflict prevention/crisis management emerged as a shared priority among security organizations, particularly after the failure to prevent war in the Balkans. Yet instead of the emergence of a system of burden-sharing, security cooperation between organizations developed incrementally, and on a case-by-case basis. Cooperation in conflict prevention between the EU and the OSCE and NATO was slow to develop, and has had mixed results. It is argued that better dialogue and cooperation between the EU and the OSCE and NATO could serve to strengthen the EU's role, as well as improving the prospects for international cooperation on pressing security challenges.

The changing role of the EU

The EU's international role is, and has been, determined by a number of interconnecting factors, including history, identity, capability, expectations and context. The EU's role has blurred structure and agency by incorporating 'the manner in which foreign policy is both purposeful *and* shaped by institutional contexts' (Aggestam 2006: 24, emphasis added). In other words, the EU's evolving role as an actor in conflict prevention in the post-Cold War era is understood as a development shaped both by internal ambitions and opportunities as well as external pressures and constraints.

During the Cold War, the EU's role as a civilian power was largely dictated by external constraints and a lack of internal capabilities. After the failed attempt to create a European Defence Community in the 1950s, Western Europe's security identity was unequivocally linked to the US through NATO. The Atlantic Alliance provided the military security that Western Europe required. The concept of 'civilian power' Europe was suggested by Duchêne in the 1970s and referred to the political value of economic and diplomatic power as an alternative to military power (Duchêne 1972). European Political Cooperation (EPC) played a significant role in the 1970s and 1980s in establishing a European Community (EC)[2] political role based on low-key (and often lowest common denominator) diplomacy. Galtung (1973) did not welcome the emergence of the EC as a 'superpower in the making'. Other commentators argued that the EC could not be considered a significant actor until it gained military power; civilian power Europe was a 'contradiction in terms' (Bull 1982: 149).

The dramatic revision of European security at the end of the Cold War had broad implications for the EU's role and the development of the Common Foreign and Security Policy (CFSP), launched in the Treaty on European Union (TEU) in 1991. The EU's place was uncertain in the new Europe; previously it had had a distinct role, with clear boundaries represented by the Cold War division of Europe (Smith 1996). Security threats to Western Europe became less about conventional and nuclear war and more about the knock-on effects of political and economic instability in the new states of Eastern and Central Europe (Dorman and Treacher 1995). The EU, a civilian organization with economic and diplomatic strength, was uniquely qualified to develop non-military security solutions, and had pressing reasons to project stability in an expanded Europe. Yet despite the changes and progress enshrined in the TEU, the EU had a limited early role in facilitating peaceful democratic transitions in Eastern Europe, with the central role falling to the United States. As the 1990s and the CFSP progressed, the EU's role in diplomacy and economic aid increased and became linked to the promise of enlargement. Former EU Commissioner for External Relations, Chris Patten, later argued that the projection of stability was the EU's 'essential mission', and that enlargement 'is the single greatest contribution the Union can make to European – even to global – stability' (Patten 2000: 19).

Commentators recognized the connections between conflicts in Eastern Europe and integration in the West (Rummel 1996). The violent break-up of Yugoslavia arguably had the greatest influence on the evolution of EU foreign policy and conflict prevention in particular, highlighting its limitations and accelerating change. Failures in diplomacy provided a catalyst for EU conflict prevention as the political, economic and human costs of conflict were underlined. One commentator coined the phrase 'normative power Europe' as a new way of understanding the EU's transformed international role: the EU's impact was not simply about capabilities, but also about ideational impact and the promotion of norms (Manners 2002).

Ironically, the EU's role as a civilian actor was increasingly deemed insufficient to cope with the full range of security challenges that emerged in the post-Cold War period. The issue of military capabilities came back onto the agenda as EU member states recognized that the Union could offer peacekeeping and peace building services that were distinct from NATO and surpassed the capacity of the OSCE. Serbian violence against Kosovans during 1998, coupled with the Franco-British St Malo summit, during which the UK government dropped its objection to the development of an autonomous EU military capacity, were key factors in this development (see the chapter by Petrov in this volume). The EU took over the crisis management functions of the Western European Union (WEU)[3] in 1999 and launched the ESDP. The EU's role was increasingly blurring the boundaries of civilian and military, and the concept of conflict prevention became a way of unifying EU external objectives.

Conflict prevention as a unifying external policy

Conflict prevention policy in the EU originated in the development policy sphere during the early 1990s. It increasingly became more associated with the CFSP and the CSDP as the European Commission's Directorate-General (DG) for External Relations extended its policy competences, and as the Council of the European Union developed competences in early warning and civilian and military crisis management (see Stewart 2008a). By the early 2000s, conflict prevention featured in EU external policy as a 'cross-cutting' issue to be mainstreamed into Community programming, as well as a civilian and military objective of the CSDP.

The EU increasingly perceived and marketed itself as a rounded security actor, combining long and short-term civilian and military competences for conflict prevention purposes. However, this was challenging institutionally as well as normatively: it exacerbated existing institutional tensions between the Council of the European Union and the European Commission, and shifted the EU away from its traditional role as a civilian power. For some analysts, the development of the ESDP could not be reconciled with the EU's role as a civilian power (Smith 2000; Treacher 2004). Yet, in many ways, the development of the EU as a pseudo-military power was a pragmatic response to the changing security environment. As civilian crisis workers relied on military protection, and military forces undertook humanitarian tasks, it became more important to develop comprehensive responses to crises, incorporating military and civilian personnel. It was widely accepted, particularly in the aftermath of the Kosovo crisis, that military means were often necessary to prevent violence and war when diplomacy failed (Bildt 2000). The EU's foreign policy therefore developed as a result of both internal institutional ambitions and changing external demands for EU crisis response. The commitment to conflict prevention at the institutional and normative levels also served to justify the EU's transition from civilian to integrated civilian-military actor.

Developing a comprehensive approach to conflict has nevertheless been challenging for the EU. The Union needs to coordinate civilian and military capacities from the early planning and analysis stages through to the operational stage in any EU mission. It has been argued by the author elsewhere that the EU has prioritized its military means over the development of longer-term competences (Stewart 2006; 2008a). While 'preventive engagement' was a central feature of the 2003 European Security Strategy (Council of the European Union 2003d), the unreflective development of military competences risks undermining the EU's role as a conflict prevention actor, since a comprehensive approach is crucial if the EU is to maintain its legitimacy as a hybrid civilian-military organization. The failure of the EU to prevent the recent conflicts in Georgia (2008) and Gaza (2008–9) is a reminder that the exercise of careful diplomacy and the extension of influence can be more powerful foreign policy tools than the ability (but not the will) to deploy troops.

The lack of comprehension in EU conflict prevention policy has implications for the breadth and value of EU cooperation with other organizational actors. The record of the EU's cooperation with a traditionally military actor (NATO) and a civilian organization (OSCE) sheds further light on the EU's conflict prevention role. Before addressing this inter-institutional cooperation, we briefly discuss the context and institutional complexity of the practice of conflict prevention in post-Cold War Europe.

EU conflict prevention in a pan-European context

As conflict returned to the European continent as an actual or potential threat, crisis response became an expanding institutional policy area in an increasingly institutionalized context. The difficulties of post-conflict reconstruction in South Eastern Europe led to a widespread approval of conflict prevention in particular as an approach preferable to dealing with the financial and human costs of violent conflict (Carnegie Commission on Preventing Deadly Conflict 1997, Munuera 1994; Rummel 1996; Clement 1997; Brown and Rosecrance 1999, Hill 2001; Van Tongeren *et al.* 2002; Björkdahl 2002). The EU's adoption of conflict prevention as a security strategy therefore did not occur independently of wider developments in the European security architecture. The EU was influenced by other governmental and non-governmental organizations, as well as by the expectations of European citizens in both the West and in the former East.

Institutional complexity

With institutional adaptations and enlargements, post-Cold War Europe became the most institutionally complex region of the world. The growing institutional complexion emerged not as a result of grand design or consensus, however, but as a result of the short-term political decisions and preferences of national governments. Unlike the initially questionable future of NATO, the EU clearly had a key role to play in the reshaping of Europe; it was the nature and extent of the EU's role that was in question. The OSCE lost its centrality after it presided over the signing of the Conventional Forces in Europe arms reduction treaty by members of NATO and the Warsaw Pact. All organizations responded to the new environment with institutional proliferation – creating new units and mechanisms – and by expanding their jurisdiction and objectives. However, adaptation was not accompanied by a division of tasks or labour. The OSCE, despite its pan-European focus and membership, did not become the central or coordinating European security organization, and its political crisis in recent years as a result of the withdrawal of the cooperation of the Russian Federation has underlined its lesser role (see Stewart 2008b). On the other hand, the 2004 enlargement of the world's most powerful military alliance and the world's most economically successful regional organization, and their shared membership, have undoubtedly contributed to the endurance and influence of NATO and the EU.

The overlapping of organizational memberships and competences was a new development in European politics. During the post-Second World War period, the competences of international organizations were clearly separated. NATO was concerned with military security and the EC was largely concerned with economic integration in Western Europe, and trade and development relations with the third world. The UN was the universal organization responsible for the maintenance of international peace and security, with the CSCE[4] (from 1975) providing pan-European back up in the field of civil, political, and minority rights. While there was inevitably some overlapping of security concerns during the Cold War, especially with growing political integration at the European level, the separation of responsibilities meant that cooperation was rarely an issue. Mitrany (quoted in Cosgrove and Twitchett 1970: 51) emphasized the difference between the UN and the EC/EU as international actors, citing the EC's 'divisive' role internationally as precluding any role in the prevention of war. The EC was a Western European organization, supported (and, in some analyses, propped up by) the US, while the UN gained peacemaking legitimacy through its global membership. This situation was transformed in the post-Cold War era. The European Union and its representatives were, by the early 2000s, citing conflict prevention as one of the organization's main external objectives. Differences and dividing lines between roles and responsibilities were no longer clear. The need to adapt from the particularities and predictability of the Cold War era to meet the security challenges of the 1990s was urgent. Yet the complexity of the security challenges and the incremental nature of adaptation failed to produce an optimal European security system. The development of the EU's post-Cold War relationships with NATO and the OSCE demonstrate this.

EU cooperation with NATO

While NATO and the EU both originated in the early days of the Cold War, the organizations were far apart in terms of ethos and practice (although analysts of the Realist school of International Relations [e.g. Waltz 1979] argued that the military security provided by NATO allowed the EC to exist). NATO shaped the EU's role during the Cold War, and it has also continued to shape the development of ESDP in the post-Cold War period. NATO's existence may no longer dictate the type of security role the EU adopts, but it has impacted on, and to some extent, constrained, the development of the EU as a crisis management actor. The EU's move into the crisis management terrain has also impacted on NATO's post Cold War remit: ambitions in crisis management were overlapping, but a clear division of labour has been thwarted by politics and disagreements about the nature of the EU's changing role. The EU-NATO relationship has therefore been complicated by the fundamental strategic significance of the partnership, which has been particularly important for the new Central and Eastern European states.

NATO's competences are narrow compared to the EU, and unlike NATO's earlier relationship with the defence-oriented WEU, the organizations are not natural partners. It does not have a wide role in conflict prevention: while it has assumed the language of stability projection, NATO's remit is primarily short-term military crisis management, and this has been the focus of the EU-NATO relationship. EU-NATO relations were therefore crucial in the elucidation of the EU's full range of operational tasks ('Petersberg tasks'). NATO negotiations with a largely civilian organization such as the EU have not been without problems, despite the fact that after the twin EU-NATO May 2004 enlargement, and the EU 2007 enlargement, EU member states made up 21 of the 26 NATO member nations.

Nevertheless, the 'Europeanization' of NATO (Cottey 1998: 56), illustrated by the Combined Joint Task Forces (CJTF) concept and the promise of enlargement of the NATO area across the European continent, tied the objectives and the fortunes of the EU and NATO together. From the joint objective of stabilization in Eastern Europe and the Balkans, NATO-EU cooperation moved up a gear when EU ambitions to undertake military operations became clear. NATO dialogue with the EU proper began after the Union decision taken at the 1999 Cologne European Council to adopt the crisis management role of the WEU. This decision represented the culmination of the 1990s debate among EU member states about if and how to develop an EU crisis management capability, and was facilitated by the arrival of the UK New Labour Party onto the political scene. The British receptivity to an EU capacity, crystallized by the Franco-British agreement at St Malo in 1998, resulted in real progress for the CSDP.

The Berlin Plus discussions originated in the 1996 NATO Ministerial Council meeting in Berlin, which allowed for WEU use of NATO assets. The Washington Summit of 1999 extended this to EU CSDP operations, allowing for 'assured EU access to NATO operational planning; use of NATO capabilities and assets; NATO European command options for EU operations; and adaptation of NATO defence planning system to incorporate availability of forces for EU operations' (Quille 2003: 7). US misgivings about the development of EU crisis management competences were compounded by objections by non-EU NATO members (mostly Turkey) about the protocols for EU access to NATO assets. The arrangements were finalized in 2002 after the Greek, and then the Turkish governments, dropped their objections. In the meantime, a deeper partnership between the organizations had been developing in joint NATO-EU *ad hoc* working groups, where security policies and modalities for cooperation were discussed. Additionally, the organizations agreed on regular joint Ambassadorial/ Ministerial level and North Atlantic Council (NAC)-Political and Security Council (PSC) meetings (NATO 2001).

The December 2002 'EU-NATO Declaration on ESDP', as part of the final Berlin Plus agreement, declared the establishment of a 'strategic partnership' between the organizations (NATO 2002). This relationship, it was declared, is founded on a mutually reinforcing partnership; effective mutual consultation; equality and due regard for the decision-making autonomy of both organizations; respect for member states' interests; respect for the principles of the UN Charter; and the 'coherent, transparent and mutually reinforcing development of the military capability requirements common to the two organizations' (NATO 2002: para. 2). The real extent of equality between the organizations is questionable: it is the EU that relies on NATO assets for crisis management, not the other way around. Furthermore, while US governmental rhetoric frequently (and confusingly) calls for the 'strengthening of the European pillar', the Bush administration did not hesitate to exploit EU member state disagreements in the run up to the war in Iraq in 2003. An Assembly of the WEU report claimed that the removal of the WEU as the link between the EU and NATO has led to a competitive relationship between the organizations, noting that 'with few exceptions, the European Union authorities avoid using the word "cooperation" to describe relations with NATO and/or the United States' (WEU 2004: 15). Nevertheless, it is in the interest of the US administration to maintain good relations with European allies, and therefore the relationship is framed in partnership terms by both the EU and NATO.

In July 2003, the EU and NATO agreed on a 'Concerted Approach for the Western Balkans' (European Union 2003a). The agreement followed the successful EU takeover from NATO (using NATO assets) of military crisis management in

Macedonia. Recognising that the endgame for the Western Balkan countries is integration into Euro-Atlantic organizational structures, the agreement cites the EU-NATO partnership as the key factor in ending conflict in the region (interestingly, no mention of the UN and the OSCE), and identifies conflict prevention and crisis management as one of six core areas for cooperation.[5] Cooperation will be ensured by regular meetings between the organizations and their institutions, and security information will be exchanged. This document proclaimed a partnership between the organizations in the Balkans that presumably could be developed for similar objectives in other countries or regions. A closer look at cooperation between the organizations throws light on the changing nature of security roles in Europe.

EU-NATO cooperation in conflict prevention

The language of long-term stability and democracy promotion can be identified in the documents of both organizations, indicating at least a rhetorical consensus on these issues. Documents such as the aforementioned EU and NATO 'Concerted Approach for the Western Balkans' indicate that the organizations are working together to promote long-term conflict prevention, even though most joint initiatives are operational. The organizations' joint enlargement in May 2004, and the joint strategy of enlargement to the Western Balkans, also indicates an agreement to coordinate to enhance stability in Europe by bringing many of the same former communist countries into European and transatlantic institutions.

Nevertheless, problems in EU-NATO cooperation indicate tensions in the partnership that have impacted on the roles of both organizations. Early warning competences are crucial for longer-term stability projection, and it can be assumed that intelligence sharing would be to the benefit of both organizations. However, while NATO's Situation Centre has links to the EU's Situation Centre (SITCEN), NATO would only agree to information exchange with the EU after tight security arrangements were in place (Andréani *et al.* 2001: 36). This was reached in March 2003 in the EU-NATO Security Agreement, which represented the final document under the Berlin Plus arrangements, and entails the release of security information by the High Representative for CFSP to NATO on CSDP matters. How much information NATO shares with the EU is unclear, however, as is whether this arrangement brings any added value to the early warning capacity of either organization. Problems in intelligence sharing have also been evident on the ground, particularly in Bosnia during the handover of NATO's Stabilisation Force (SFOR) to the EU mission (EUFOR). The ongoing dispute between Turkey and Cyprus has also stymied early warning cooperation between the organizations in Kosovo and Afghanistan: formal agreements on intelligence sharing between NATO and EU staff have been blocked (Keohane 2009).

Early warning cooperation has been boosted by the threat of global terrorism, particularly as NATO's objectives became increasingly focused on supporting the US-led 'War on Terror'. In April 2004, the 26 members agreed on a 'Declaration on Terrorism' including the establishment of a Terrorist Threat Intelligence Unit, which was operational by the June 2004 Istanbul Summit. Additionally, NATO pledged to step up information sharing with the EU on terrorism and the proliferation of weapons of mass destruction. Yet it remains to be seen if this focus will be beneficial to wider conflict prevention. Information sharing appears to be narrowly focused on military and terrorist activities, and it is difficult to see how this could enhance anything but a restricted range of security concerns. NATO's focus on intelligence cooperation for terrorist prevention serves to illustrate the different approaches of the two organizations, with the EU tending to take a less military-centric attitude to early warning.

The 'double-hatting' of military representatives (where EU Alliance members send the same representative to the EU and NATO Military Committees) aids coordination between the organizations. Indeed, the EU's military structure is modelled on that of NATO (see Chapter 6 in this volume). While this is pragmatic and avoids duplication, it could hamper the EU in developing its own military doctrine, encompassing views of a wider variety of member states that may go beyond the concerns of the Alliance. Moreover, it has not prevented problems. For example, PSC-NAC meetings have been blocked by resistance from Turkey and France and currently formal meetings only deal with Berlin Plus operations such as EUFOR in Bosnia. Other key issues such as NATO-EU cooperation in Kosovo and Afghanistan have been kept outside these formal meetings.

The double-hatting of NATO officials for EU-led operations has therefore meant that NATO military doctrine and practices have greatly influenced the development of the EU as a military actor (see Ana Juncos' chapter in this volume). This has generated some controversy. Giovanna Bono (2004) suggests that NATO has too much influence in EU operational planning and military thinking. Others have asked, 'how far should [the EU] defer to expertise coming from an organization whose aims may not always coincide with its own?' (Andréani *et al.* 2001: 69). Indeed, there is evidence to suggest that the organizations have different crisis management visions. Mawdsley and Quille argue, 'although the EU and NATO are not different in their global ambitions, their organizational outlook makes them emphasize distinctly different military needs and visions of combat intensity' (Mawdsley and Quille 2004: 15). The EU emphasizes multilateralism and has a more holistic approach to security, while NATO does not always seek partnerships and practices operations of high intensity.

A pragmatic model of cooperation between the organizations has failed to emerge. There was, for example an attempt to reach an agreement on a 'Berlin Plus reverse' i.e. the EU providing civilian support to NATO military missions (following the Afghanistan model). Opposition from the European Commission as well as from France meant that this proposal was dropped. The relationship has been beset by further political problems. EU enlargement rendered cooperation with NATO more difficult because of the need for non-NATO EU states to be member of NATO's 'Partnership for Peace' programme (a particular problem for Turkey in the case of Cyprus' membership). This led to the inauguration of 'informal dinners' to keep the discussions going (Keohane 2009). As already mentioned, the Iraq war strained Alliance relations, leading to proposals from France,

Germany, Belgium and Luxembourg for an autonomous EU operations unit in Brussels. Discussions of a 'mutual assistance' clause in the context of the EU Constitutional Treaty debate, a provision retained by the Lisbon Treaty, led to further fears that NATO could be undermined (Keohane 2009). The change in French policy towards NATO under President Sarkozy (France rejoined NATO's military command structures in 2009) is, at least, one positive step towards enhanced cooperation between NATO and the EU.

These political issues have affected practical cooperation on the ground. While the transference of peacekeeping duties in the Western Balkans from NATO to the EU went fairly smoothly, cooperation in theatres where both organizations are operating (i.e. when the Berlin Plus arrangements are not in place), such as Kosovo and Afghanistan, are more difficult. Cooperation between the EU's Rule of Law Mission in Kosovo (EULEX) and NATO's military crisis management force (KFOR) has faced opposition from Turkey. This has impacted negatively on the smooth running of international civilian and military support missions in Kosovo. The continued lack of formal agreements between the organizations has also limited the effectiveness of the EU police training mission (EUPOL) in Afghanistan, which overlaps with the mandate of NATO's International Stabilisation Force (ISAF) (see Chapter 8).

The 'strategic partnership' between the organizations is, at best, tenuous. EU dialogue with NATO is shallow and restricted; the organizations, on occasion, reinforce each other rhetorically and diplomatically. Julian Lindley-French's assessment of NATO-EU institutional meetings in 2003 is still relevant: they 'all too often . . . appear to resemble summer diplomatic garden parties in which polite small talk is exchanged while the weeds growing in the corner are ignored. There needs to be far more intensive interaction between officials of the two organizations on a day-to-day basis across the security spectrum' (Lindley-French 2003).

The relationship between the EU and NATO will continue to be characterized by the limitations imposed by high-level politics, as well as differences in crisis management approaches between the organizations. The EU's role in European security has been both bolstered and restrained by its crucial, but problematic, relationship with NATO. As long as member states continue to disagree about the scope and functions of the CSDP, this situation is likely to persist.

EU cooperation with the OSCE

The OSCE is an intergovernmental organization with a consensus-based, non-legally binding decision-making procedure, aiming primarily to prevent disputes between and within its participating states. It is therefore a different type of organization from the EU, which practices its foreign and security policy not within, but beyond, its borders. Unlike the OSCE, the EU has power and influence in its ability to attract members and offer tangible economic rewards for compliance with EU political and economic norms. However, EU states played a key role in the origins of the Conference for Security and Cooperation in Europe (CSCE – renamed 'organization' in 1995) in the 1970s, and the CSCE was one of the first platforms for coordination of European foreign policy within the 'European Polit-ical Cooperation' framework. Moreover, the agendas of the organizations' have overlapped in the post-Cold War era, to a much larger extent than the EU-NATO relationship. This means that there are functional crossovers between the organi-zations in the fields of diplomacy (e.g. delegations of representatives to mediate in disputes), civilian crisis management (e.g. border monitoring, police missions), and in more general objectives such as the promotion of democracy and human rights. All these activities can be described as conflict prevention. This cross-over of activities has had a significant impact on the respective roles of the organiza-tions in European security. The EU has gone from contributing to OSCE missions and discussing operating under OSCE mandates to operating independently as a competing conflict prevention actor in the pan-European area (Lynch 2009). This has taken place as a result of the development of EU civilian competences and because of a decline in political cooperation within the OSCE.

While the organizations worked together on an *ad hoc* basis throughout the 1990s, particular modalities for cooperation were not discussed until a concrete role in EU civilian crisis management had emerged. In February 2003, the Council of the European Union published Draft Conclusions on EU-OSCE cooperation in conflict prevention, crisis management and post-conflict rehabilitation (European Union 2003b). The document identified five key areas of 'enhanced cooperation': exchange of information and analyses, cooperation on fact-finding missions, coor-dination of diplomatic activity and statements (including consultations between special representatives), training and in-field cooperation. The modalities for cooperation are concentrated on the political level and include meetings between the 'Troikas' and briefings by the High Representative for CFSP and the Commis-sioner for external relations to the Permanent Council in Vienna. Also included is field level cooperation between EU personnel (e.g. High Representative, heads of EU crisis management operations, European Commission delegations) and OSCE field missions and personal representatives, and staff to staff contacts between the General Secretariat of the Council of the European Union, the European Commis-sion and the OSCE Secretariat and institutions. The first formal staff-level meeting between the OSCE Secretariat and EU institutions took place in Vienna in May 2003. Despite the formalization of EU and OSCE relations in 2003, 'enhanced' cooperation has not brought many visible results. The ongoing political dead-lock within the OSCE, largely as a result of the withdrawal of cooperation of the Russian Federation and several close allies, has contributed to blocking the devel-opment of an active EU-OSCE partnership (Stewart 2008b).

EU-OSCE cooperation in conflict prevention

On-site dialogue and cooperation between OSCE Mission offices and European Commission Delegations takes place in states where dual presence exits, although the extent of this cooperation is variable and difficult to measure. Most of the dialogue takes place in EU candidate or associate states, for example, formerly in the Baltics, and now mainly in the Balkans. In South Eastern Europe OSCE missions work with EU representatives, helping host countries in the context of the EU Stabilization and Association Agreements – for example on issues such as judicial reform, democratization, and human rights. According to the 2003 OSCE Annual Report, EU-OSCE cooperation 'has been successful in providing a climate conducive to stabilization, normalization, and ultimately integration in the Euro-Atlantic structures' (OSCE 2003). OSCE offices have contact with the EU Special Representative for the South Caucasus (appointed in 2003) and the Special Representative for Central Asia (appointed in 2006). The granting of EU candidate status resulted in the ending of OSCE missions in Estonia and Latvia. This pattern is being repeated in the Balkans: the OSCE mission to Croatia closed in 2007. Arguably, the withdrawal of OSCE missions in anticipation of EU membership has been premature in the Baltics, where there are ongoing problems with Russian minorities, and possibly in Croatia too (see Stewart 2008b). As the EU has expanded, the area in which the OSCE operates has shrunk. This, at least to some extent, has created tensions between the organizations, and a fear by OSCE personnel that the EU is taking over its role (Bailes *et al.* 2008).

Despite difficulties, cooperation between the organizations in the field for long term conflict prevention takes place, although it is difficult to assess the extent and effectiveness of this dialogue. Successful inter-organizational coordination will often depend on the individual diplomats and officials on-site. It may also depend on the nature and number of EU representatives on the ground: whether this is a Delegation, Special Representative, a head of a crisis management or monitoring mission, or some combination of these. This is important, since there is likely to be various points of contact, and successful coordination with the OSCE may depend on internal coordination among the EU actors present. The reform of EU overseas representation featured in the 2009 Lisbon Treaty (the EU External Action Service) could vastly improve the coordination of EU external policy in third countries, since it aims to bring together EU actors on one site. However, the devil is in the detail, and, at the time of writing, member states have not yet made any decisions about how it will work, or what services will be merged. In any case, national embassies will still continue to exist alongside EU Delegations.

The mechanisms for information exchange and cooperation for early warning between the OSCE's Conflict Prevention Centre and the EU SITCEN are largely *ad hoc* (Doyle 2002). This reflects the familiar problem of how to share potentially sensitive information. The OSCE's openness is not reciprocated by the Union. The EU receives restricted information from the OSCE but is unwilling to share information with non-EU/non-NATO members. OSCE officials have requested greater cooperation, but the EU (the PSC in particular) is reluctant to create more structured dialogue and prefers to work on an *ad hoc*, case-by-case basis. This, in fact, could be interpreted as going against the commitments made in the 2003 EU-OSCE Council Conclusions for enhanced cooperation in the exchange of information and analyses. The situation has not changed, and it does not bode well for the development of cooperation on fact-finding missions.

The EU's development of civilian crisis management competences has led to increased cooperation with the OSCE in election monitoring and police missions in particular. The EU has worked closely in crisis management with the OSCE in both Kosovo and Macedonia, where a partnership has been facilitated by the extent and nature of international involvement. In both these cases the international community has been instrumental in brokering peace agreements/ cease-fires, and administering their implementation. This has entailed meetings and dialogue between representatives of international organizations from the beginning. The international spotlight on these countries has encouraged and necessitated cooperation.

Cooperation in the South Caucasus and Central Asia has been slow to develop as a result of the lack of a clear EU strategy in these areas and as a consequence of resistance to organizational intervention by local governments. There is little indication that cooperation between the EU and the OSCE on the Balkans scale will take place again: especially since the withdrawal of the OSCE office and monitoring mission in the South Caucasus state of Georgia in 2008. The Russia-Georgian war in August 2008 led to the consolidation of Russian control over the Georgian *de facto* territories of Abkhazia and South Ossetia and the subsequent vetoing by Russia of OSCE and UN presence in the region. This leaves the relatively inexperienced EU Monitoring Mission[6] as the only international presence near the *de facto* states. Given the international community's failure to prevent the August war (despite clear warning signs of rising tensions between Georgia and Russia), the task of preventing further conflict will be challenging, and the future status of the *de facto* states is uncertain.

In summary, despite the fact that the EU and the OSCE practice conflict prevention activities in the same countries around Europe, the declining prestige of the OSCE has meant that formal modalities for cooperation have not been capitalized on. Moreover, the EU's prioritization of dialogue at the headquarters level between senior officials in Brussels and Vienna may be the wrong focus in light of the nature of OSCE activity, which is largely field-based. A pragmatic culture of cooperation needs to be fostered between actors on the ground, so that dialogue becomes common practice. High-level diplomacy at respective headquarters is not enough. The EU's development as a security actor has had negative implications for the OSCE's role, however unintended. Pan-European security would be better served by a common perception of partnership rather than competition.

Concluding remarks

The role of the EU in conflict prevention has been shaped by both internal factors and external context. By the end of the 1990s, EU member states and institutions had internal ambitions to develop a comprehensive approach to security, surpassing the EU's traditional civilian role. Conflict prevention was therefore developed as a policy reflecting the EU's changing role, and unifying external civilian and military ambitions. On paper, the EU has gradually developed a comprehensive conflict prevention policy, ranging from long-term to shorter-term competences. However, combining military and civilian means has been internally problematic, and evidence suggests that EU conflict prevention has been increasingly operationalized to the detriment of stability projection. Recent conflicts in the EU's neighbourhood demonstrate the need for a longer-term commitment to the prevention of disputes and indicate that the EU has failed to strike the correct balance between its short and long-term policy objectives.

The impact of the external context on the EU's role cannot be easily separated from internal drivers. In the years following the end of the Cold War, the EU was perceived as being crucial in the development of peace and stability in a reunited Europe, and the desire for the expansion of the EU's external competences was further catalysed by the failure to prevent the violent break-up of Yugoslavia. The EU followed other European organizations in its adoption of conflict prevention rhetoric and mechanisms, and the policy was identified as a key area for multi-lateral cooperation. However, inter-organizational cooperation progressed in an incremental and *ad hoc* manner, driven by necessity rather than by planning or multilateral consensus. The EU's internal divisions and complexities coupled with its ambitious external objectives have had a negative impact on cooperation with other security actors. EU dialogue with NATO is focused on short-term military objectives, lacks substance, and shows few signs of being a 'strategic partner-ship'. The EU's relationship with the OSCE should be positive, given the long-term conflict prevention remit of the OSCE. Yet EU cooperation with the OSCE is not adequately comprehensive, despite the convergence of the organizations' objectives.

The EU's relationship with both the OSCE and NATO therefore tends to reflect short-term priorities rather than support longer-term objectives. The restricted nature of cooperation also prevents the EU from fulfilling its potential role as the leading European security organization, and damages prospects for long-term pan-European stability. The EU could enhance its role and make a more significant contribution to conflict prevention by extending the depth and range of cooperation with other European actors. This is particularly important at a time when international security cooperation is strained because of the breakdown of cooperation within the OSCE, and the proliferation of conflicts close to the EU's borders. This reorientation would, however, require member states to make some fundamental decisions about the scope and purpose of EU foreign policy, and to find consensus on divisive issues, such as enlargement and EU relations with the Russian Federation. Only then will the EU be able to secure its role as the leading conflict prevention actor in the pan-European area.

Notes

1 Conflict prevention is a notoriously difficult concept to define (see also Chapter 1; Stewart 2003; Ackermann 2003). EU conflict prevention capacities are broadly defined here and categorised as follows: long-term (structural) policy aimed at addressing root causes of conflict, medium-term early warning and analysis competences, and finally short-term civilian and/or military crisis management (operational).

2 Previously to its reincarnation as the European Union in the Treaty on European Union (TEU) in 1991, the organization was known as the European Community (EC) or the European Economic Community (EEC).

3 The WEU is a military alliance based on the Brussels Treaty signed in 1948 by the UK, France, Belgium, the Netherlands, and Luxembourg (and joined by West Germany and Italy in 1954).
4 The OSCE was known as the Conference for Security and Cooperation in Europe (CSCE) until December 1994.
5 The other areas are defence and security sector reform, strengthening the rule of law, the threat of terrorism, border security and management and arms control and the removal of small arms.
6 The EU Presidency brokered a ceasefire after the five-day war and sent several hundred civilian monitors to patrol the borders between the de facto states and Georgia proper. The Russian Federation has recognised Abkhazia and South Ossetia as independent states, increased its troop presence in both regions, and has yet to pull back its troops to the pre-conflict lines, despite agreeing to this in the ceasefire agreement.

Part II
Institutions

4 Introducing governance arrangements for EU conflict prevention and crisis management operations

A historical institutionalist perspective

Petar Petrov

Introduction

The development of the European integration project has always been tightly related to the design and development of its unique institutional architecture (Peterson and Shackleton 2002: 2). A policy domain where existing institutions have been reformed and new ones created from scratch in the last couple of decades has been the Common Foreign and Security Policy (CFSP), including the Common Security and Defence Policy (CSDP). This chapter looks from a historical institutionalist perspective at the institutional dimension in the development of the CSDP – the latter is seen in this chapter as a manifestation of the long-debated idea of introducing robust conflict prevention and crisis management capabilities in the EU's foreign policy toolbox (Howorth 2007a; Cameron 2007). Thus, when addressing the introduction of the CSDP as a distinctive policy area between 1999 and 2000, this chapter in fact analyses the institutional logic behind the introduction of governance arrangements for EU conflict prevention and crisis management operations in that period. The leading argument is that the introduction of these governance arrangements between 1999 and 2000 came as a result of an evolving and path dependent process rather than on the grounds of carefully planned and executed design. Informed by insights from historical institutionalism, this argument builds on the understanding that after the unsuccessful attempts for the institutionalization of European security and defence cooperation in the 1950s and 1960s, a process of incremental policy and institutional change developed from the early 1980s onwards and visibly intensified through a series of critical moments between 1991 and 1998. In the context of another critical moment – the crisis in Kosovo (1998–99) – the formal introduction of the CSDP came as a result of a combination of complex stimuli for reform, which built on each other's effects and led to a major policy development (critical juncture) that crystallized in the agreements in Cologne (1999), Helsinki (1999) and Nice (2000). In all this, the institutional factor mattered in providing the structural context and the expertise for introducing the new governance arrangements for conflict prevention and crisis management operations.

Along the lines of the new institutionalist scholarship (Bulmer 1994: 355; Hall and Taylor 1996: 938; Armstrong and Bulmer 1998: 52), this analysis defines institutions as both formal structures based on written formal procedures and informal bodies based on internal norms and conventions which provide unwritten, but equally important rules of behaviour and codes of conduct.

First, the chapter presents the historical institutionalist perspective on institutional change and development over time. Second, it addresses the security projects in the 1950s and 1960s and the re-introduction of security and defence matters on the European political agenda from the mid-1980s up until 2000. In doing so the chapter offers a historical institutionalist analysis of the main factors that led to the formal introduction of governance arrangements for EU conflict prevention and crisis management operations in the second pillar. Last, the analysis briefly looks at the latest developments in the governance structure of the CSDP and offers conclusions on the role of the EU as a conflict prevention and crisis management actor.

A historical institutionalist perspective on institutional change

This analysis supports the view that any research on the development of particular set of governance arrangements has to take into account the process of institutional change and development over time (Armstrong and Bulmer 1998). The necessity of an approach which is sensitive to both the historical process and the policy institutional dimension justifies the application of historical institutionalism. Historical institutionalism is not regarded as a new grand theory, but rather as a middle-range or meso-level theory, capable to unravel many processes in the daily EU policy-making, which might remain hidden from the research agenda of neofunctionalism or intergovernmentalism (Thelen and Steinmo 1992; Bulmer 1994, 1998; Peterson and Shackleton 2002).

Compared to both the rational choice and sociological strands of new institutionalism, the value of the historical institutionalist approach is that it focuses on the very institutional dimensions of a particular policy area and aims at capturing the temporal and structural rationale behind its development (Thelen and Steinmo 1992; Hall and Taylor 1996; Schmidt *et al.* 1999). It focuses on the institutions themselves and traces their unique historical development and the way in which this influences both actors' preferences and policy outcomes (Schmidt *et al.* 1999: 2). Pierson (2004) particularly emphasizes the ability of historical analysis to present a 'moving picture' of institutional development, which is contrasted to the 'snap-shot' approach of the rational-choice theories and the rational-choice institutionalism respectively.

Although scholars rightly observe the macro-historical bias in historical institutionalism (Schmidt *et al.* 1999) and its preoccupation with path dependency and institutional stability (Thelen and Steinmo 1992; Gorges 2001), recent research has demonstrated that transformative changes may occur based on micro-scale reasons such as incremental institutional adaptation through accumulation and reinterpretation of norms and practices, increased actors' interactions and changes in the cultural aspects of institutions (Burch *et al.* 2003). It is namely the ability of historical institutionalism to present a moving picture of institutional change and development *over time* by grasping the temporal dimension of institutions that informs its application in this analysis.

Between path dependency and incrementalism

From a strictly historical institutionalist viewpoint, once established, institutional arrangements are usually stable and hard to change. This is thanks to the prevalence of path dependency in the course of institutional development (Pollack 1996; Pierson 1996; Peters 1999). Path dependency rests on the observation that initial institutional choices 'become self-reinforcing over time' (Pierson 1996: 145). Closely related is the notion of institutional lock-ins described as situations in which institutions and policies become rigid and very difficult to alter, even in the face of a changing policy environment (Pollack 1996: 432–42).

However, scholars have been aware that even in the context of a stable polity, change may still occur through adaptation – seen as adding new activities (or dropping old ones) without examining (or questioning) the fundamental premises of the original design or worrying about their coherence with existing ends (Haas 1990: 3). This denotes the process of incremental institutional change, viewed as one of the usual ways in which institutions evolve (Thelen and Steinmo 1992; March and Olsen 1996; Burch *et al.* 2003). Alternatively, change may also occur as a result of a major shift or crisis that leads to a systemic shock to the polity (Collier and Collier 1991). Such a change is usually associated with the notion of innovation, which denotes not simply adjustments to, but an explicit alteration of existing structures (March 1991: 71).

Critical moments and junctures

Closely related to the aforementioned is the notion of critical juncture. It symbolizes the moments when substantial institutional change takes place, creating a specific context or a 'branching point' that marks the beginning of a qualitatively new path of institutional development (Hall and Taylor 1996: 942). Collier and Collier define critical junctures as 'a period of significant change, which typically occurs in distinct ways in different countries [. . .] and which is hypothesized to produce distinct legacies' (1991: 29). Critical junctures can be triggered by either external factors (e.g. crisis brought by wars) or internal ones (ongoing institutional developments and growing density of institutional structures/procedures) and can vary in duration from relatively quick transitions to longer policy or regime periods (Collier and Collier 1991: 32).

Bulmer and Burch take a step further by distinguishing between a critical moment and critical juncture (1998). The former is present when 'a perceived opportunity arises for significant change' – this is usually in the context of an event which raises a general expectation that a significant change will follow (Burch *et al.* 2003: 8). Formerly rigid institutional patterns come under pressure and become more malleable. Actors within an institution may be expected to acquire a new or improved position before the 'window of opportunity' provided by the critical moment is closed (Burch *et al.* 2003: 8; cf. Thelen and Steinmo 1992: 17). This opportunity might not be realized and exploited, in which case the moment might appear to be just one stage in an overall process of self-contained incremental change. However, if 'such opportunities are realized', this marks the emergence of a critical juncture insofar as the latter incorporates 'a clear departure from previously established patterns' (Bulmer and Burch 1998: 7; cf. Burch *et al.* 2003: 8).

Incremental transformative change

In addition, there are studies of the 'uncharted analytical space' between evolutionary and revolutionary change, discovering that incremental institutional change may also lead to transformative results over time. Burch *et al.* (2003) studied the handling of the UK European policy under the ongoing project of devolution in Britain and suggested the bridging concept of incremental transformative change – a process of incremental developments which 'through accumulation and interaction may bring transformative changes on institutions and institutional frameworks' over time (Burch *et al.* 2003: 3, 7). In other words, 'institutional changes which are incremental in nature may accumulate in such a way that the sum of these changes is to establish a change in pattern distinctively and qualitatively different from that which previously existed' (Burch *et al.* 2003: 8).

Overall, the concept of incremental change and the notions of critical moments and junctures are important insofar as they offer a more nuanced reading of institutional development over time. The analysis sees the three concepts as complementary, since within periods of incremental developments major external shocks (critical moments) may still take place. Moreover, this may lead to the intensification of ongoing institutional changes and ultimately to the crystallization of a substantial institutional reform (critical juncture). The previous incremental changes may play an important role because they may have created fertile ground for greater acceptance among institutions and political actors of the introduction of far reaching reforms. These historical institutionalist concepts form the backbone of the analytical framework that leads the empirical analysis discussed later.

Key moments in the development of Europe's security and defence outlook: 1952–2000

The CSDP and related governance arrangements for conflict prevention and crisis management operations were formally established by the Treaty of Nice in December 2000. However, this did not happen in isolation but in relation to a number of projects and institutional developments in this policy domain. The process, which opened the way for introduction of distinctive conflict prevention and crisis management tools, was not linear and planned, but slow, contested, and incremental that later visibly intensified to produce a decisive policy change. After a period of stasis, this process was reinvigorated in the 1980s, went through a series of critical moments in the 1990s and culminated as a critical juncture with the agreements in Cologne (1999), Helsinki (1999) and Nice (2000) that established new governance arrangements for conflict prevention and crisis management operations. The analysis later presents the historical narrative of these developments and links it with the historical institutionalist perspective on institutional change and development over time.

The European Defence Community project

It is important to note from the outset that the matters of crisis management and conflict prevention per se, as introduced by Cologne (1999) and the Gothenburg (2001) European Councils respectively (see Chapter 1 in this volume), did not feature as defined objectives in the projects and initiatives suggested between the 1950s and the mid-1990s. However, these projects are explicitly addressed in the analysis later as they offer the opportunity to observe the dynamics in the overall development of the European security and defence cooperation. This is important as it sheds light on the type and character of the institutional logic that led to the decisive institutional reform between 1999 and 2000.

In the early 1950s, the growing pressure for finding ways to provide for Germany's and Italy's post-WW2 rearmament and re-integration to the emerging West European security framework created a suitable context for the idea of establishing a European Defence Community (EDC). It was largely a French initiative, launched by Jean Monnet and the French Foreign Minister René Pleven. The Pleven Plan, which gave the substance for the EDC treaty (27 May 1952), envisaged the establishment of a purely supranational community in the field of security and defence. The organizational framework consisted of an integrated European army; common planning; integrated command; an integrated defence industry and a common budget (Fursdon 1980). The envisaged institutions were a Board of Commissioners (equivalent to today's European Commission), a Council of Ministers, an Assembly and a Court of Justice. They possessed respectively the executive, coordination, monitoring, controlling and judicial powers, which would have made them influential political actors capable of governing the EDC far beyond the member states' reach (Fursdon 1980; Nuttall 1992).

The fact that the proposed EDC was going to be organized on a purely federalist basis was a condition, which decisively alienated Britain from signing the treaty and remained a thorny issue in the ratification process (Fursdon 1980; Duke 2000). This, together with several crucial domestic and international developments,[1] led to a decisive reorientation of the French position regarding the EDC treaty. Eventually, the French National Assembly voted against the EDC treaty on 30 August 1954, which in practice stopped the ratification process and put the project for an integrated European army on hold.

The Western European Union

With the failure of the EDC, the issue of the German and Italian rearmament and reintegration in the Western European security and defence framework remained unresolved. However, it was not long before a suitable formula was suggested by the British Prime Minister Anthony Eden – to use the provisions of the Brussels Treaty (1948) as a basis for creating a European organization competent in security and defence issues. The legal framework of the new organization was adopted by the Nine-Powers conference held in London and Paris (September-October 1954) (Duke 2000: 38). Among other developments (the end of the German occupation; and invitation to Germany to join NATO), the conference amended and broadened the original Brussels Treaty to provide for the accession of Germany and Italy, and thus created the Western European Union(WEU) (Modified Brussels Treaty 1954; Duke 2000: 39).

By definition, the WEU was a defence Union and similarly to NATO, one of its most important features was the provision of mutual defence guarantees should any member state be attacked by an external aggressor. However, Britain, the US and the majority of the European Community member states considered NATO as the main institutional framework responsible for the security and defence of Europe, while the WEU was mostly seen as the convenient intergovernmental forum for discussing security matters with Germany and Italy. After fulfilling its immediate tasks of guaranteeing the German rearmament and integration in the Euro-Atlantic security order, the WEU was gradually marginalized and lost political visibility up until the mid-1980s (Duke 2000: 55; Nuttall 1992).

The Fouchet Plans

Another attempt to organize the European states into their own security organization was initiated in the early 1960s by the French president De Gaulle in the framework of the Fouchet Plans. The initiative aimed at establishing a European political community, covering security and defence policy, based on purely intergovernmental principles (as opposed to the federalist structure of the EDC). Consultations with NATO and the possibility to include new member states became part of the 'Fouchet I' Plan which led to its approval (Nuttall 1992; Duke 2000). However, at the beginning of 1962, the French President personally made crucial amendments, removing the references to NATO and the accession of new member states. The result was the 'Fouchet II' Plan. This unexpected turn, together with the French veto on Britain's application for membership of the European Economic Community in 1963, alienated the other member states and led to the failure of the proposed intergovernmental political cooperation.

In summary, for a considerable period of time – between the mid-1960s and early 1990s – the issues of security and defence were not legally endorsed as an integral part of the wider process of European integration. Moreover, the domains of conflict prevention and crisis management were not even mentioned in the proposed projects in this period. However, several important observations regarding the institutional logic behind the development of European security and defence cooperation could be made at this point. The impasses reached with the demise of the EDC and the Fouchet Plans led to the establishment of a particular policy and institutional outlook that effectively placed the domain of security and defence cooperation outside the European integration process. The member states were reluctant to institutionalize such a policy in either supranational or purely intergovernmental governance framework. In addition, the US completely dominated the provision of security and defence in Europe in this period. Thus, NATO remained the main forum for discussing issues of security and defence, whereby the WEU remained a convenient, but largely dormant organization. As a result, EC member states did not discuss matters of security and defence within a structured format of political cooperation until the mid-1980s. However, although this may seem to have introduced inertia and immobility in the domain of foreign policy cooperation as a whole, this analysis claims that there was another, much more nuanced process that soon started to evolve. This was a process of incremental and informal institutional development, which started with the re-introduction of the security and defence issues on the EC/EU political agenda from the mid-1980s onwards. In particular, it became visible in the context of the European Political Cooperation (1970–90) (Reynolds 2005; Smith, M.E. 2004b).

The European Political Cooperation

The European Political Cooperation (EPC) started as an informal and strictly intergovernmental process among the member states aimed at better coordinating their responses to important international events. In its first 17 years, the EPC operated under the 'report-format approach' and was more 'a private agreement among the foreign ministers' without any legal codification (Nuttall 1992: 11).[2] However, the more the EPC evolved, the more visible was the increase of coordinated European actions in the field of foreign policy. Particularly in the 1980s, the EPC activities expanded in both number and functional scope (medium and long-term common positions; managing crises and resolving conflicts) and gradually started to include security issues. The member states engaged in security cooperation in the context of the Conference for Security and Cooperation in Europe (CSCE) and even considered taking security-related actions 'against a number of non-EU states' (Smith, M.E. 2004 b: 52). These developments, together with the reinvigoration of the WEU in 1984,[3] demonstrated a gradual re-introduction of security issues on the European political agenda that steadily built up momentum in the following years.

The peak of the EPC process was marked by its legal codification in the Single European Act (SEA) in 1986, which formally recognized it as a part of the overall EC development. For the first time, the Community policies and the EPC were put under a single legal framework, although they were still regarded as distinct and parallel institutional arrangements (Nuttall 1992; Duke 2001). A small permanent Secretariat (five national seconded diplomats and a head) was established in Brussels (Dijkstra 2008: 5). At that time, it was separate from the EC Council Secretariat and mainly had the task of providing administrative assistance to the Presidency in implementing the EPC activities (SEA 1986: Art.30.10g). In addition, the member states agreed on introducing closer cooperation mechanisms between the EPC machinery on one hand and the Commission and the European Parliament

(EP) on the other (SEA, Arts.30.3b and 30.4). The SEA particularly mentioned the security aspects of the EPC emphasizing that cooperation in matters of European security was integral to the development of a European foreign policy identity (SEA 1986: Art.30.6a).

Thus despite the explicitly cautious approach in the 1970s and 1980s, the security aspects of foreign policy cooperation were addressed in the context of the late EPC process and then officially mentioned in the Single European Act. In the context of the reinvigoration of the WEU in 1984, this tendency was further strengthened by the WEU's formal endorsement as the defence arm of the European Union in the Maastricht Treaty.

Maastricht: a 'critical moment' for introducing the ESDP?

With the Treaty on European Union (TEU), signed in Maastricht in 1991, the idea for developing European security and defence policy received stronger impetus. The negotiations leading to the signing of the treaty happened in the context of the Gulf War and the outbreak of the first inter-ethnic conflicts in former Yugoslavia. The US provided the bulk of the military and logistical assets and capabilities for handling these crises while the EU member states were largely unable to contribute with adequate forces and logistics. This demonstrated the strong dependence of the Europeans on the US and NATO which created strong stimuli for the introduction of security and defence components to the proposed Political Union in the 1991 Intergovernmental conference (Duke 2000: 82, 85). The treaty formally established the Common Foreign and Security Policy and mentioned for a first time in the history of European integration the possible framing of a common defence policy, which in the future might lead to a common defence (TEU 1992: Title V, Art.J.4.1). The WEU was recognized as 'an integral part of the development of the Union' and as capable 'to elaborate and implement decisions and actions of the Union which have defence implications' (TEU 1992: Art. J.4.2).

This strengthened language in the treaty clearly demonstrated the growing importance of security and defence issues. Compared to the developments from the mid-1980s, the questions addressed in 1991 regarded not simply the strategic nature of security and defence matters – i.e. whether they should become part of the broader European foreign policy cooperation as debated in 1986. This time, the institutional aspects of the new policy were also addressed – i.e. whether the EU should take over WEU's structures, procedures and wider expertise in crisis management and what institutional adaptations and/or innovations were needed within the existing European institutions.

Certain institutional adaptations regarding the CFSP domain took place in the European Commission. Its position and importance in the CFSP process were much strengthened compared to the EPC period as it could now have a greater say in the decision making, implementation, funding, ensuring compliance and evaluation of various CFSP activities (Smith, M.E. 2004 b: 187). In response, the departing President Delors, converted the EPC Unit of the Secretariat General into a new Directorate General for External Political Relations (DG IA) entrusted to handle all EU external political relations including the CFSP (Spence 2006: 370). In 1995, Commission President Jacques Santer, further strengthened the Commission administrative capacity in the CFSP domain by reorganizing all the external relations DGs along geographical lines and giving them competence over the economic and political aspects in their respective geographic area (Spence 2006: 187). Similarly, the EPC Secretariat received broader responsibilities – assisting not only the Presidency, but also the Council of Ministers. It was merged with the Council Secretariat, thus becoming 'a Community institution [and] a central administrative resource' in CFSP matters (Spence 2006: 188). More specifically, the previous EPC secretariat was integrated in the newly created Directorate General for External Relations (DG-E) and became known as the CFSP Unit, responsible for the political aspects of the CFSP (Dijkstra 2008: 5).

The institutional developments discussed earlier clearly demonstrated the growing re-introduction of the issues of security and defence on the EU political agenda and the related creation of new structures and procedures. Seen from the EPC perspective, these developments were visibly incremental as they built on each other and created a permissive context for the introduction of further changes in the domain of security and defence.

As discussed earlier, the historical institutionalist concept of 'critical moments' denotes the emergence of events and/or circumstances that create strong opportunities for institutional reforms to occur, which may or may not materialize into a substantive policy change. At the beginning of the 1990s, the end of the Cold War and the outbreak of the first conflicts in former Yugoslavia exposed the need for the European Community to strengthen its political presence in the international arena. The logical next step was the negotiation of the Maastricht Treaty and with it – the creation of a political union, the introduction of the CFSP and the unprecedented mentioning of the possible establishment of a European security and defence policy. In the context of external conflicts and already ongoing re-introduction of security and defence matters, the member states started to increasingly acknowledge the need to strengthen their foreign and security credentials on the international arena. In this context, the Maastricht Treaty could be seen as a critical moment for the introduction of robust crisis management and conflict prevention arrangements. Yet, this possibility failed to materialize due to a lack of internal stimuli for reform (sufficient institutional expertise and explicit political will among the member states) at this stage. During the negotiations of the Amsterdam Treaty (1996–97), the momentum for making practical steps in this direction grew once again.

The Treaty of Amsterdam: introducing further institutional changes in the CFSP domain

The amendments to the TEU agreed at the Amsterdam Summit in 1997 introduced further improvements in the existing institutional arrangements regarding the CFSP. The negotiations leading to the new Treaty took place in the context of continuing ethnic and territorial conflicts in former Yugoslavia, which again painfully demonstrated the inability of the EU to step up militarily and offer leadership in crisis management (Jorgensen 2002: 211).

Five years before Amsterdam, the WEU ministers agreed on the Petersberg Declaration (June1992), which defined the types of operations that the WEU was prepared to undertake both independently and under the aegis of the EU. These became known as the Petersberg tasks and ranged from conflict prevention to robust crisis management missions: 'humanitarian and rescue tasks, peacekeeping tasks, tasks of combat forces in crisis management, including peacemaking' (Petersberg Declaration, 1992: Part II, 4). The Amsterdam Treaty fully incorporated the Petersberg tasks in Article 17(2), which in practice meant that the EU explicitly defined and formalized the type and scope of its future crisis management and conflict prevention operations. It also envisaged closer coordination and consultation with NATO which was a continuation of an earlier initiative launched at the NATO Berlin Summit on 3 June 1996. In Berlin, the two defence organizations signed an agreement (Berlin Agreement) according to which the WEU could borrow military assets, command capabilities and logistics for conducting crisis management operations on behalf of the EU.

The institutional set-up of the CFSP was further elaborated. On one hand, the member states agreed on the introduction of the post of High Representative for the CFSP, who was also appointed as the Secretary General of the Council Secretariat (HR/SG). The role of the High Representative has been very important in introducing a stronger representation of the Union in the field of foreign and security policy and for facilitating consensus on policy issues within the Council (Howorth 2007a: 66). On the other hand, the treaty established the Policy planning and early warning unit (also known as the Policy unit) with the main function to assist the High Representative in analysing situations and suggesting policy options in both the CFSP and CSDP matters (Treaty of Amsterdam 1997, Declaration 6). It was set up in parallel to the Secretariat's CFSP Directorate and started functioning as an extended cabinet of the High Representative (Missiroli 2004: 62). The Policy unit was seen as a valuable addition to the CFSP (and later to the ESDP) as it professionalized the analysis of external developments and potential crises (Missiroli 2004; Howorth 2007a).

The Commission responded to the new developments in this domain by introducing relevant reorganizations in its external relations portfolios. The most significant was the creation of a separate CFSP Directorate General, widely known nowadays as DG RELEX, which replaced the previous DG IA. DG RELEX consisted of four new units whose core tasks directly corresponded to the type of activities the EU was preparing to undertake under the Petersberg tasks (Spence 2006: 372).[4]

Overall, by 1998 one could observe a visible process of increased discussion of the security aspects of foreign policy cooperation and relevant institutional developments in this respect. Developments such as the formalization of the WEU as the defence arm of the EU, the inclusion of the Petersberg tasks as Article 17 TEU; the expansion of the Council Secretariat and the Commission plus the creation of the High Representative and the Policy unit denoted the continuous development of incremental institutional changes. Moreover, these changes kept the momentum of institutional and functional expansion in the domain of foreign and security policy alive and thus continued creating a favourable context for the institutionalization of crisis management and conflict prevention arrangements.

However, the negotiations leading to the Amsterdam Treaty represented another critical moment when decisive institutional change (introducing specific policy instruments, procedures and structures for conflict prevention and crisis management operations) could potentially occur, but in fact did not materialize. Similarly to the situation in Maastricht, among the main reasons behind the failure of the Amsterdam Treaty to introduce decisive reforms was the fact that despite the ongoing incremental developments in the domain of security and defence matters, until 1998, the CSDP project lacked a decisive internal momentum that could have transformed the early critical moments into a critical juncture. The combination between growing institutional expertise and emergence of strong political leadership would have meant bringing the area of foreign and security policy onto a distinctively different level of institutional development – i.e. one comprising the military aspects of crisis management and arrangements for coherent use of cross-pillar economic and political instruments of conflict prevention.

The St Malo 'revolution': just another critical moment?

Between 1999 and 2000 a qualitatively different situation developed in which internal and external stimuli coupled to produce not simply a possibility for significant change but namely an opportunity that was practically realized (Bulmer and Burch 1998). A new critical moment emerged in the aftermath of the crisis in Kosovo. The latter served as a strong external stimulus for the EU to undertake decisive institutional reforms within the CFSP domain because most member states were disappointed with the EU inability to step in militarily and offer viable alternatives to the US preferred option of air strikes in Kosovo (Grant 1999; Hoffmann 2000).

A decisive role in this respect was played by the Franco-British relationship that crystallized in the Joint Declaration on European Defence, signed by the French President Jacques Chirac and the new British Prime Minister Tony Blair, in Saint Malo (4 December 1998). The declaration emphasized that the international aspirations of the EU needed to be backed up by 'credible military forces, the means to decide to use them and a readiness to do so in order to respond to international crises' (St Malo Declaration §1 and 2, in Rutten 2001: 8). In particular, it pointed to the need of developing relevant European capabilities for the planning, command and conduct of 'military action where the Alliance as a whole is not engaged' (Rutten 2001: 8–9). An important contextual factor for the development of active Franco-British cooperation in the CSDP domain was the Kosovo crisis (March 1998 – June 1999). Reportedly, both France and the UK expressed frustration and saw the lack of EU military capabilities as the main reason for the Union's weak performance in the crisis (Bono 2002: 29–30; also Grant 1999; Hoffmann 2000).

St Malo represented a real breakthrough in the development of the ESDP. The summit has been defined as 'a watershed' event (Howorth 2000a: 769), which represented a 'sea change' (Rutten 2001: 8) and 'a profound re-configuration' (Whitman 1999: 9) of the British attitude and principle position to the development of the ESDP. Apart from ending the UK consistent opposition to any discussions of defence matters (Howorth 2001: 769), St Malo also demonstrated that the UK government under Blair accepted the urgency and legitimacy of an EU security capacity on both political and military levels.[5] In addition, the British support for the creation of the ESDP opened new possibilities for the actual development of the EU as a security actor having both the institutional capacity to take political decisions and the necessary military capacity to implement them (Howorth 2000a; 2000b; 2007 a).

Apart from the context provided by the crisis in Kosovo, all this came in a moment when the idea of developing a stronger political role for the Union on the international arena was rapidly gaining greater support within the European political circles (Howorth 2007a). It also coincided with the growing popularity of the concepts of humanitarian intervention, conflict prevention and crisis management, which particularly appealed to EU's affinity to 'multilateral internationalism' (Howorth 2007a: 54). In such a context, many in Europe accepted the idea that the development of strong crisis management capabilities – to deal with regional and intrastate conflicts – and not the development of a European army responsible for the territorial defence of Europe was at stake (Howorth 2007a: 55–57).

In short, the combination between the external stimuli provided by the Kosovo crisis and the ability of the Union to capitalize on these opportunities (i.e. active Franco-British leadership) became instrumental for reaching important political decisions in the following couple of years. The convergence of interests among the EU member states happened in the context of the continuing institutional developments since the 1990s onwards and led to further intensification of the debate on formally institutionalising robust conflict prevention and crisis management arrangements. From Vienna through Cologne and Helsinki, to Sintra, Santa Maria da Feira and Nice both the military and civilian aspects of crisis management and conflict prevention were increasingly present on the EU's political agenda and dealt with by both the representative and expert CFSP structures. The issue density was high and every Council meeting (both formal and informal) and/or relevant expert committee in the Council Secretariat dealt with a growing number of policy, institutional and technical proposals. The latter were important as they provided the expert basis for the discussions and further specified the concrete proposals regarding the role of the EU in conflict prevention and crisis management. This expert input then re-appeared in all European Council Summits between 1999 and 2000 thus providing the substance of the political decisions taken in this period.

The post-St Malo effect: Towards a critical juncture

The European Council in Vienna (10–11 December 1998), welcomed 'the new impetus given to the debate on a common European policy on security and defence' and stated the need of reinforcing the CFSP with 'credible operational capabilities' (Presidency Conclusions (76), in Rutten 2001: 13). In the next two years, the decisions in Vienna were backed up by a series of EU summits that demonstrated an unprecedented consensus introducing robust EU conflict prevention and crisis management capabilities.

The Cologne Summit (3–4 June 1999) defined a number of institutional and procedural steps for achieving this goal: the takeover of the WEU; the introduction of regular meetings of the General Affairs Council including the defence ministers; setting-up new politico-military bodies and specialized military committees; elaborating criteria for usage of either NATO or national headquarters for EU-led operations, etc. (Cologne European Council, Presidency Report, in Rutten 2001: 44). These decisions were reaffirmed at the next EU Summit held in Helsinki (10–11 December 1999) where the member states approved in principle the creation of new political and military bodies – established as interim bodies from March 2000 – responsible for the planning and implementation of crisis management operations.[6] The Summit introduced the Helsinki Headline Goal for creating EU Rapid Reaction Forces (RRF) by 2003, which were largely seen as a pool of forces and capabilities that the EU could resort to if and when needed (Oakes 2000). Also, under the insistence of the neutral and specifically the Nordic member states, Helsinki called for the establishment of a 'non-military crisis management mechanism [. . .] to coordinate and make more effective the various civilian means and resources in parallel with the military ones' (Helsinki European Council, Presidency Conclusions, Part II, par.28).

Two months after the Summit, the EU defence ministers met in Sintra, Portugal to discuss the steps to be taken in achieving the Headline Goal. They adopted the Toolbox Paper and the Food for Thought Paper both of which specified the key technical aspects of the Helsinki Headline Goal (see Rutten 2001: 94–117; Bono 2002). The background preparation of these documents demonstrated the early signs of a developing informal working relationship among experts and officials across EU capitals and the experts situated in Brussels regarding security issues – e.g. in the summer of 1999 James Hatfield from the British Ministry of Defence initiated the expert process of specifying the Helsinki decisions (the Hatfield exercise) (Rutten 2001: 94).

The next European Council in Santa Maria da Feira (19–20 June 2000) affirmed the goal of developing both civilian and military means for crisis management and approved the setting-up of a Committee for Civilian Aspect of Crisis Management. The importance of this Summit was that by setting the civilian dimension of the ESDP and deciding on the areas of cooperation between NATO and the EU, it finalized the conceptual background and main principles of the new policy area. This opened the way for the formal introduction of the CSDP by the Treaty of Nice.

The Nice Treaty on European Union was agreed by the Heads of state and government between 7 and 9 December 2000. The painful realization of the military ineffectiveness of the EU during the Kosovo crisis and the unprecedented support to the CSDP by Britain resulted in a situation in which 'the EU could, with no controversy and in the shortest time, reach a unanimous decision on the new ESDP committees' (Müller-Brandeck-Bocquet 2002: 266). The Treaty endorsed all previous suggestions on the ESDP, and thus substantially strengthened the role of EU role in this domain (Bono 2002: 20).[7] One of the significant Treaty changes in this respect was that the EU officially took over the WEU functions in crisis management and became directly responsible in security and defence matters (Duke 2001: 159). The takeover of the WEU also meant that the EU officially imported some of its relevant structures (the Satellite Centre in Torrejon and the Institute for Security Studies) and its expertise for planning and conduct of crisis management operations.[8]

In ensuring that the EU was able to effectively administer and manage its new security and defence tasks, the member states expanded the Council General Secretariat and officially endorsed the Helsinki decisions for the creation of interim politico-military structures (Political and Security Committee, Military Committee and Military Staff) with a view of making them permanent in due course (Duke 2001: 160; Juncos and Reynolds 2007). Directorate General E within the Council General Secretariat merged its two distinct units for foreign policy (trade/development and CFSP) into a bigger structure – Directorate General External Economic Relations, Politico-Military Affairs (Dijkstra 2008: 8). It also expanded in terms of personnel and new/restructured directorates, working groups and units responsible for administering and providing expert advice in the preparatory, planning, conduct, and monitoring stages of EU-led crisis management and conflict prevention operations (for more on the Council Secretariat's units and functions see Chapter 5). The continuous expansion of both the Commission and the Council Secretariat from the 1991 onwards, coupled with the explicit creation of new specialized politico-military bodies was one of the explicit signs that Nice moved the debate on the CSDP on a distinctively different level – the process of its actual institutionalization (Oakes 2001: 20).

The new structures, together with the High Representative, the Policy Unit, the Situation Centre, the Satellite Centre, the Committee for Civilian Aspects of Crisis Management and the new/reformed directorates and units in the expanded Council General Secretariat represented the main structures that formed the basis of the governance machinery for conflict prevention and crisis management operations. In addition, the General Secretariat circulated among the member states' delegations at Nice suggestion for standard crisis management procedures which were fully adopted later (Council of the European Union 2003b). Moreover, shortly after Nice, in the context of the early planning of the first EU-led military operations, an *ad hoc* and informal body for intra-institutional coordination – the Crisis Response Coordination Team – became part of the governance arrangements for conflict prevention and crisis management operations. Initially, this body operated under largely unwritten procedures and codes of conduct and only later its role was spelled out in an internal document of the Council Secretariat (Council of the European Union 2003b: Annex 2 to Annex 31–34; also Gordon 2006: 352). Similarly, in the context of the first EU-led military crisis management operations (EUFOR Concordia and Artemis) other structures and procedures first operated on *ad hoc* and informal basis and only later were formalized. In fact, this movement from *ad hoc-ness* and informality to stabilization and formalization of structures and procedures was one of the main characteristics of the early process of institutionalization of the CSDP governance arrangements. Examples include the EU-NATO and EU-UN liaison bodies and coordination procedures in 2002–3 and the EU Staff Group in SHAPE HQ, firstly established on an *ad hoc* basis for EUFOR Concordia and later formalized for EUFOR Althea.[9]

The unprecedented creation of permanent structures and standard operating procedures shed light on the progress that the Union made since the St Malo Declaration. The continued expansion and specialization of both the Council and the Commission in the domain of conflict prevention and crisis management together with the expert input behind the decisions in Cologne, Helsinki and Nice undoubtedly demonstrated that the continuous institutional developments and specialization were contextual factors that mattered for bringing substance behind the governance arrangements for conflict prevention and crisis management operations.

In addressing the main argument of this analysis, it becomes clear that the emergence of the EU as a conflict prevention and crisis management actor was not the result of a linear and carefully planned process, but an incremental and often contested process of institutional development over time. In short, over a considerable period, institutional incrementalism led to expansion of the expertise of the Commission and the Council Secretariat in conflict prevention and crisis management and stable presence of the security and defence issues on the EU's political agenda. Thus, it could be argued that the increased institutional development and specialization from the 1980s onwards persisted, and grew over time thus creating a dynamic of its own. This development was further intensified by the effects of major external crises and provided the institutional context for growing awareness among the member states of the need to support further reform of the CFSP. The combined effect of these factors eventually led to a highly visible policy change. The latter crystallized between the EU Summits in Cologne and Nice and was codified with the creation of the CSDP in the Treaty of Nice. This was a clear expression of an effective change in the domain of the European security and defence matters insofar as the creation of the CSDP and the explicit introduction of new crisis management capabilities was unprecedented in the overall process of European integration. Moreover, the new governance structures and procedures, involved new competences and expertise regarding an entirely uncharted territory for the EU – the planning and conduct of crisis management operations. All this confirms that the critical moment provoked by the Kosovo crisis was not missed, but further developed thanks to the unique combination of internal and external stimuli for decisive policy and institutional reform that led to the series of agreements in Cologne (1999), Helsinki (1999) and Nice (2000) and culminated with the treaty codification of the CSDP in 2000 (critical juncture).

Since the Nice Treaty the institutional dimension of the EU conflict prevention and crisis management capabilities continued to rapidly evolve. New developments included the creation of EU-UN (2003) and EU-NATO (2006) permanent liaison mechanisms; and the introduction in 2004 of the 'Athena' mechanism for financing the common operational costs of military operations. In 2004, the European Council adopted the Military 'Headline Goal 2010' which included four new proposals: the establishment of the European Defence Agency (established in July 2004) to coordinate the creation of an integrated European defence market; a Civil-Military Cell as an integral part of the EU Military Staff offering joint civil military planning options (2005); a stand-by facility in Brussels – Operations Centre – for the strategic operational command and control of crisis management operations (2007); and EU Battle Groups (operational since 2007) comprising 1500 troops each with full logistical support. In February 2008, with the launch of the Security Sector Reform mission in Guinea-Bissau, another key structure was created – the Civilian Planning and Conduct Capability (CPCC) – a de facto Operational Headquarters for the strategic command and control of specifically civilian missions.

Most recently, the Lisbon Treaty created the position of High Representative for Foreign Affairs and Security Policy who is also a vice-president of the Commission and who will manage the European External Action Service formed by a combination of Council Secretariat, Commission and national seconded officials. The Treaty also extends the remit of the Petersberg tasks to disarmament, advice and assistance missions in both conflict prevention and crisis management operations (Art. 43 TEU). It introduces a 'mutual assistance clause' (Art.42.2), a mutual solidarity clause (part V, title VII, Art.222) and permanent structured cooperation among a group of member states in defence matters (Art. 42.5).

Overall, the continued expansion of structures and procedures in the field of EU conflict prevention and crisis management demonstrates the ambitions of the EU in asserting itself as an influential foreign policy actor. The scale of these changes also buttresses the unprecedented reforms that were unleashed between 1999 and 2000 and confirms their distinctive character.

Conclusion

This analysis revealed a visible process of incremental policy change that underpinned the various institutional adaptations and innovations that took place from the mid-1980s onwards in the domain of foreign and security policy including matters of conflict prevention and crisis management. The introduction of the CSDP in the period between the EU summits in Cologne and Nice represented a critical juncture from the pre-existing order in the sense that it was an *institutionalized* and *European* policy in contrast to the US/NATO domination in European security and defence matters in the previous decades. However, after the Nice Treaty introduced the new governance arrangements for conflict prevention and crisis management operations, the main question became how best and quickly to operationalize them. This is a very important aspect insofar as it provides the opportunity to assess in detail the workings of these arrangements and shed light on the inter-institutional dynamics as well as the role of institutions in shaping the planning and conduct of the respective operations. Thus, the present analysis on the factors that led to the formal introduction of the CSDP only reveals the macro-picture in the development of the EU conflict prevention and crisis management profile. In contrast, analyses on the post-design phase open up the micro-picture, which may reveal further aspects in the ongoing institutionalization of this domain (see Chapters 5 and 6). Ultimately, this could not only shed light on the development of the CSDP proper, but also provide a better understanding of the evolving nature of the EU as an international actor. With the Lisbon Treaty being currently fully in force, the EU has created the necessary conditions for engaging in crises around the globe by applying better inter-institutional coordination, using all the instruments at its disposal and planning missions on the basis of a joint civil-military approach. However, how successfully the new institutions (e.g. the European External Action Service) implement their mandate will be crucial as this may have far reaching effects on the international credibility of the EU as a conflict prevention and crisis management actor.

Notes

1 In 1953, the stepping down of Schuman as the French Foreign Minister left the EDC project without a dynamic and strong political leadership, a succession of unstable French cabinets under Pinay, Mayer and Laniel further weakened the sense of a lack of political leadership (Duke 2000: 31). Furthermore, Stalin died in March 1953, the War in Korea ended in July, the Indo-China war worsened in early 1954 and Britain openly opted for staying outside the EDC, all of which defused the sense of crisis and urgency that underpinned the initial rationale for the creation of the EDC (Duke 2000: 31–33; also Fursdon 1980).

2 The three reports that constituted the EPC process until its legal codification under Title III of the SEA were adopted in: Luxembourg (27.10.1970), Copenhagen (23.07.1973) and London (13.10.1981). They were never submitted to parliamentary scrutiny and the authority to agree on them never exceeded the framework of the member states' Foreign Ministries (Nuttall 1992: 11).

3 In the Rome Declaration (October 1984), the WEU member states unequivocally expressed their willingness to contribute to the European security and the strengthening of NATO by reactivation of the WEU activities. This was followed by The Hague 'Platform on European Security Interests' (October 1987), which emphasized the necessity of reinvigorating the WEU to ensure greater European effort in the security and defence domain and strengthen the European pillar within NATO. Between 1987 and 1998, the WEU member states took part in a number of humanitarian and crisis management operations deployed in diverse geographical locations such as the Persian Gulf and the Balkans (Duke 2000; WEU 2000).

4 These were the Security Unit, the Conflict Prevention and Crisis Management Unit, the CFSP Counsellor's Unit and the European Correspondent Unit (Spence 2006).

5 However, Britain perceived the development of the CSDP as a part of a wider process of strengthening NATO (Whitman 1999; Howorth 2000b; 2007a).

6 These were the Political and Security Committee, the EU Military Committee, and the Military Staff complemented by the creation of a Situation Centre and the transfer of two WEU bodies to the EU – the Satellite Centre in Torrejon, Spain and the Institute for Security Studies in Paris (the last two were later established as EU agencies).

7 It added a number of Annexes on the CSDP whose implementation was not subject to ratification. These annexes are known as Presidency Report on the ESDP (Rutten 2001: 168–209).

8 Interviews with EU officials, Brussels, June-July 2007.

9 Interviews with EU and NATO officials, Brussels and Mons, May-July 2007. See also Chapter 6 in this volume.

5 Conceptualizing the EU as a civil-military crisis manager

Institutional actors and their principals

Nadia Klein

Introduction[1]

The civil-military crisis management of the European Union (EU) is characterized by the interplay between the EU member state principals, on the one hand,
and their EU agents on the other hand. The policy under scrutiny here, EU crisis
management, lacks a generally accepted definition (Boin *et al.* 2006: 488–89; see
also Chapter 1). Thus, the boundary between 'EU crisis management' and other
activities in the field of EU foreign policy is often elusive. Crucially, while EU
crisis management activities are primarily associated with the Common Security
and Defence Policy (CSDP) in the second pillar, there are also crisis management
instruments in the first, i.e. the Community pillar. For the purpose of this chapter, EU agents are defined as the EU administrations composed of EU officials
in opposition to the EU institutions composed of national government representatives, i.e. the principals. These agents encompass the supranational European
Commission as well as administrative and executive structures of the Council of
the European Union such as the General Secretariat of the Council,[2] headed by the
High Representative for the Common Foreign and Security Policy (CFSP), and
the EU Special Representatives with their support staff.

  In contrast to the rich literature on the role of supranational actors in the
EU's first pillar policies (cf. Christiansen 1997, Cram 1994, 1997, Laffan 1997,
Pollack 2003), the impact of CSDP-related agents is under-researched and hardly
specified. At the same time, there is a broad consensus among practitioners and
analysts that inter-institutional turf battles represent a major obstacle for carrying
out a consistent EU crisis management (cf. Gomez and Peterson 2001: 55, Ioannides 2006: 81, Khol 2006: 127, Spence 2006: 392–93). Moreover, some authors
have recently argued that the Commission and especially the Council Secretariat
play increasingly proactive roles with regard to the formulation of and decision-
making in the Union's foreign policy (Keukeleire and MacNaughtan 2008: 90,
Drieskens 2007, Vanhoonacker and Dijkstra 2007).

  Therefore, this study focuses on the following research question: What impact,
if any, do EU agents have on the formulation and implementation of the Union's
civil-military crisis management? The chapter starts from the assumption that EU
agents such as the Council Secretariat and the Commission can be conceptualized

as rational competence-maximizers (Cram 1994: 199, Pollack 2003: 34–39). Under certain conditions, they are expected to pursue autonomous preferences distinct from or even in contradiction to their principals' preferences.

The principal-agent approach, as developed within rational choice institutionalism, and the bureaucratic politics approach provide suitable tools in order to investigate the conditions under which EU agents actually influence the policy-making in the field of crisis management. In particular, they shed light on the mechanisms established by the principals to control their agents and on conflicts among the agents. Thus, the chapter explores the following two hypotheses:

Hypothesis I: The higher the level of delegated authority, and the higher the principal's monitoring and sanctioning costs, the more the agent will use its competences to pursue autonomous preferences in EU crisis management. The collective principal's capacity to sanction the deviating agent depends on two factors: the decision threshold and the availability of alternative options in a given moment.

Hypothesis II: The more competences of different agents overlap, the more institutional competition will be and the more restrained will be each agent's room for manoeuvre.

The hypotheses take into account two different perspectives regarding the control of agent behaviour. Hypothesis (I) focuses on *principal-agent* relationships and highlights the characteristics of monitoring and sanctioning in the Union's crisis management. In the following, this perspective will be called 'vertical control'. Hypothesis (II) provides an alternative explanation for actual agent autonomy by focusing on the – often neglected – dimension of *agent-agent* relationships. This will be called 'horizontal control'. It is argued that only by taking into account the mechanisms of both vertical and horizontal control, the impact of EU agents can be fully assessed. A discrepancy can be observed between an overall limited delegation of executive powers to EU crisis management agents on the one hand, and their significant impact on the policy-making on the other hand.

The argument is developed as follows: the second section of the chapter points at current gaps in the analysis of EU foreign policy, namely the lack of explanatory concepts for analyses from a short-to mid-term perspective. The third section develops a conceptual framework which allows assessing both vertical and horizontal mechanisms of control. In particular, it adapts the principal-agent approach for the field of EU crisis management, referring to a comprehensive understanding of delegation and the limited availability of oversight mechanisms. Most importantly, the difficulties of sanctioning deviating agents are highlighted: given the characteristic unanimous decision-making in crisis management, the respective agent can easily exploit conflicting preferences among the EU member states. The fourth section outlines the delegation of competences to the Council Secretariat and the European Commission, focussing especially on the increasingly politicized role of the former. Then, the actual autonomy of these two institutional actors is illustrated both for the planning and the implementation stage. This includes examples from the EU military operation EUFOR Tchad/Central African Republic and EU missions in Bosnia and Herzegovina, which represent cases of one sidedness and agent slippage, respectively. The conclusion summarizes the main findings and points to future avenues for research, mainly with regard to the current re-structuring of the institutional set-up under the Lisbon Treaty.

State of research: the double lack of concepts

Dealing with EU crisis management, the researcher with a theoretical focus is confronted with a double lack of concepts: first, a general lack of conceptual work in the field of EU foreign policy (Strömvik 2005: 10–17, Tonra and Christiansen 2004: 4), and second, a lack of concepts focusing on the day-to-day policy-making. Regarding the latter, in the literature on EU foreign policy, the reasons for the *creation* of CSDP in 1999 have been discussed under various theoretical perspectives (Bretherton and Vogler 2006: 189–214, Link 2001, Reynolds 2005, Sjursen 2004, Webber *et al.* 2004). As different as these approaches are in terms of explanatory factors and levels of abstraction, they are all based on a *long-term* research perspective. This perspective is hardly applicable to explain the daily policy-making of EU crisis management and to specify the respective role of EU agents. This is not to say that in-depth studies cannot reveal some evidence e.g. for historical institutionalist core concepts such as path dependency, lock-ins and the concept of unintended consequences (see Petrov's chapter in this volume). This study does not question the explanatory power of long-term oriented approaches but, given the fast development of EU crisis management institutions since 1999, it argues that there is a strong need for complementary approaches, based on a short-to mid-term perspective. As outlined later, rational choice institutionalism and the bureaucratic politics approach provide suitable concepts for the specific research question of this chapter.

It should also be noted that in the conceptual debate on CFSP/CSDP, the term 'Brusselization' (Allen 1998, Howorth 2001) has often emphasized the specific role of new permanent, Brussels-based EU bodies. It denotes the transfer of foreign and security policy functions to the EU level (Smith 2004a: 741). The term also hints at some form of specific integration quality, lower than the supranationality in the Community pillar, but 'beyond traditional intergovernmentalism' (Howorth 2001: 787).[3] Despite the enduring attractiveness of this term in the recent debate, the concept has not been further developed. Beyond the basic functional argument that the Brusselization process will be enhanced by the need for 'rapid decision-making and efficient implementation' (Howorth 2001: 765), the conditions for, as well as the mechanisms and implications of that process have not been explored yet. In particular, the role and power of EU agents have not been theorized – which is the main aim of this chapter.

Theorizing principal-agent and agent-agent relationships: Mechanisms of vertical and horizontal control

Vertical control

Rational choice institutionalism assumes that rational actors behave strategically on the basis of a fixed set of preferences, reacting to institutional incentives and constraints (Aspinwall and Schneider 2000: 13–15, Hall and Taylor 1996, Pollack 2004). The principal-agent (PA) approach focuses on a specific set of institutional incentives and constraints, namely the principal's instruments to monitor and sanction the agent. Basically, '[a]gency relationships are created when one party, the *principal*, enters into a contractual agreement with a second part, the *agent*, and delegates to the latter responsibility for carrying out a function or set of tasks on the principal's behalf' (Kassim and Menon 2003: 122).

A principal is defined as an actor being able to 'both grant authority and rescind it' (Hawkins *et al.* 2006: 7). As PA scholars point out, the definition of 'the principal' depends on the peculiarities of the respective political setting (Dehousse 2008). With regard to EU crisis management, this chapter identifies (a) the European Council, composed of the EU heads of state and government, (b) the Council of the European Union, composed of the relevant national ministers, (c) the Committee of Permanent Representatives (COREPER), and (d) the Political and Security Committee (PSC), the latter composed of national permanent representatives, as formations of one collective principal.[4] This chapter is interested in the principal-agent interaction which begins after the EU member governments conceived as a collective principal have delegated to the Council Secretariat or the European Commission the task to plan or to implement an EU crisis management action. Thus, the analysis focuses on post-delegation agency drift in order to assess the actual influence of EU agents in this policy field.

It is the tension between the persistent authority of the principal and the inbuilt agency losses (Hawkins *et al.* 2006: 24) that constitutes a puzzling political phenomenon. While the principal is driven to reduce agency losses by controlling the agent's autonomy, a total control of the agent would jeopardize the added value of delegation. This means, rational principals seek a balance between granting their agents enough authority for the efficient fulfilment of delegated tasks and controlling their agents in order to reduce agency costs. In the delegation literature, this balance is expressed by the term 'discretion' (Epstein and O'Halloran 1999: 26–27, Pollack 2003: 26–29). It refers to the *officially delegated* policy-making authority *taking into account possible constraints* for the use of this authority. Thus, if a high level of delegated authority is combined with strong control mechanisms for the respective agent, the overall level of discretion, i.e. the agent autonomy, is considered to be rather low.

The mechanisms to control agent behaviour represent the core of each PA analysis. *Ex ante* control is carried out by defining the 'scope of agency activity, the legal instruments available to the agency, and the procedures to be followed by it' (Pollack 2003: 27). The literature further distinguishes two basic monitoring strategies: the direct 'police-patrol' oversight and the indirect 'fire-alarm' oversight, carried out by affected third parties (Lupia and McCubbins 1994: 97, McCubbins and Schwartz 1984: 166). Though, effective control depends not only on the principal's capacity to monitor agent behaviour, but also on the capacity to sanction agent behaviour in the case of agency slack. Sanctions include the control over appointments and budgets, and the possibility of overriding agency behaviour through new legislation or the revision of mandates (Hawkins *et al.* 2006: 30–31, Pollack 2003: 27). In the case of a *collective* principal such as the Council of the European Union, composed of 27 member state representatives, the capacity to sanction is first and foremost linked to the capacity to aggregate the diverse preferences (Lyne *et al.* 2006: 46). Thus, the rules of decision-making, namely the thresholds for joint decisions represent a major factor in PA analysis.

Applied to the study of EU crisis management, the PA model has to be adapted. The four most important specifications are the following: first, rational institutionalist analysis is based on a functional understanding of delegation. This means that EU governments create institutions according to their policy preferences in order to lower transaction costs. The principal especially wants to benefit from the expertise of a specialized agent. Though, in the field of EU security policy, policy-relevant expertise is largely produced by and exchanged among the member states. In a strict sense, crisis management agents hardly possess any information which is not available to the member states. The agents dispose, however, of a specific procedural expertise and overview, namely regarding the operational planning in Brussels. Moreover, there is *per se* an informational advantage as regards ongoing missions in the framework of the CSDP and the work of EU Commission delegations on the ground (first-hand information).

Second, in methodological terms, it is appropriate to apply a comprehensive understanding of delegation which takes into account both primary and secondary EU law (March and Olsen 1998: 953, Pollack 2003: 9, Schimmelfennig 2004: 82). The development of EU crisis management is characterized by major decisions at the level of the European Council, namely the summits in Cologne, Helsinki (both 1999), Nice (2000) and Brussels (2003), and subsequent refining decisions at lower levels. In this policy field, principals typically delegate non-binding, or 'soft' powers to the Commission and to the General Secretariat. A narrow understanding of delegation – based only on the provisions of primary law – would therefore neglect significant acts of delegation.

A third specification refers to the issue of monitoring: given the fact that EU crisis management is implemented in third countries *outside the Union*, the range of possible oversight procedures is essentially limited to police-patrol instruments. This means that the collective principal directly monitors agent behaviour via the Council's advisory and steering committees. These Council bodies represent also the focal point of the comprehensive reporting system for CSDP agents on the ground. In contrast, the concept of fire alarms refers to a more or less elaborated *decentralized* system of rules and procedures that enable affected citizens or interest groups to examine agent behaviour and, eventually, to blame agents for the violation of the principal's goals (McCubbins and Schwartz 1984: 166). Such a reliable, 'external feedback system' simply does not exist when the EU intervenes in a country in crisis.

Finally, a fourth specification refers to the issue of sanctioning. CSDP principals dispose of a variety of sanctions. For example, the Council of the European Union controls the appointments of the EU Special Representatives and the civilian and military heads of mission. Moreover, at least in theory, many agent mandates can be easily revised on the basis of Council decisions. In the CSDP context, however, the application of these sanctioning mechanisms is limited because of two reasons. First, it requires a decision by a *collective* principal. Thus, conflicting preferences among the member states might be exploited by the agents, especially under the condition of unanimous decision-making. This means, if any of the member state principals 'is made better off by the agent's shirking, then that principal will block the application of sanctions' (Pollack 2003: 43, also Hawkins *et al.* 2006: 21). Therefore, the (rather counterintuitive) assumption can be deduced that once established, EU agents dispose of a comparatively large room for manoeuvre especially in the intergovernmental field of CSDP. Furthermore, the availability of alternative policy options limits the principal's capacity to sanction its agent (Hawkins *et al.* 2006: 24). Especially the ultimate sanction, i.e. the withdrawal of agent authority (the end of the PA relationship), can only be applied if either the principal is willing and capable to take over the agent's functions, or if there is another agent available to replace the shirking agent.

On the basis of these considerations, the following hypothesis (I) on vertical control can be developed: the higher the level of delegated authority, and the higher the principal's monitoring and sanctioning costs, the more the agent will use its competences to pursue autonomous preferences in the EU's crisis management. The collective principal's capacity to sanction the deviating agent depends on two factors: the decision threshold and the availability of alternative options in a given moment.

Horizontal control

Keeping the internal perspective on constraints and incentives provided by the EU framework, an alternative explanation regarding agent autonomy can be derived from focusing on the relationships between the agents, i.e. *horizontal* relationships. To date, agent-agent relationships and their impact on agent autonomy have been largely neglected in PA analysis (Hawkins and Jacoby 2006). However, the very concept of rational competence-maximizing agents points at the potential relevance of agent interaction. Most importantly, it introduces the notion of competition into the analysis: the range of competences and related resources is finite within any given institutional framework. Therefore, given the primary interest of organizational survival, agents behave rationally when they compete for available resources – eventually at the cost of other agents' competences and influence (Peters 1992: 121). The rational interest to defend their 'territory' (Downs 1967: 215) creates conflicts ('turf wars') – even if at large, the interaction might be characterized by co-operation (Downs 1967: 216, Hill 2003: 92). Consequently, the inherent competition of agent-agent relationships can be conceptualized as an indirect mechanism of control, a form of mutual restraint, or as 'horizontal control'. It is argued that agent competition represents a particular relevant factor in a policy field such as civil-military crisis management which is characterized by the involvement of multiple agents.

The concept of horizontal control draws on core concepts of the bureaucratic politics approach and adapts them for the analysis of EU agent influence. The bureaucratic politics approach has been developed for the analysis of national (foreign) policies (Allison and Zelikow 1999, Downs 1967, Halperin 1974, Hill 2003: 85–92). It assesses the relative influence of main decision-making actors, i.e. top government officials, with regard to a certain policy outcome. Individual preferences, intermingled with the official's bureaucratic position within the executive, account for this outcome. An actor's relative amount of influence depends both on its bureaucratic position and the institutionalized rules of bargaining (Jäger and Oppermann 2006: 118). In contrast to this study's focus on the influence of *institutional* agents, the bureaucratic politics approach focuses on the individual as the unit of analysis. It is assumed, though, that the variety of individual preferences is strongly related to the respective organization's basic interests such as survival and growth. The central role of organizational interests in the approach provides sufficient common analytical ground to refer to selected bureaucratic politics concepts in order to model the interaction of institutional agents in EU crisis management.

There are two assumptions of particular relevance. First, given its interest of survival, organizations evaluate policy options in view of the implications for their capacity to carry out delegated tasks effectively. Organizations will reject decisions which, as a result, limit their own performance and effectiveness. In contrast, they will favour those policy options whose implementation depends on the functions provided by the respective organization (Downs 1967: 213–16, Halperin 1974: 26–27). This study therefore assumes that the European Commission and the Council Secretariat favour policy options in crisis management which are closely related to their respective competences. In the same vein, while acknowledging the existence of *intra*-institutional conflicts (Christiansen 2001), it is argued that, analytically, a significant amount of organizational interests allows treating the two agents as unitary actors (Klein 2010).

Second, the bureaucratic politics approach claims that political power is dispersed among governmental actors trying to put forward their preferences within the internal bargaining process. Crucially, the institutional rules provide bureaucratic actors with specific bargaining resources (Halperin 1974: 105). These resources include the power to influence the agenda, especially through a formal right (or even monopoly) of initiative, participation and voting rights in central decision-making and advisory committees, implementation and evaluation authority, rights of consultation and information, and the control over operational resources (Allison and Halperin 1972: 50–53, Allison and Zelikow 1999: 278–81 and 300–302).

Based on these assumptions, the following hypothesis on horizontal control (Hypothesis II) can be developed: the more competences of different agents overlap, the more institutional competition will be and the more restrained will be each agent's room for manoeuvre. Thus, equally based on a rationalist framework, Hypothesis II provides an alternative explanation of variation in agent influence related to the effects of *horizontal* control as opposed to the mechanisms of *vertical* control as hypothesized earlier.

The EU's civil-military crisis management: institutional architecture

After outlining the core concepts for the analysis, this section introduces the legal basis for EU crisis management and presents its main actors, namely the bodies of the collective principal (European Council, Council of the European Union, Permanent Representatives Committee, Political and Security Committee) and the two main agents, i.e. the Council Secretariat and the European Commission. As Agnieszka Nowak (2006: 10) has pointed out, the 'EU contribution to crisis management is primarily associated with the [ESDP]', i.e. civilian and military instruments in the framework of the intergovernmental second pillar. Article 17(2) of the Treaty of the European Union (TEU) lists 'humanitarian and rescue tasks, peacekeeping tasks and tasks of combat forces in crisis management, including peacemaking' – the so-called 'Petersberg tasks'. The *European Security Strategy* (European Council 2003) further extended this catalogue by stressing the need for a comprehensive civil-military approach in the field of crisis management and conflict prevention. According to the Strategy, relevant political, diplomatic, military and civilian, trade and development activities need to be carried out more coherently (European Council 2003: 13). At the conceptual level, the *European Security Strategy* has served as the core reference document for the ongoing set-up of EU crisis management. While its merely 14 pages do not deal with institutional details, its claim for coherence has unfolded a dynamic which has had an impact on the development of both instruments and procedures. In particular, EU agents have referred to the principle of coherence in order to support their claim for extended rights of participation, both during the planning and the implementation stage.

The EU military structure, firmly based in the second pillar, faces a more fragmented civilian counterpart (Figure 5.1). First, after the creation of the CSDP in 1999, structures for the civilian aspects of crisis management have been established within the second pillar. Second, the European Community traditionally supports countries in post-conflict situations (art. 177(2) TEC; see also section on the European Commission later).

Since the creation of the CSDP in 1999, the European Council is the leading body for the shaping of the EU's civil-military crisis management. Especially at the beginning, the EU heads of state and government did not only define the 'principles and general guidelines' (Art. 13(1) TEU) for the CSDP, but formulated rather precise guidelines (European Council 1999a,1999b, 2000a, 2000b, 2000c). Legally, the Council of the European Union is the principal decision-making body for major operational ESDP questions such as the launch of ESDP missions or the appointment of the respective Head of Mission (Art. 13, 14 TEU). In this context, the Council's main decision preparation body, the Permanent Representatives Committee (COREPER) (Art. 207 TEC), plays a limited role. De facto, ESDP decisions are prepared, discussed and taken by the Political and Security Committee (PSC) which was established on a permanent basis by the Treaty of Nice (2000) (Duke 2005). The PSC is composed of member state ambassadors

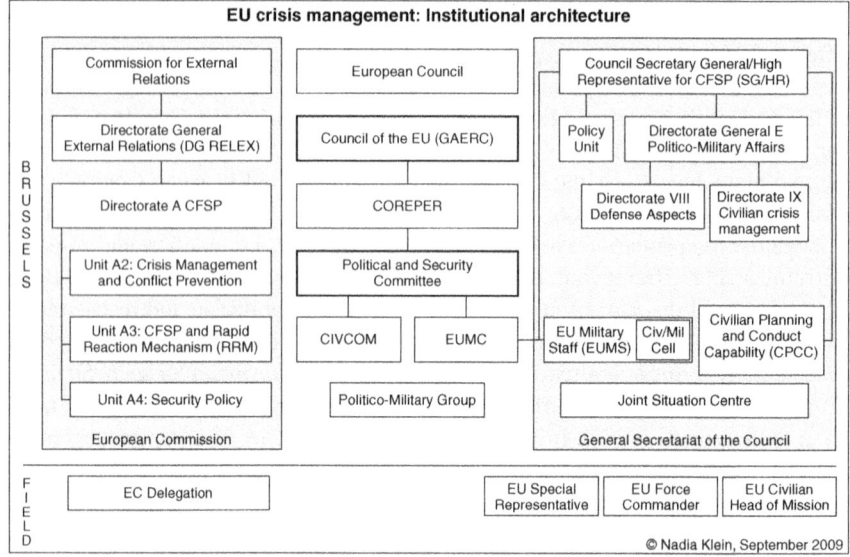

Figure 5.1 EU crisis management: institutional architecture prior to the entry into force of the Lisbon Treaty

and meets at least twice a week. For its decisions, the PSC takes into account the advice of the Committee for Civilian Aspects of Crisis Management (CIVCOM) as well as the advice of the EU Military Committee (EUMC). Moreover, the PSC is supported by the Politico-Military Group (PMG) which serves as a forum to examine military-related issues (Cameron 2007: 40–59). The two advising committees and the PMG are composed of national representatives and shall help to find a consensus among the principals.[5] To sum up, in the Union's civil-military crisis management, the bargaining among the member state principals essentially takes place at the level of the European Council and the PSC, including its advising bodies. The principals have delegated three major functions to their crisis management agents: agenda management, operational planning and management, and the external representation of the Union.

Delegation to the Council General Secretariat and the European Commission

The Council Secretariat: The fragmented agent

The role of the Council General Secretariat has changed fundamentally with the creation of the European Security and Defence Policy. Traditionally, the Secretariat assists the Council of the European Union with regard to organizational tasks (art. 207 TEC). By fostering a more operational EU foreign policy the EU member states have for the first time entrusted the Council Secretariat with executive tasks (Christiansen and Vanhoonacker 2008: 760). Within the Secretariat, several bodies are responsible for the planning and implementation of crisis management. The Secretary-General/High Representative for the CFSP (High Representative) shall assist the EU Presidency and the Council 'in matters coming within the scope of the [CFSP], in particular through contributing to the formulation, preparation and implementation of policy decisions' (TEU, Art. 26). Furthermore, the High Representative shall contribute to the CFSP 'when appropriate and acting on behalf of the Council and at the request of the Presidency, through conducting political dialogue with third parties' (TEU, Art. 26).

The High Representative's institutional resources related to crisis management action comprise his personal staff, i.e. his cabinet, and the Policy Unit. Composed of approximately 30 personnel, the main task of the Policy Unit is to develop policy options for central questions of EU foreign policy, including crisis management (Regelsberger 2004: 34–35). The High Representative can further appoint Personal Representatives to deal with specific issues such as human rights in the area of CFSP or the status of Kosovo (Cameron 2007: 51). Under the authority and the operational direction of the High Representative, a number of EU Special Representatives represent and promote the policies of the EU with regard to a specific country or region. EU Special Representatives on the ground are closely involved in the Union's crisis management activities, fulfilling a broad range of diplomatic, advising and co-ordinating tasks, depending on their area of deployment.[6]

Within the Secretariat's Directorate-General External and politico-military affairs (DG E), there are two directorates dealing with crisis management: Directorate VIII 'Defence aspects', composed of 25 personnel, and Directorate IX 'Civilian crisis management', composed of 17 personnel.[7] Directorate VIII is not involved with the daily conduct of EU operations; it mainly deals with basic planning documents for EU operations and military capabilities. In contrast, Directorate IX has focused both on horizontal concept development and the task of conducting civilian missions on a daily basis, especially with regard to EU police missions. In autumn 2007, the chain of command for civilian missions was re-organized and approximately three quarters of the then Directorate IX staff were transferred to a new body within the Secretariat: the Civilian Planning and Conduct Capability (CPCC), initially set-up with 55 personnel.[8] The CPCC, composed of an Operations Unit and a Mission Support Unit, and headed by a Civilian Operations Commander, is responsible for civilian command and control (Council of the European Union 2007a: 13). The CPCC reports directly to the High Representative. Directorate IX has remained responsible for overarching issues such as civilian capabilities and training exercises as well as the preparation of concepts.

The EU Military Staff (EUMS), including the Civilian/Military Cell,[9] provides the High Representative and the EU bodies with military expertise. In particular, the EUMS is tasked to perform early warning, situation assessment and strategic planning (Council of the European Union 2008). It is composed of approximately 200 personnel.[10] The EUMS is a Directorate-General within the Council Secretariat; it works under the military direction of the EU Military Committee. As a

Council Secretariat department, it is at the same time directly attached to the High Representative.

The Council Secretariat and the Commission are formally involved in all stages of the policy cycle of EU crisis management. Since the ESDP became operational in 2003, the delegation of tasks to EU crisis management agents, and especially to the Council Secretariat, has become increasingly politicized. The debate on the allocation of competences is closely linked to the so-called 'Hampton Court process' and the concept of Civil-Military Co-ordination (see later).

The politicized role of the Council Secretariat

At the Hampton Court EU summit in October 2005, the heads of state and government asked the High Representative, Javier Solana, to develop proposals in order to improve *inter alia* the Union's crisis management structures in terms of greater coherence and efficiency. Overall, Solana's proposals aimed at strengthening the Council Secretariat's planning and conduct capacities – and at strengthening the High Representative's competences to direct them. Thus, a high-level Crisis Management Board under Solana's chairmanship was aimed to tie together the relevant expertise of a re-structured and further strengthened Council Secretariat. The creation of a Civilian Operations Commander was part of this set of proposals. The following intense controversy between Solana and the member states as well as among member states[11] can serve as a general indicator that the EU member states acknowledge the Council Secretariat's (informal) influence on the policy-making. In principal-agent terms, the controversy illustrates the difficulties for the principals to find a balance between granting their central crisis management agent the necessary discretion in order to render the policy-making more efficient on the one hand, and keeping the necessary control in order to prevent agent slack on the other hand.

This so-called Hampton Court follow-up process was closely related to the debate on Civil-Military Co-ordination (CMCO) within the Union. CMCO is an internally-oriented, EU-specific concept aiming at improving intra- and inter-pillar co-ordination between its civilian and military instruments at all levels (political-strategic, operational, tactical). The status quo is characterized by subsequent EU Presidency initiatives on various CMCO aspects and resulting 'living documents' on these issues.[12] In this context, government officials of the EU member states congruently alluded to the Council Secretariat and its autonomy to take up a certain proposal or not.[13] Thus, even if the Secretariat does not dispose of a formal right of initiative, it can rely on its procedural power to procrastinate or to bring forward certain (own) proposals, depending on its organizational interests. Thereby, the Secretariat exerts an indirect form of agenda-setting power which does not necessarily fit with the planned agenda-setting of the respective EU Presidency. While the EU Presidency and the Council Secretariat work closely together on a daily basis, a situation which allows the former to closely *monitor* the latter (a form of police patrol oversight, see earlier), the principal has hardly any possibility to immediately *sanction* the agent with regard to its agenda-setting activities.[14]

The agenda-setting power of the High Representative has further increased with the implementation of the Lisbon Treaty which foresees a right of initiative of the High Representative and the establishment of the External Action Service.

Operational planning in the CSDP context

Regarding the agents' influence on operational crisis management, the so-called Crisis Response Co-ordination Team (CRCT) is an interesting case in point. In the early planning phase of a mission, the CRCT should institutionalize civil-military co-ordination at the Brussels level by bringing together all relevant agents. The CRCT is a body without decision-making powers, composed of senior officials from the Commission and the Council Secretariat. It should meet *ad hoc* whenever necessary in order to prepare the Crisis Management Concept and to ensure coherence between civilian and military instruments during the implementation phase (Council of the European Union 2003b: 31–34).

On the civilian side, after the Council has agreed on the Crisis Management Concept, the Civilian Planning and Conduct Capability (CPCC) develops civilian strategic options. On the basis of the options selected by the Council, the CPCC is tasked to prepare the Concept of Operations. On the military side, the EUMS develops military strategic options. On the basis of the options selected by the Council, the EUMS is tasked to prepare the initiating military directive. This directive serves as a guiding document for the drafting of the military Concept of Operations by the operation commander at the selected operational headquarters.[15] All CSDP planning documents have to be endorsed by the collective principal, namely by the Political and Security Committee and the Council. Therefore, at first sight, the operational planning and management activities of the Council Secretariat seem to be closely controlled and steered by the member states.

The European Commission: The expanding agent

In terms of autonomy and influence, the European Commission benefits from its financial resources and the fact that it can be hardly sanctioned in the field of crisis management. There is a variety of relevant financial instruments of the European Community (EC), in addition to the budget line for the Common Foreign and Security Policy (European Commission 2001b). Importantly, the Commission not only manages these EC instruments, it also proposes them in the first place, based on its sole right of initiative in the Community framework (Streinz 2003: 190–204). Overall, Commission activities have become increasingly relevant in the field of crisis and humanitarian assistance (Smith 2006: 329).

First, there has been a broad range of sectoral EC crisis management tools. The most important sectors have been disaster response and civil protection, democracy, human rights and the rule of law and rehabilitation and reconstruction (Gourlay 2006: 51–56). From 2001 to 2006, the 'Rapid Reaction Mechanism' (RRM) provided flexible, short-term Community funding for crises-related activities up to the duration of six months. There was no geographical limitation for RRM activities (Council of the European Union 2001). While the Commission had to inform the Council before taking a decision under the RRM Regulation, no further sanctioning mechanisms were foreseen. Thus, in order to ensure rapid action, the comitology procedure – the system of oversight committees by which the EU member states traditionally control the Commission's work – was not applied for RRM decisions. The RRM was programmed by the Crisis Management and Conflict Prevention Unit which has been located within Directorate A 'Crisis Platform and Policy Co-ordination in CFSP' of the Directorate-General for External Relations (DG RELEX). This unit has served as the main link between relevant Commission services and the Council bodies in crisis management issues.

Second, the Commission has carried out crisis management-related activities funded by long-term geographic instruments (Gourlay 2006: 57–60). In the Western Balkan countries,[16] under the CARDS (Community Assistance for Reconstruction, Development and Stabilization) programme (2000–2006), the Commission funded *inter alia* projects to support police and justice reforms (Gourlay 2006: 59, Ioannides 2006: 71–72), which should have complemented respective short-term CSDP missions. In practice, though, given the elusive boundary between short-term post-crisis intervention and long-term institution-building, overlapping mandates and the resulting rivalry of the involved EU agents have characterized the planning and implementation of crisis management (discussed later).

In 2007, the external assistance of the European Community was streamlined, replacing most of the existing thematic and geographical instruments (European Commission 2004b). For example, from 2007 onwards, CARDS and other pre-accession instruments have been replaced by the Instrument for Pre-Accession Assistance (IPA). IPA focuses mainly on institution building and economic development in the Western Balkans. Since 2007, funding related to crisis management and security aspects in the region has been based on the new Instrument for Stability, which has replaced the Rapid Reaction Mechanism (European Parliament and Council of the European Union 2006). In this context, the duration of and the budget for measures which are not subject to time-consuming – and, from the Commission's perspective: restraining – comitology procedures have been significantly extended.[17]

Informational asymmetries

Before turning to the analysis of the *actual agency* of the Council Secretariat and the Commission, based on the competences outlined earlier, the remainder of this section will have a closer look at the flow of information in the framework of EU crisis management. A basic factor in PA analysis is the information asymmetry in favour of the agent (Pollack 2003: 26). This information asymmetry is particularly acute when the principal is located in Brussels and its agent acts on the ground. In host countries of EU crisis management activities such as Bosnia and Herzegovina (BiH), the respective EU Special Representative (EUSR) fulfills two functions 'under the authority and operational direction of the High Representative' (Council Secretariat 2007: 1): first, s/he externally represents the Union with regard to local or international actors in his or her area of responsibility. Second, s/he internally co-ordinates the activities of other EU actors on the ground, depending on his/her respective mandate. Especially smaller EU member states with limited diplomatic resources depend on the EUSR as a provider of information. The EUSR is requested to report on a regular basis to the Council of the European Union, the PSC and various Council working groups. On the basis of a joint action, EUSRs are appointed and dismissed by the Council. Similarly, the Council decides upon an EUSR's specific budget and staff (Grevi 2007). Overall, the formal control of the EUSR can be characterized as 'police patrol' oversight.

Regarding Community crisis management activities, the situation is significantly different. In general, there is a structural-based informational asymmetry between the Commission and the EU member states. Whereas the Commission has no decision-making power within the CSDP framework, it is nevertheless 'fully associated' (TEU, art. 18(4)). This means that it is represented in all relevant CSDP committees, including a limited presence in the EU Military Committee (Council of the European Union 2002). Consequently, the Commission is well informed about crisis management debates within the second pillar. In contrast, since the principals are not present during internal Commission meetings, they are less aware of the crisis management debate within the Commission.

Agency in Brussels and in the field

The following examples illustrate how the Council Secretariat and the Commission have used their competences and in how far their autonomy has actually been restrained by control mechanisms (vertical control) and overlapping mandates (horizontal control).

As outlined earlier, the CRCT is composed of CSDP agents and represents a CMCO-triggered inter-pillar co-ordination tool for the planning process. To date, its *ad hoc* meetings have had a formal character; institutional competition inhibits substantial co-ordination. Consequently, the drafting of the different parts of a given Crisis Management Concept has been done separately and added afterwards.[18] There is no evidence that the currently limited influence of the CRCT is due to any principals' control mechanisms. In line with the theoretical assumptions underpinning Hypothesis II, in the planning phase of crisis management, the bodies of the Council Secretariat and the Commission are preoccupied with defending and extending their respective area of competence. They leave it up to their principals, i.e. the PSC ambassadors, to ensure co-ordinated civil-military crisis management activities. In terms of agent autonomy and agenda-setting power, the 'real test' would come if the PSC were confronted with an elaborated Crisis Management Concept based on a *consolidated* position of the involved EU agents.

Yet, CSDP agents' contributions to the operational planning do matter. The planning input is not neutral, but biased by agent-specific interests and preferences: '[n]otably the Council Secretariat, but also the Commission, leave their distinctive marks on the shape of many ESDP operations' (Björkdahl and Strömvik 2008:

24, Vanhoonacker and Dijkstra 2007: 3). In this context, there are two important factors: (1) the decision threshold and (2) the availability of alternative options under time pressure (Wagner 2003: 583).

The example of the EU military operation EUFOR Tchad/RCA illustrates the relevance of these two factors. Thus, the analysis of the respective operational planning reveals how agents – in this case the EU Military Staff (EUMS) and DG-E VIII – are able to put their views forward, even against the position of several EU member states. During summer 2007, the EUMS and DG-E VIII prepared the Council's decision on 15 October 2007 to launch a military operation in Eastern Chad and North Eastern Central African Republic (EUFOR Tchad/RCA) (Council of the European Union 2007b). The operation's main objective was to protect and support refugees in the context of the crisis in Darfur. Given its rather civilian focus, there was an intense debate among EU member states regarding the added value of launching a costly military CSDP operation.[19] The strong French position in favour of the operation was backed by the EUMS/DG-E VIII preparatory work: rather one-sided, all four strategic options proposed to intervene militarily. Even if *de jure*, the Political and Security Committee could reject the strategic options developed by the preparatory bodies entirely, de facto, given the characteristic shortage of time, it hardly does. Thus, in the case of EUFOR Tchad/RCA, the EUMS/DG-E VIII took advantage of the political constellation and influenced the decision-making process by restricting its proposals to the realm of its core competence, i.e. a military EU intervention.[20]

Similarly, the evidence points to the fact that the Council Secretariat cannot only influence significantly the planning, but also the implementation of crisis management. In general, crisis management mandates are to a certain extent voluntarily vague in order to provide the actor in the field with the necessary flexibility to carry out its tasks. At the same time, it provides the agent with a certain leeway to interpret its mandate according to its own interests. Within the limits of its respective mandate, the EU Special Representative can be regarded as a powerful agent because of its co-ordinating role among EU actors. An illustrative example for the EUSR's autonomy in Bosnia and Herzegovina (BiH) can be drawn from the debate on the pooling of functional expertise such as legal, political and media functions under the EUSR guidance. A proposal from 2005 by the then-EUSR for BiH, Paddy Ashdown, to bring functional expertise of the EU Police Mission (EUPM) under the EUSR competency (Penksa 2006: 13), was in line with the conceptual debate in Brussels on the role and competences of the EUSR (Council of the European Union 2006b: 8). However, in the case of BiH, in 2006, the then new EUSR, Christian Schwarz-Schilling, and the EUPM Head of Mission, Vincenzo Coppola, agreed *not* to pool the aforementioned functions but to keep the current set-up of separated in-house expertise for operational reasons. Afterwards, Brussels was officially informed about the non-pooling via the regular review process.[21] It is important to stress that the final decision was taken by the EU agents (EUSR and the Head of the Police Mission) in Sarajevo and not by the political-strategic level in Brussels. The incident might be interpreted as a form of agent slippage with regard to the collective principal's aggregated preferences as expressed in the related Council document (Council of the European Union 2006b).

Conclusion

This study has explored the impact of the Council Secretariat and the European Commission on the formulation and implementation of the Union's civil-military crisis management. Drawing on the principal-agent and the bureaucratic politics approach, the chapter has developed a conceptual framework to analyse the role of these institutional actors in a short-to mid-term perspective. Most importantly, this framework allows taking into account both direct and indirect mechanisms of agent control: direct mechanisms of monitoring and sanctioning set up by the collective member state principal (vertical control), as well as effects of agent competition which indirectly limit agent autonomy and influence (horizontal control).

In sum, a certain discrepancy can be observed between an overall limited delegation of executive powers to CSDP agents, and their significant autonomy regarding the implementation and even the formulation of the EU's crisis management policy. Hypothesis I on vertical control has stated that the higher the principal's monitoring and sanctioning costs, the more the agent will use its competences to pursue autonomous preferences in EU crisis management. The analysis of the role of the EU Special Representatives confirms the hypothesis: the respective police-patrol monitoring system does not lead to micro-management by the collective principal. In contrast, as shown in the case of Bosnia and Herzegovina, the EUSR can use its discretionary power to take decisions which might even contradict the principal's position. This can be explained by high sanctioning costs in terms of the decision threshold in the Council (unanimity) and the salient position of the EUSR on the ground (lack of alternative options).

Overall, the Council Secretariat can be characterized as a fragmented agent with limited formal decision-making power but multifaceted forms of implementation and agenda-setting power. The actual agency of the Secretariat's bodies is based on their central role in the mission planning process in Brussels and on their presence on the ground, namely via the EUSRs. The Commission can be characterized as an expanding agent whose influence is mainly based on the management of EC financial resources. With the establishment of the Instrument for Stability in 2007, the overall amount of 'comitology-free' funding has been significantly increased. This can be interpreted as an expression of the principal-agent tension: in order to ensure rapid crisis management measures, the EU member states have loosened their regular oversight mechanisms *vis-à-vis* the Commission. As a by-product, they have reduced their capacity to sanction the Commission in the case of agency slack.

At the same time, though, evidence points to the fact that the two agents are constrained by strong mechanisms of *horizontal* control. Thus, as outlined in Hypothesis II, EU crisis management is characterized by bureaucratic rivalry as a result of overlapping mandates. The competitive interaction of the agents in the context of the CRCT can serve as an illustrative – but by far not the only – example in this regard. Generally spoken, the comprehensive policy approach of CMCO has provided the relevant EU agents with a comprehensive de facto right of participation, which in turn leads also to intense institutional turf battles.

The complementary analytical perspectives applied in this study have allowed drawing a comprehensive picture of the Council Secretariat's and the Commission's actual influence on EU crisis management. The principal-agent approach helps to clarify why EU member states delegate powers to EU agents and how the agents use these powers under the conditions of vertical and horizontal control. A caveat has to be made, however, with regard to the approach's basic assumption of unitary institutional agents. While evidence indicates that in many cases two distinct sets of organizational interests can be identified, thereby justifying the modeling of two distinct actors, in some cases, *intra*-institutional conflicts may prevail (Christiansen 2001). Thus, the approach hardly captures explanatory factors below the level of the organizational units as defined initially.

Future research on principal-agent and agent-agent interaction in crisis management might build on and refine the concepts outlined in this chapter, namely on the basis of thorough case studies. With the Lisbon Treaty having entered into force on 1 December 2009, it will be furthermore interesting to observe in how far the envisaged (partly) fusion of the structures of the Council Secretariat and the Commission in the framework of the European External Action Service may modify their capacity to influence the EU's crisis management. On the basis of this study, one might expect that agent influence will be further enhanced as a result of limited horizontal control.

Notes

1 The chapter is based on the author's book (Klein 2010). The research was carried out with the kind support of the joint research programme 'European Foreign and Security Policy Studies' of the foundations Compagnia di San Paolo (Italy), Riksbankens Jubileumsfond (Sweden), and Volkswagen-Stiftung (Germany).
2 As highlighted by Christiansen and Vanhoonacker (2008: 767), the Council Secretariat is not an official EU institution in the formal understanding of the Treaties.
3 In this context, see also the notion of 'intensive transgovernmentalism' (Wallace 2005: 87).
4 The notion 'collective principal' does not imply any expectations about the *content* of relevant preferences, but it underlines the process of preference aggregation. It is argued that EU agents essentially are confronted with the *aggregated* preferences of its collective principal becoming manifest in the Union's primary and secondary law (Lyne *et al.* 2006: 46, Pollack 2004: 146). Accordingly, it is assumed that at a given moment EU member governments' preferences and the existing decision-making institution have interacted to produce a single executive preference ruling out possible alternatives. For details, see Klein 2010.
5 Interviews with EU officials in Brussels in 2005, 2006 and 2007.
6 There are Brussels-based or 'travelling' EUSRs such as the EUSR for the African Great Lakes Region and the EUSR for the Middle East Peace Process, and field-based EUSRs such as the EUSR in FYROM and the EUSR in Bosnia. For a detailed overview see Grevi 2007: 157–59.
7 All figures based on 'EU Whoiswho', http://europa.eu/whoiswho/public/index.cfm? (accessed August 2009).

8 Interview with an EU official, Brussels, October 2007.
9 The Civilian/Military Cell (Civ/Mil Cell) should contribute to strategic planning, especially with regard to joint civil-military operations (Khol 2006: 131).
10 Email interview with an EU official, December 2009.
11 The controversy was based on two letters with institutional reform proposals sent by Javier Solana to the EU heads of state and government on 14.12.05 and 13.06.06. Interviews with EU officials and EU member state officials, Brussels, January and October 2007. While the Civilian Operations Commander has been established in 2007, other, more far-reaching reform proposals on the establishment of four 'blocks' within the Council Secretariat (assessment, policy development, mission planning and implementation) have not been implemented at the time of writing.
12 See, for instance, the Tri-Presidency initiative on CMCO with the focus on planning (UK II/2005 (Council of the European Union 2005b)), management (Austria I/2006 (Council of the European Union 2006b)) and situational awareness (Finland II/2006 (Council of the European Union 2006d)).
13 Interview with a Swedish government official, Stockholm, April 2007, on the Swedish initiative in 2005 and 2006 to establish integrated 'Civilian Response Teams' (CRT). Interviews with German government officials in Berlin, July 2006, British government officials in London, October 2006, and French government officials in Paris, November 2006.
14 As a result, depending on their diplomatic resources, some Presidencies had tried to control the process by drafting most proposals on their own. Interview with an EU official, Brussels, October 2007.
15 Interviews with EU officials, Brussels, May 2006 and January 2007.
16 The Western Balkan countries are Albania, Bosnia and Herzegovina (BiH), Croatia, Serbia, Montenegro, Kosovo (under the United Nations Security Council Resolution 1244), and the former Yugoslav Republic of Macedonia (FYROM).
17 Art. 6 of the Instrument for Stability foresees no comitology procedures for 'exceptional assistance measures' with a financial amount of less than Euro 20 million with a duration of up to 24 months. For details, see Klein 2010.
18 Interviews with EU officials, Brussels, November 2005 and May 2006. See also Khol 2006: 129–30.
19 The reference amount for the common costs was fixed at Euro 99, 2 million.
20 Interviews with EU officials, Brussels, October 2007.
21 Interviews with EU officials, Sarajevo, June 2007.

6 The other side of EU crisis management

A sociological institutionalist analysis

Ana E. Juncos

Introduction

Long criticized for being unable to deal with conflicts in its neighbourhood, since the end of the 1990s, the European Union (EU) has concentrated its efforts in building an effective military crisis management capability through the institutionalization of its Common Security and Defence Policy (CSDP). A lot of attention has been paid to the origins and the formal institutionalization of the CSDP (see also Chapter 4), while the performance and day-to-day development of this policy remains a less studied subject. Without neglecting the role of the member states and external events in explaining the origins of the CSDP, this chapter looks at how institutions have shaped the design and performance of military crisis management operations. In line with previous chapters in this section, this chapter highlights the significance of institutions in EU crisis management, but it does so from a different theoretical perspective, that of sociological institutionalism. This chapter argues that sociological institutionalism can be helpful in illuminating some of the puzzles surrounding this policy and, in particular, the design of crisis management institutions and missions, the performance of institutions, and its impact on the policy substance and implementation. In support of this claim, the chapter looks at different factors, building on the insights of sociological institutionalism and organization theory, *inter alia*, institutional isomorphism, organizational routines and socialization processes.

The analysis presented in this chapter shows how informal institutions, culture and norms have affected the design and performance of EU crisis management. It also draws attention to the impact of institutions on processes of preference formation. First, it argues that the design of institutions and EU operations such as EUFOR Althea has more to do with institutional constrains, mimesis and the professionalization of the field than with the rational decisions and preferences of the member states. This explains the similarities between EU and NATO's institutions and operations. Second, although the member states formally control the decision-making process and thus the monitoring and implementation of EU military operations, their capacity to shape day-to-day outcomes is undermined by the logic of existing organizational routines and the role of implementing agents. Finally, a sociological institutionalist approach, as the one adopted in this contribution, also sheds light on processes of socialization whereby the institutional environment within which EU crisis management is embedded might have an impact on actors' preferences and identities.

The empirical evidence used in this chapter is drawn from the planning and implementation of EUFOR Althea. This operation, launched in December 2004 in Bosnia and Herzegovina (hereafter Bosnia), constitutes so far the largest and longest running EU military operation. This mission is being carried out with recourse to NATO assets and capabilities, according to the Berlin Plus arrangements. The EU expressed its readiness to take over from the NATO mission in Bosnia as early as December 2002 (European Council 2002). One year later, and after the EU had successfully taken over the NATO operation in Macedonia, preparations for EUFOR Althea started in Mons and Brussels. However, the launch of the mission had to await NATO's official announcement at the Istanbul Summit in June 2004 that operation Stabilization Force (SFOR) would be concluded (North Atlantic Council 2004).[1] The transfer of authority from SFOR to EUFOR took place on 2 December 2004. EUFOR took over the job with approximately 7,000 troops, the same number as SFOR had in December 2004. Essentially, the same forces which contributed to SFOR were present in EUFOR (the soldiers just swapped their badges for the insignia of the European Union Force), but with the major difference that there were no US troops. In May 2007, following a previous Council decision, EUFOR Althea was downsized. At the time of writing (February 2010), a total of 2,000 troops remain in the country. The operation mandate was amended to include non-executive capacity building and training tasks as part of the EU's contribution to security sector reform in the country in January 2010. Given political situation in the country, a final date for withdrawal has not been agreed yet among the member states.[2] The empirical evidence gathered about this operation will be used to support the main theoretical arguments and to illustrate the potential of sociological institutionalism to contribute to an understanding of the role of institutions in EU crisis management.

To demonstrate the usefulness of this theoretical perspective, the chapter proceeds as follows. It first introduces the core analytical tenets of sociological institutionalism, an approach that, it is argued, can overcome some of the weaknesses of rationalist and intergovernmentalist explanations of EU crisis management. It then examines three factors identified in the sociological institutionalist literature: institutional isomorphism, organizational routines and socialization processes. It is argued here that the analysis of EU crisis management could benefit from an application of these three concepts. This argument is supported with empirical evidence drawn from the case study of EUFOR Althea. Finally, the chapter discusses some of the flaws of this approach and outlines a future research agenda.[3]

Competing explanations of EU crisis management

Theoretical explanations of the origins and development of EU crisis management (and the CSDP) have frequently relied on rationalist and intergovernmentalist approaches. The member states, and in particular, the Big Three (France,

Germany and the UK), have often been singled out as the key actors in the establishment of the EU crisis management structures following the decision agreed at St Malo and then endorsed at the European Councils of Cologne, Helsinki and Feira, and at the 2000 Intergovernmental Conference. In particular, the change of strategy of the UK regarding European defence has been mentioned as one of the factors explaining the St Malo agreement (Howorth 2004; Whitman 1999). External events such as the Bosnian or the Kosovo crisis or changes in the structure of the international system have also been mentioned as explanatory factors in the emergence of CSDP (Everts 2002; Hyde-Price 2006; Howorth 2004; Pond 1999; see also Chapter 4). From a realist perspective, the creation of CSDP institutions is seen as a purposive act of rational decision-makers and these institutions reflect the interests of the most powerful EU member states. In line with French and British preferences, CSDP has thus remained an intergovernmental policy. From this perspective, the possibility of changes in member states' preferences and a common identity emerging from cooperation within EU institutions is rather limited (Gordon 1997/1998; Lindley-French 2002).

Notwithstanding the validity of intergovernmental and realist explanations of CSDP, it can be argued that 'grand bargains' among the member states at EU summits take place in a particular institutional context that constrains the range of available options and shapes actors' preferences (Smith 2004b). In many cases, while CSDP institutions are the result of the member states' decisions, they are not necessarily the products of conscious design or they do not develop in the way foreseen by their creators. Besides, although the member states remain the 'masters of the treaties', their capacity to shape political outcomes *in between* intergovernmental conferences is undermined by the autonomous activity of CSDP organizations and the implementing agents (see also Chapter 5). When it comes to the day-to-day implementation of the CSDP, the institutional environment within which EU crisis management is embedded can also be said to have an impact on actors' preferences through processes of socialization. This understanding of EU crisis management is heavily reliant on the insights from the 'new institutionalist' research agenda, and namely, sociological institutionalism.

Sociological institutionalism emerged as a reaction to rationalist accounts in political science where individuals were often portrayed as atomistic and utility-maximizing. Instead sociological institutionalism stresses the centrality of 'routines, procedures, conventions, roles, strategies, organizational forms and technologies around which political activity is constructed [as well as] beliefs, paradigms, codes, cultures, and knowledge that surround, support, elaborate, and contradict those roles and routines' (March and Olsen 1989: 22). Unlike rational choice institutionalism, sociological institutionalism embraces a broader conception of institutions including informal rules and 'culture', as well as bureaucratic organizations. From this perspective, institutions are not only arenas in which politics take place, but also determine the distribution of resources, and provide the institutional memory, i.e. they are a repository of routines and practices. More specifically, for March and Olsen (1998: 948), institutions might define 'appropriate behaviour for specific groups of actors in specific situations', in other words, legitimize certain ways of doing things. In this light, institutions represent the 'rules of the game' (North 1990: 83).

In the following sections, I will assess the added value of sociological institutionalism in the analysis of EU crisis management. In particular, I will discuss three concepts that have been identified in this literature – institutional isomorphism, standard operating procedures and socialization processes – to explain the design, performance and impact of institutions.

The design of institutions: institutional isomorphism

An important contribution of sociological institutionalism to the study of EU crisis management is its focus on culture and legitimacy when explaining the design of institutions which contrast with the rationalist view of institutions and bureaucracy. According to rational choice institutionalism, institutions are considered to be consciously created in order to facilitate cooperation and solve collective action problems (Pollack 1997; Tsebelis 1994). The Weberian view of bureaucratic organizations is also one of rationality and efficiency. The move towards more similar organizations in our modern society is said to be the result of an effort of bureaucratic organizations to increase efficiency in performing their tasks (Hall and Taylor 1996: 14). From a sociological institutionalist perspective, however, institutions, and in particular, the similarity between organizations in the same field can be explained by reference to legitimacy, rather than effectiveness.

The concept of isomorphism coined by DiMaggio and Powell (1991) seems particularly helpful in this regard. This concept posits that instead of diversity in institutional designs, one should expect similarity and homogenization of organizational fields (DiMaggio and Powell 1983). According to DiMaggio and Powell, isomorphic processes can make 'organizations more similar without necessarily making them more efficient' (1983: 147). Institutions are not designed in a particular way to fit particular requirements or tasks, they are not designed on a *tabula rasa*; they are modelled on other institutions to enhance legitimacy rather than to improve performance. DiMaggio and Powell distinguish three mechanisms of institutional isomorphism: coercive, mimetic and normative.

Coercive isomorphism stems from external pressures (e.g. new laws or regulations) or dependence on other organizations. Mimetic isomorphism would result from uncertainty. When there is uncertainty or goals are ambiguous one can expect organizations to model themselves on other organizations. As mentioned before, the adoption of such models can also have a ritual aspect: enhancing legitimacy of the new organization by adopting the models of other organizations that are perceived as more legitimate or successful (DiMaggio and Powell 1983: 152). Finally, normative isomorphism stems from the professionalization of that organizational field. Mechanisms such as education, the establishment of professional networks, as well as the filtering or transference of personnel from one organization to another 'create a pool of almost interchangeable individuals who occupy similar positions across a range of organizations and possess a similarity of orientation and disposition that may override variations in tradition and control that might otherwise shape organizational behaviour' (DiMaggio and Powell 1983: 153). In sum, these three mechanisms might explain why organizations within the same field tend to look alike.

Although this model has been originally applied to economic and social organizations, much can be gained by applying this concept to other areas such as political or security institutions (see for instance Radaelli 1997; Smith 2004b). Imitation of EC procedures has already been mentioned by M.E. Smith (2004b: 240–44) to explain some of the features of Common Foreign and Security Policy (CFSP) institutions. In the case of EU military crisis management, one could look at NATO's structures and procedures to explain its current configuration. As expected from this perspective, when it comes to dealing with crisis management, the EU has modelled itself following NATO's procedures, already familiar to most of the EU member states – twenty-one of the twenty-seven EU member states are also NATO members and another five member states are Partnership for Peace members. The decision-making process for the launching of a military operation follows the so-called Crisis Management Procedures (Council of the European Union 2003b) which describe the procedures for the planning, implementation and evaluation of an EU crisis management operation (military or civilian in nature) and which are very similar to that of NATO. The same can be said of the EU's rules of engagement that follow closely those that are used in NATO operations.[4] When it comes to EU institutional structures, resemblance between the EU and NATO is also striking: a politico-military body at ambassadorial level, assisted by a Military Committee composed by the representatives of the Chief of Defence and supported by a military staff. Although some differences remained – for instance the Political and Security Committee (PSC) did not originally have a permanent chair as is the case with the North Atlantic Council, the member states had certainly taken NATO decision-making structures into account when establishing the PSC, the EU Military Committee and the EU Military Staff (for more on this, see Reynolds 2007).[5]

Arguably, NATO's institutional arrangements were taken as a model for EU crisis management not only because there were obvious gains in future co-ordinating arrangements and harmonization of military capabilities, but also because it was perceived as a 'successful' institution, even by those member states that were more reluctant about the role of the Alliance in European security.[6] One could argue that the three mechanisms identified by DiMaggio and Powell (coercive, mimetic and normative) have facilitated the homogenization of European security governance. First, one can point to the dependence of the EU when it comes to NATO planning and assets. This dependence has fostered the need to establish interoperable forces and capabilities through the Headline Goal process. Second, one could also argue that the EU has adopted structures and processes similar to those in NATO because, in an uncertain environment, many policy-makers perceived this model as an effective one, irrespective of whether this was the best model for the type of security organization that the EU wanted to become (see also Stewart's in this volume). In this way, by copying NATO arrangements, the EU would try to increase its legitimacy in the security field. Finally, normative isomorphism can also be identified in this case. If one looks at the officials and troops that are participating in NATO and EU operations, one can discover a high degree of transfer of personnel from one organization to the other, something that is not only allowed, but also encouraged by the member states. This filtering process facilitates harmonization of procedures and capabilities. Usually, these officials have very similar training and background and undergo anticipatory socialization to common expectations about their personal behaviour, common jargon, and even appropriate style of dress.

As DiMaggio and Powell argue, this isomorphic process may take place even without evidence that it increases effectiveness. In other words, '[n]one of this, however, insures that conformist organizations do what they do more efficiently than do their more deviant peers' (1983: 154). However, in medium long term, it might well increase effectiveness precisely because of the homogenization of structures and procedures. According to them, '[t]his similarity can make it easier for organizations to transact with other organizations, to attract career-minded staff, to be acknowledged as legitimate and reputable, and to fit into administrative categories that define eligibility for public and private grants and contracts' (DiMaggio and Powell 1983: 153). For instance, in the case of EU-NATO cooperation, isomorphism might well lead to increasing interoperability of forces and procedures, which could in turn increase the effectiveness of these organizations when dealing with international crises under Berlin Plus.

The performance of institutions: an (inefficient) organizational logic

Sociological institutionalism has its roots in sociology and organization theory (Peters 1999: 26) and it has incorporated many of the insights from these disciplines. What these studies highlighted was the fact that, in contrast to rationalist approaches to institutions, the activities of organizations often deviated from the original purposes of their creators; that their routines and procedures made them resistant to change and innovation; and that organizations were usually conflictual and loosely coupled (Allison and Zelikow 1999; Brunsson and Olsen 1998; Pressman and Wildavsky 1973). In sum, this perspective captures well the independent dynamics affecting institutions that sometimes make them rather ineffective, producing unintended results.

In order to understand the way organizations perform, we must first introduce the concept of organizational routines, also known as standard operating procedures (SOPs), which refers to 'those specific rules of behaviour that are agreed upon and (in general) followed by agents' (Lowndes 2002: 103) or 'the routines for dealing with *standard* situations' (Allison and Zelikow 1999: 178, emphasis in the original). In a context of uncertainty and complexity, organizations rely upon SOPs. Organizations fit problems, no matter the specificities of a particular situation, into 'standard' solutions or SOPs. These institutional routines are ordered into institutional programmes and repertoires that are then applied to a specific situation. SOPs allow for concerted action by the members of a given organization in response to a problem. On the downside, SOPs are difficult to change and the routinization of organizational action means that, as a result, organizational behaviour can be at times reactive, inappropriate or too formalistic (Allison and Zelikow 1999: 169–70).

On the other hand, to better deal with uncertainty, there is a tendency among organizations to fragment and divide issues according to areas of responsibility (Allison and Zelikow 1999: 166). This compartmentalization of responsibilities, with different organizations/units being responsible for different policy areas, facilitates their task and specialized attention to a specific problem, but it also makes coordination more difficult. Unintended consequences might be the result of the complexity of joint action (Pressman and Wildavsky 1973). In large organizations, the existence of contradictory and overlapping routines and rules at different levels increase the chances of clashes and problems. Moreover, organizations might try to colonize or take control of new areas of activity (Pressman and Wildavsky 1973: 181, note 76). This process of colonization or exploration can also be expected in the interactions between different EU organizations (Schroeder 2007).

Finally, an organizational approach points at the possibility that officials might use their expertise and exploit their autonomy from the principals when operationalizing the broader objectives set up in the organization's mandate into concrete tasks (Allison and Zelikow 1999). In this way, organizations dispose of certain autonomy when it comes to the implementation of the mission. Political decisions might also deviate from original objectives because of the dysfunctional performance of institutions. This does not always occur, and in general organizations increase the capacity of political leaders, but political masters should be wary of the possibility of unintended consequences and dysfunctional behaviour by institutions. For all these reasons, one may expect that the implementation of the mission's objectives will differ from the original intentions of its political masters.

The impact of institutions: socialization processes

Even though rationalist approaches admit that actors' strategies can be modified as a consequence of institutional arrangements, they deny that institutions affect actor preferences. Interests are instead considered to be exogenously formed and to remain fixed. Hence EU-level institutional environments such as CFSP institutions are considered to have no impact upon the definition of national preferences since these are considered to be formed in a domestic context external to the institution itself and no changes would be expected to occur as a result of such routine interactions in Brussels (Moravcsik 1993). By contrast, for sociological institutionalists, institutions shape not only actors' strategies, but also their preferences and identities (Checkel 2001; Lewis 2005). Institutions involve a normative dimension, prescribing norms of behaviour, and a cognitive one, giving meaning to the world and determining its interpretation and the limits of the thinkable (Hall and Taylor 1996: 15). For sociological institutionalists, individual choices and preferences cannot be understood 'outside of the cultural and historical frameworks in which they are embedded' (DiMaggio and Powell 1991: 10). Thus, the process of preference formation is endogenous, shaped by individuals' involvement in institutions. This argument follows the so-called 'logic of appropriateness' coined by March and Olsen: actors do not try to calculate the consequences of their actions in cost-benefit terms according to the 'logic of consequences', but instead 'actors associate certain actions with certain situations by rules of appropriateness' (March and Olsen 1984: 741).

It is through socialization processes that individuals grasp those 'rules of appropriateness'. Socialization has been broadly conceived in the literature as a force shaping 'the practices, perceptions and interests of policy makers, including any possible redefinition of self-interest' (Manners and Whitman 2000: 7–8) or a 'process by which social interaction leads novices to endorse expected ways of thinking, feeling and acting' (Johnston 2001: 493). From this viewpoint, the institutions in which people act have a 'deep' impact shaping not only actors' behaviours, but also their preferences and identities, leading to an internalization of rules and norms (i.e. norms would become taken for granted by actors). One could expect therefore that interactions within EU institutions would facilitate socialization processes which may not only shape the process of goal selection and actors' strategies, but also lead, in the longer term, to a reconstitution of actors' preferences and identities. This is also the case in the security realm where 'CFSP might be better understood in terms of identity creation than as an exclusively rationally-based exercise in national self-interest' (Tonra 2003: 738). From the previous account, it seems clear that sociological institutionalism can offer useful avenues to investigate the policy design and implementation of EU crisis management.

A sociological institutionalist analysis of EUFOR

This contribution uses the case of EUFOR Althea in Bosnia as the primary test case for the theoretical approach. The empirical evidence presented here shows how sociological institutionalism can explain the design, performance and impact of EU crisis management institutions.

Borrowing from NATO: the design of EUFOR

Beginning with the design of institutions, EUFOR Althea was essentially modelled on the previous NATO-led operation SFOR. During the planning phase, the transfer of operational procedures and practices from NATO was of paramount importance. Most of the planning relied on the intelligence and assessments of SFOR on the ground and NATO Headquarters in Mons (Brussels) and EUFOR basically inherited SFOR's Operational Plan. The EU staff involved in the early planning of operation Althea spent an enormous amount of time coordinating with NATO Headquarters.[7] According to a former EUFOR official, 'while the mobilization of NATO expertise facilitated the work of the planners, it also narrowed the room for operational innovation' (Bertin 2007: 63). In other words, dependence on NATO planning and capabilities helps explain similarity between the two missions, following the aforementioned mechanism of coercive isomorphism.

Certainly mimetic isomorphism also played a role in the design of EUFOR. Since SFOR was perceived as a 'success' by the Bosnian authorities and population, the EU military operation was to perform the same key and supporting tasks as SFOR. EUFOR took over with the same troop levels as its predecessor to ensure a smooth transition and boost its credibility. In spite of this, EUFOR also wanted to be recognized as 'different' and a way to do so was taking over new tasks such as the fight against organized crime.[8] The resulting EUFOR was a very robust one with similar tasks to SFOR and an even tougher approach to organized crime. Finally, normative isomorphism can also be mentioned here. The fact that many officials in charge of EUFOR had previously taken part in NATO missions (including SFOR) or had been seconded to NATO Headquarters cannot be underestimated and certainly facilitated the transfer of NATO procedures and practices to the EU operation.

Other features of SFOR were also retained by EUFOR among them, the creation of Liaison and Observation Teams and the establishment of a paramilitary police force, the Integrated Police Unit. To facilitate coordination with the civilian authorities and population, EUFOR established 46 Liaison and Observation Teams living in rented houses among the Bosnian population. They were deployed at potential hot-spots and served (and still do) as an 'early-warning system'. This practice was based on the Civil-Military Cooperation Concept of SFOR which was to provide the operational commanders with intelligence, including information about the political and social context where the operation takes places (NATO 2000; Packett II *et al.* 2005: 71). One can also point at the experience of the EU Monitoring Mission in Bosnia which had monitoring teams deployed around the country.[9]

For its part, the creation of the Integrated Police Unit, which took over from its predecessor in SFOR, the Multinational Specialized Unit, shows clearly the difficulties EUFOR faced in trying to innovate, as well as the weight of previous institutional legacies. From the outset, some countries argued that the Integrated Police Unit should not be located under the chain of command of the military mission, but under the EU Police Mission. According to these member states (Nordic countries, Spain and France),[10] 'such a reorganization would have been in line with EU concepts, according to which police officers assigned to international mission should be placed under civilian command' (Bertin 2007: 63; see also Council of the European Union 2003a). Italy, by contrast, was very keen on the establishment of this type of force within EUFOR (it was already the main contributor to the paramilitary force in SFOR).[11] Due to the divergent views amongst the member states, the final decision drew heavily on the past SFOR practice. The member states agreed to set up a paramilitary police contingent under EUFOR command, but only consisting of forces from those few member states willing to contribute to it.

Organizational routines and practices: an implementation perspective

Insights from sociological institutionalism also offer useful perspectives on the performance of the mission. In the case of EUFOR Althea, organizational routines determine formal and informal channels of communication and the way information flows within the mission. Formal provisions in the Joint Action ensure internal coherence and strategic direction from Brussels to Sarajevo. The political control of the operation lies with the Council, with the assistance of the High Representative for the CFSP. For more day-to-day management, the PSC exercises political control and strategic direction of the operation. Regarding the operational command of the mission, and, in line with the Berlin Plus arrangements, NATO's Deputy Supreme Allied Commander Europe (DSACEUR) has been appointed as Operation Commander. The Operation Commander reports directly to the PSC and Defence Ministers when appropriate and to the joint PSC-North Atlantic Council meetings. The chain of command goes from the EU Operational Headquarters in SHAPE (Mons, Belgium) down to Naples where an EU Command Element has been established. These formal SOPs and the existence of double-hatted posts in Mons and Naples have ensured coordination between the EU and NATO at the strategic and tactical level. However, at the political level, SOPs proved of no use due to a Turkish veto which has put formal discussions on hold at PSC-North Atlantic Council meetings. Hence informal mechanisms of coordination in theatre became key to solve political disagreements in Brussels. For instance, an informal agreement between the NATO and EUFOR Commanders was achieved by which, they agreed to share the authority to vet senior Bosnian officers and to authorize the movement of weapons in the country. They also agreed on a division of tasks between the two organizations.[12]

SOPs also determined other aspects of the implementation of the mission, including EU-NATO arrangements for contingency plans, the troops' code of conduct – know in military jargon as the 'rules of engagement' – and issues relating to national caveats. The mission's SOPs aim to help develop a common doctrine, but recognising the diversity of each national contingent in terms of tactics, techniques and procedures (Packett II *et al.* 2005: 70). While these SOPs ensure coordinated action and minimize confusion in an uncertain environment, sometimes they are too inflexible or inadequate for a particular situation. For instance, the rules of engagement might require changes to adapt to new circumstances on the ground. If these are significant changes, the Force Commander will have to communicate them to the Operational Commander who will have to do the same at the political level. Given the protracted decision-making process in the EU, this whole process might take too long in an emergency situation. Concerns about this problem were expressed in the case of the EU operation in Congo in 2007.[13]

National caveats (domestic laws that limit the way in which a national contingent can contribute to international peacekeeping forces) have also affected the performance of the mission, although in this respect, EUFOR is not very different from other international missions. The French troops, for instance, are not allowed to participate in crowd control operations, nor can they use dogs or bullets. The Dutch caveats are also significant in the fight against organized crime and corruption, and German troops are not allowed to use tear gas and need approval from the Bundestag for several types of operations. Usually these caveats are announced by the member states before the operation begins, but it may happen that sometimes they are not communicated to the Force Commander or that they are established once the operation has started, for instance, as a result of changes in the rules of engagement. In this case, the Force Commander will only find out later on that he or she cannot dispose of some troops and will need to introduce changes to the mission's programmes. This was the case with EUFOR's activities in the fight against organized crime where the Force Commander only discovered some of the national caveats after the mission was launched.[14]

For its part, complexity of joint action helps explain, for instance, some of the problems that EUFOR encountered when implementing its mandate (Pressman and Wildavsky 1973). Different EU bodies have different routines and organizational culture, not to mention the existence of different rules and strategies at different levels within the same organization (at the political, strategic and tactical levels). Thus, fragmentation of the EU activities on the ground introduced some strains in the implementation of the operation. Even though the need for a coherent action was acknowledged from the outset, problems did not take time to materialize. A case in point refers to the fight against organized crime and the coordination between EUFOR and the EU Police Mission (EUPM). In theory, the mandates of the two missions did not clash. Whereas the EUPM's mandate aimed at long-term capacity-building of the police forces, EUFOR focused on short-term deterrence. The first had a non-executive mandate (monitor, mentor and inspect); the latter an executive one with enforcement tools to be used if appropriate. However, as a result of the existence of some grey areas between the EUPM and EUFOR's mandates, tensions between the two missions did not take time to appear, especially due to, what some EUPM officers considered, an intrusive attitude on the part of EUFOR.

The first EUFOR Commander, General Leakey, expressed his personal commitment to play a significant role regarding this issue (Leakey 2006), making clear from the beginning EUFOR's expansionist strategy. Since EUFOR key tasks were easily performed (the country has not experience major threats to security in the last 15 years), resources were left available to expand activities to other domains. Once EUFOR took over from SFOR, several operations were launched to support local law enforcement agencies in fighting illegal activities such as weapons smuggling, drug trafficking and illegal logging. Although EUFOR officials stressed that these operations were not meant to usurp local efforts, this assertive approach generated some criticism amongst EUPM and other EU officials for exceeding its mandate.[15] As one EUPM official put it, 'by sending EUFOR here with 7,000 soldiers stopping cars, closing borders, arresting people [. . .], it is conflicting with our mandate'.[16]

With regard to the role of the implementing agents, the Joint Action (Council of the European Union 2004a) and the Operational Plan, adopted at the political level, specified EUFOR tasks, troops, capabilities and rules of engagement. One could expect therefore the implementation of EUFOR to follow a linear process and stick to the provisions agreed by its political masters. However, after a closer look at EUFOR implementation, this claim needs qualifying at least. This is because the implementing agents have certain degree of autonomy to adapt the general objectives stated in the mission's Operational Plan to the specific circumstances on the ground. As we have noted before, the Force Commander may introduce operational changes in the mission's mandate or rules of engagement as a result of changes in the environment or unintended consequences, although if these changes are substantial, the PSC will have to approve them. All in all, the Operational Plan has to be flexible enough to give the Operations Commander and the Force Commander the necessary room of manoeuvre but without leading to excessive micromanagement from the ground.

There are situations where it is possible for the implementing agents (the Force Commander) to deviate from the original intentions of the member states. The role of EUFOR in the fight against organized crime can be mentioned here as an example. At the political level, while most of the member states agreed on the importance of dealing with organized crime in Bosnia, they diverged on the appropriate strategy to be used. As mentioned before, it was finally agreed the creation of an Integrated Police Unit and the inclusion of organized crime as a supporting task of EUFOR, but for many member states, it had to remain so: a supporting task which should not determine the size of the force.[17] However, from the beginning, it was obvious that at the implementation level, the Force Commander had a different view on the matter and saw organized crime as one of the main tasks of EUFOR (Leakey 2006). The proactive role played by EUFOR from December 2004 showed not only the clashing objectives between the political and tactical levels, but also the difficulties of the political level to control the implementing agents.

A different case might be that of the national seconded officials to the Council Secretariat (DG-VIII and EU Military Staff) who play an important role in the drafting of the documents during the planning and implementation of military operations. Although the administrative level does not enjoy as much autonomy as is the case in the design of civilian crisis management operations, the EU Military Staff and officials from DG-VIII do have some room of manoeuvre to incorporate their input in the planning of the operation because they have the expertise, maintain the institutional memory and draft all the documents that will be adopted at the political level. But, in general, Council Secretariat officials are very careful to take into account the member states' positions and produce documents which are 'potentially flyable'.[18] They help achieve consensus since they know what the potential red lines are. According to one EUMS official, 'because we sit very close to these guys and we sit in all the committees, we pick up fairly quickly the political nuances and the issues that are running'.[19]

Institutionalized interactions: socialization processes and EUFOR

Finally, if we take the case of EUFOR Althea, a focus on socialization processes allows for an analysis of the impact of norms and EU institutions in the launch of the mission. A first question relates to why the member states agreed to launch this operation. In this regard, a sociological institutionalist perspective would point at the importance of values and identities in explaining this decision. In support of this argument, one could argue that 'national interests', understood in terms of vital security interests or economic interests, cannot explain why the member states adopted this decision. In fact, there was no need for the EU to take over from NATO. A NATO operation could have stayed in the country for two or three years more, even without US troops on the ground. Factors other than material, security-related considerations were thus important in this case. Two motives help account for the EU's decision to launch CSDP operations in Bosnia. First, a desire on the part of the EU member states to test and develop EU crisis management capabilities (i.e. its desire to strengthen the EU's global role) in a 'controlled environment', and second, a shared responsibility towards the future of Bosnia, symbolized by the prospect of EU membership. After the fiasco of UNPROFOR (mainly a European force), this new force epitomized the EU's desire to rebuild its credibility in the region, as well as on the world stage, thus making it clear that CSDP was not simply a talking shop.[20] In sum, this was justified as a decision to pursue collective rather than national interests.

Looking at socialization processes at the micro-level reveals the role played by national representatives and EU officials in Brussels-based institutions. A case in point is the role played by the PSC. Negotiations in this committee show how socialization processes can help national representatives to reach a compromise. This is possible because national representatives are concerned by their reputation and credibility in the group and they will try to avoid isolation. As a group, PSC ambassadors want to be seen as 'effective' and will try to adopt as many decisions as possible in order to ease the burden of the Foreign Affairs Council. In sum, they are committed to 'make the system work' and they also share expectations about appropriate behavior within the PSC (Lewis 2006: 20). The role of the PSC in forging consensus among the member states has been discussed elsewhere (Howorth 2007b: 21–22; Juncos and Reynolds 2007; Meyer 2006: 132–35). In relation with EUFOR, the PSC was an arena for negotiations between the British and the French regarding EU-NATO cooperation (see also Meyer 2006: 135) and also on the role of the Integrated Police Unit. In the first case, even though all the member states initially agreed on the use of Berlin Plus, there were some disagreements on the way the particular distribution of tasks and intelligence-sharing would take place, with the UK and France leading two opposing camps. After negations in the PSC, an agreement was reached to allow NATO to maintain a Headquarters with around 200 staff to support defence reform, counter-terrorism and the detention of persons indicted for war crimes. However, to symbolize the primacy of EUFOR on the ground, the EUFOR Commander would be a three star general, while the US Commander in charge of NATO Headquarters was only a two star general. The PSC was also the scenario for discussions regarding the role and composition of the IPU. As mentioned before, a compromise was reached to set up a paramilitary police contingent, but only consisting of forces from those few member states willing to contribute to it. Furthermore, the composition and status of the IPU would be submitted to regular revision by the PSC.

Yet, more research needs to be done to determine whether, in this particular case, EU institutions have had a deep impact on individuals leading to internalization of norms. As noted elsewhere (Juncos and Pomorska 2006), some intrinsic characteristics of the CFSP domain might suggest that socialization in this policy domain has mainly followed a logic of strategic calculation (Checkel 2005). High rotation levels and the often narrow margin of manoeuvre of national diplomats in Brussels are mechanisms established by the capitals in order to prevent them from 'going native'. Even if internalization of norms is not ruled out in the long term, what it is often observed in the case of national representatives dealing with ESDP and EU crisis management is that they adopt practices, such as consensus-building or the co-ordination reflex because of strategic reasons. The long term perspective of negotiations means that complying with the rules of the group may result from a rational cost-benefit calculation. For instance, compromising on an issue today might help achieve another issue of major importance in future negotiations. Furthermore, since frequent and repetitive contacts take place amongst the same individuals, national representatives have an incentive to maintain their reputation and credibility within the group by following its rules. The final section reviews other aspects of sociological institutionalism which would require some theoretical and methodological refinement and outlines a future research agenda.

Conclusion: weaknesses and a future research agenda

From the previous account, it is clear that sociological institutionalism has potential to contribute to a better understanding of different aspects of EU crisis management. These insights are particularly useful when analysing the design and implementation of EUFOR showing that EU crisis management does not always follows a 'rational plan'. With its emphasis on rules and norms and a continuous questioning of the 'rationality' of institutional design and performance, it can illuminate many aspects of EU crisis management for which rationalist and intergovernmental explanations seem inadequate or incomplete. For instance, sociological institutionalism can help explain the striking similarities between NATO and EU institutions and operations. It is also useful in exploring organizational routines and processes that account for many features surrounding the implementation of EU crisis management. Finally, a focus on socialization processes sheds light on the impact that EU institutions have on the policy process and, arguably, on the policy substance.

Critics of sociological institutionalism have however pointed at this approach's tendency to neglect human agency. Since some institutions become taken for granted, and in so doing determine the preferences and identities of individuals, this can make the possibilities for agential response very limited within this approach. It therefore has been criticized for its determinism in 'writing actors out of the script' and treating them as 'cultural dupes' (Tonra 2003: 735). However, sociological institutionalism can also incorporate a role for agency as it is often the case that actors are socialized in different environments simultaneously and they will have to choose between competing or shared allegiances. This involves a degree of strategic action in interpreting the meaning of the institutional environment (Finnemore and Sikkink 1998; Peters 1999: 26). Moreover, agency is not the

main concern here since an over-emphasis on agency is precisely what sociological institutionalism approaches seek to counter.

Sociological institutionalism has also been criticized for its failure to explain
innovation (Hall and Taylor 1996). The fact that some institutions can become
taken for granted, determining actors' preferences and identities, can in turn limit
agent's ability to introduce institutional change. According to Hall and Taylor
(1996: 8), 'institutions are resistant to redesign ultimately because they structure
the very choices about reform that the individual is likely to make'. For this reason,
institutions are perceived as being quite resistant to change and hence the problem
of sociological institutionalism to explain it. Yet, one could argue that sociological
institutionalism does not entirely reject the possibility of change or redesign of
institutions, but foregrounds incremental change by pointing at the importance of
institutional legacies. Innovation, or a fundamental alteration of existing structures
(March 1991), would be very unusual and often the result of critical junctures or
external shocks (Skocpol 1979; see also Petrov's in this volume).

There are also some methodological challenges regarding the operationaliza-
tion of this approach. A first challenge refers to the issue of internalization of
norms: has a norm been internalized and to what extent, or is it only followed
according to strategic calculations? Second, and related to the former, in practice,
it is difficult to distinguish between the logic of consequences and the logic of
appropriateness. As noted by Lewis (2006: 9), in the cases of the EU presidency
and the Council General Secretariat 'it is notoriously difficult to cleanly separate
instrumental motivations from noninstrumental/ appropriateness ones'; these two
logics become 'intertwined'. These challenges however do not make the analysis
of socialization less pertinent, but on the contrary encourage more research to
determine in which instances national representatives and EU officials are more
likely to follow a logic of appropriateness or otherwise.

Despite the potential of sociological institutionalism to contribute to the study of
EU crisis management, there are only few studies that have exploited this potential
(Schroeder 2007). In particular, we still need more in-depth empirical research to
test some of the aforementioned claims. For instance, the concept of isomorphism
can be aptly applied to the design of different components of EU crisis management, including the development of its civilian capabilities. In the latter case, more
research needs to be done on whether and how the EU has followed other organizations' experiences when designing its own police and monitoring missions (e.g.
the United Nations or the OSCE). The study of EU crisis management would also
profit from a development of the literature on organizational processes and organizational culture, both at the EU and at the national level.

Furthermore, there are few studies of the socialization process in EU crisis
management or in a CSDP more broadly. There have been several studies on
the PSC and the CFSP Council Working Groups (Howorth 2007b; Juncos and
Pomorska 2006; Juncos and Reynolds 2007; Meyer 2006). These studies have
noted the impact of Brussels-based institutions on actors' behaviours. As a result
of participation in these institutions, national representatives have adopted the
groups' rules and norms, including consensus-building and a co-ordination reflex.

Yet, the impact of socialization on national interests and on the policy substance still remains a matter of controversy. More research looking at specific policies or cases needs to be conducted to offer a more definitive account of the nexus between national interests and Brusselization. Another promising research avenue refers to the role of epistemic communities, looking in particular at the role of experts and national representatives in EU committees and institutions (for more on this see Davis Cross 2008; Howorth 2004). Sociological institutionalism can also be helpful in tracing how social representations determine the shape and functioning of EU crisis management institutions (Mérand 2006). In sum, there are still many worthy and interesting research questions that deserve attention and that would benefit from a perspective inspired by sociological institutionalism. The hope is that this chapter serves to provide some pointers in this direction.

Notes

1 NATO had operated in the country since 1995 when it first deployed 60,000 troops under the Implementation Force (IFOR). In 1997, IFOR was replaced by SFOR with 30,000 troops.
2 For more information about the operation, see http://www.euforbih.org/ [last accessed: 15 August 2010].
3 In addition to secondary sources, this chapter draws on 35 semi-structured interviews conducted with EU officials and national diplomats between March 2005 and June 2007. The author would like to thank the many officials who gave their time to discuss their work. To maintain the anonymity of the interviewees, neither their name nor their positions are disclosed.
4 Interview with an EU official, Brussels, May 2007.
5 With the entry into force of the Lisbon Treaty, the PSC is chaired by a permanent representative of the High Representative for Foreign Affairs and Security Policy (Treaty of Lisbon, Declaration 9).
6 Interview with a French national diplomat, May 2007.
7 Interview with an EU official, Brussels, November 2005.
8 The first Force Commander, General Leakey, used to characterize EUFOR as 'new and distinct' operation when comparing to SFOR (Leakey, 2006: 60). The slogan of EUFOR ('From Stabilisation to Integration') also sought to emphasize the added value of EUFOR.
9 Interview with an EUPM official, London, January 2006.
10 While the Nordic countries were reluctant to the idea of paramilitary police forces as such, France and Spain, even though they do have paramilitary police forces, resisted their use within a military chain of command.
11 Interviews in Brussels and Sarajevo, 2005–6.
12 Interviews with EUFOR officials, 2007.
13 Interview with an EU official, Brussels, May 2007.
14 Ibid.
15 Interviews with EUFOR, EUPM and EUSR officials, Sarajevo, 2005.
16 Interview with an EUPM official, Sarajevo, May 2005.
17 Interviews with national diplomats, Brussels, January 2006.
18 Interview with an EU official, Brussels, November 2005.
19 Ibid.
20 Interviews in Brussels, 2005–6. The symbolism of the operation can be seen from the high number of contributors (34 countries). For many countries, in particular, EU member states, participating in EUFOR was in itself important, even though they could only make small contributions.

Part III
Policies

7 The EU in West Africa

From development to diplomatic policy?

Marie V. Gibert

The European Union (EU), over the last decade, has become increasingly concerned with conflicts and insecurity in other parts of the world and has accordingly stepped up its involvement in these issues and developed a set of conflict prevention and crisis management policies. This evolution has occurred in parallel with, and is clearly linked to the emergence of a European Common Foreign and Security Policy (CFSP), and seemed to point to the politicization of the EU's external relations, until then essentially based on the European Community's (EC's) development policies and on member states' relations with third states. The Lisbon Treaty is meant to strengthen this new trend by creating a High Representative of the Union for Foreign Affairs and Security Policy, an External Action Service and transforming the European Commission delegations into EU delegations that replace the Presidency's embassies in their representation and negotiation functions. It would seem reasonable to conclude from this set of observations that the EU is attempting to become a diplomatic actor, one increasingly involved in the making of international political affairs, in possession of a good understanding of the politics of its international partners and willing to engage in political negotiations with them – hence the concept of 'politicization' used here.

This chapter analyzes how conflict prevention policies have been introduced into the EU's development agenda.[1] These policies did not emerge in a vacuum and have therefore been based on, tied to or streamlined with other, often older external relations policies, thus creating some room for gaps and inconsistencies between different policy instruments, approaches and discourses. Whereas studies of EU conflict prevention and crisis management focusing on the Brussels institutions or on other parts of the world may underline deep changes in the nature of the EU's foreign policy, this chapter will show that in Africa these changes have been more quantitative than qualitative. The introduction of a security element – in the form of an EU concern for conflict prevention and crisis management – has broadened the agenda, thus the field, of the EU's interventions, but the main philosophy behind this agenda and Europe's understanding of its relations with, and role in, Africa have evolved little. The object of this chapter is therefore to temper somewhat the current enthusiasm that sees in the EU's conflict prevention and crisis management policies a new era in the development of its foreign policy by showing that in some parts of the world, they have made little difference and may even have detrimental effects both for the states and populations involved and for the EU's external image and reputation.

In order to do so, this chapter attempts to measure the level of politicization that has effectively occurred in the EU's external relations with Africa. The continent, since the European Economic Community (EEC) started concluding preferential trade partnerships and delivering aid through its in-country delegations, has been an ideal field of experimentation, or 'laboratory' (Bayart 2004), for European consensus-finding and new external policy trends. Observations led in West Africa show that there remains an important gap, however, between the European – member states' and European institutions' – discourse in favour of a multilateral and diplomatic EU that would contribute to Africa's development, good governance and security and the reality of what essentially remains an EU 'transformational development policy' in Africa. The term 'transformational development policy', borrowed and adapted from American foreign policy discourse, is used here to underline that the main objective of the EU's involvement in Africa is to transform the continent's states according to an apparently technical agenda – or development policy. The outline of this chapter follows from these brief observations. The first part looks at the evolution of the EU's agenda in Africa over the last 15 years and underlines the many signs that could have led one to predict a politicization of this agenda through the increasing integration of governance and security concerns. The second part analyzes the institutional and political limits that have clearly hampered this politicization. The third part defines and develops the term 'transformational development policy' in order to highlight the ambiguous nature of the EU's Africa policies. Finally, the fourth and last part of this chapter underlines the other side of the coin, i.e. the highly political and transformative contents of the policies advocated by the EU – under a technical disguise – in Africa.

From development aid to conflict prevention: the politicization of the EU's agenda in Africa?

The European Coal and Steel Community, the EU's ancestor, was, under the cover of an industry revival programme, a political project from the start. Preventing war between France and Germany was the overriding objective (Page 2001: 6). This objective seemed to suffice as sole political programme for many years and on the international scene, the EC contented itself with its 'civil power' role, based on economic instruments (Telò 1998: 95), and its reliance upon the US and NATO for its security (Robert 2002). This did not prevent, however, the European Commission from slowly developing an external relations policy, in the late 1950s, when the EC began delivering development assistance to Africa (Olsen 2005: 127). These relations were essentially born from France's willingness to maintain a strong link to its – future – former colonies:

> As part of the bargain struck in 1957 in establishing the Treaty of Rome, France insisted that a special relationship be established, under part IV of

the Treaty, with selected African states and Madagascar, almost all of whom were still French dependencies, though shortly afterwards destined for independence in 1960.

(Hewitt 1989: 286)

This part of the Treaty of Rome translated, six years later, into preferential trading arrangements that were progressively expanded to other former colonies in Africa, the Caribbean and the Pacific – the so-called ACP group.[2] The EC-ACP relations were meant to symbolize both continuity and a break with Europe's colonial past – the continuity of Europe's interest and link to Africa, but a break with the highly unequal and exclusively bilateral relationship between the colonized and the colonizer.

The first Lomé Convention, which succeeded the Yaoundé conventions in 1975, was in effect hailed as a new departure in North-South relations. It was put forward as a path-breaking 'partnership of equals' and offered some major innovations by removing reciprocity in the EC's trade preference-giving and establishing a special fund, the European Development Fund (EDF). African governments held the Lomé arrangements in high esteem and EC aid was considered 'softer', both in financial terms and in general conditions, than that of the other donors or of the international financial institutions. Lomé, however, failed to fulfill its promises. The reality of the Convention was that both aid and trade provisions acted to confine ACP countries to the export of certain primary commodities (Hewitt 1989: 290), while the EC's poor institutional capacity on the ground led to only a small proportion of the aid reaching those it was supposed to benefit (Lord 2005: 119). By the end of the 1980s, the EC had managed to become an essential donor for Africa, but achieved few tangible results in most parts of the continent, which was better known for the poverty of its populations and the many political conflicts and crises that had characterized its first decades of independence, than for its economic successes.

This observation, which did not only apply to European development programmes, gave way to a new reflection on the causes of underdevelopment and, subsequently, to a new trend in development programmes. Part of the problem, it was thought, was in the nature of Africa's political regimes. Economic prosperity for all could not be achieved in non-democratic environments. The EEC, like the rest of the international community, thus added a measure of democratic conditionality to its development programmes. Lomé IV, the partnership agreement concluded with the ACP in 1990, acknowledged a close link between respect for human rights and economic development (Lomé IV Agreement 1989, art. 5). Respect for human rights, democratic principles and the rule of law then became essential elements – whose violation could lead to the partial or total suspension of development aid – in the subsequent Lomé IVbis agreement (Lomé IVbis Agreement 1995, art. 5). The Cotonou Agreement, signed in 2000 and revised in 2005, further reinforces this conditionality and defines 'good governance'[3] as a fundamental element alongside the three essential elements already defined in Lomé IVbis. With the exception of serious cases of corruption, a state facing governance problems will be provided with support and advice to improve its performance (Cotonou Agreement 2000 and 2005, art. 9).

The Washington consensus and its state-reducing strategies, which had first been meant to address the South American economic crisis and then spread to the rest of the world, were also progressively questioned. A new literature on the nature of the African state emerged, that described it, in turn, as 'failed', 'weak' (Migdal 1988), 'quasi' (Jackson 1993), 'collapsed' (Zartman 1995), or 'shadow' (Reno 1998). These different designations imply different emphases in the analysis of African states, but all underline these states' inability to appropriate the Westphalian and Weberian models of statehood. While their sovereignty is internationally recognized, they fail to impose this sovereignty on their national territories or to fulfill the developmental duties that would enhance their domestic legitimacy (European Commission 1996 and 2001a; Council of the European Union 2003d). 'Bringing the [African] state back in' (Evans *et al.* 1985) therefore became the new order of the day and development programmes comprised new sets of state reforms aiming at the improvement of state capacities. Former 'fragile states' would, through these reforms, recover their authority and eventually be able to deliver the long expected economic prosperity, as well as peace and stability. The EU, there again, willingly adopted this capacity-building trend and seconded technical assistants to the partner ministry – or 'national authorising officer', in EU jargon – in charge of administering EC aid from the EDF and implementing the projects agreed upon with the European Commission.

This first step towards a more political involvement in the affairs of sovereign, if weak, states again failed to deliver the expected results. What some had somewhat optimistically called a third wave of democratization was on the longer term circumscribed to a few isolated African states. Moreover, the end of the Cold War did not mean the end of instability in Africa, which had long played the role of a proxy field for superpower rivalry. The conflicts in Liberia, Somalia, Rwanda and Sierra Leone that ignited in the 1990s were marked by high levels of violence, their duration and a tendency to spill over in neighbouring countries. This, however, strengthened the 'state as guilty party and solution' logic. Weak African states were unable to contain rebel movements and other sources of insecurity. The answer to the problem logically followed and donors focused their attention on (re)building strong states and reforming their administrations and security sectors as a conflict prevention strategy (Caplan and Pouligny 2005: 124). The late 1990s and early 2000s thus saw the emergence of a number of pre- and post-conflict reform packages, which were expected to be both broad – all root causes of a crisis should be addressed – and technical – reforms must remain manageable and ethically acceptable in that they should not infringe the sovereignty of African states (European Commission 2001a). The EU institutions themselves have integrated these packages within the policies managed by the Commission, such as administrative or rule of law reform programmes, or by the Council, such as the ESDP missions focusing on security sector reform in the Democratic Republic of Congo (DRC) and Guinea-Bissau.[4]

As rightly underlined by the editors in the introduction to this volume, conflict prevention has thus been streamlined with other policy areas. This is clearly visible in the EU's Africa policies, where good governance, development and security are now seen as closely interlinked and jointly contributing to the prevention of new conflicts. The very first article of the Cotonou Agreement, for example, fully incorporates this comprehensive three-dimensional approach. The agreement was concluded 'with a view to contributing to peace and security and to promoting a stable and democratic political environment' (Cotonou Agreement 2000 and 2005, art. 1). The boundaries between these different concepts are increasingly blurred, thus creating the impression that when one objective is pursued, all of them are. The security sector, rule of law and administrative reform programmes managed by the European Commission and funded through the 9th and 10th EDF in Guinea-Bissau are thus meant to contribute to governance and security as well as, on a longer term, economic development, while preparing the ground for, complementing and possibly providing a follow-up to the ESDP mission, EUSSR Guinea-Bissau, which focuses on the reform of Guinea-Bissau's security sector.[5] This example also confirms that conflict prevention has been, in effect, integrated into a ready-made development policy and has had little power to modify this policy or to impose the institutional changes that were needed for the establishment of a preventive diplomacy, in particular.

The missing common European diplomacy in Africa

The observation will certainly not come as a surprise to most observers of the European foreign policy, but in spite of the emergence of the CFSP, the EU lacks a strong institutional body that would be able to implement it. Member states have clearly been more eager to develop the – often more technical and thus possibly straightforward – ESDP dimension of the CFSP than its more political and diplomatic one. The following observation, drawn by the International Crisis Group in 2001 but still valid today, underlines this gap between the EU's strong rhetorical engagement in favour of conflict prevention and management and the absence of a diplomacy that could implement this ambitious task:

> [T]he EU is staking much on the contributions of development cooperation and democratization to conflict prevention (through peace building). Although the balance is slowly shifting, this has tended to give EU conflict prevention thinking a disproportionately heavy focus on economics, human rights and democratization, to the neglect of diplomatic conflict prevention measures that seek to significantly alter the political dynamics of an emerging conflict.
>
> (International Crisis Group 2001: ii)

Strangely enough, this obvious limit is only rarely underlined and many observers seem to find natural that Africa's conflicts are essentially dealt with through a mixture of developmental and military approaches and in the near absence of political analyses and instruments.

The EU, as Africa's largest aid provider, enjoys a great deal of visibility and leverage in Africa. Accordingly, EC delegations have for 50 years been and still are aid agencies. But in spite of – or possibly because of[6] – the deconcentration process initiated in 2000, which gives them more autonomy and influence over the programmes they support, EC delegations have not developed into European embassies. They lack the financial and material means and their staff have never been granted the training that would enable delegations to lead the diplomatic and political missions – on top of the essentially technical missions in development cooperation which they currently conduct – that are so obviously entailed by the notion of 'external service'. In the absence of a real evolution of their mission and capacities, the EC delegations' role in matters of conflict prevention very much depends on the determination of the chief of delegation to encourage his/her staff to acquire capacities in political analysis and preventive diplomacy or on a member state's expressed wish that a member of staff trained in conflict prevention strategies be appointed to a delegation.[7]

For now, European member states, especially those which have a permanent in-country representation, retain the intelligence, political expertise and influence that make a strong diplomatic culture. This is especially true in West Africa, where relations with Europe are generally defined in the former colonial power's embassy. In Europe too, the EU's policies in West Africa are essentially prepared in the former colonial power's capital city and subsequently approved in Brussels. There is little European diplomacy on Africa going on between the member states' permanent representations to the EU.[8] The EU's Africa diplomacy is therefore often limited to an implicit bargaining game between the capital cities of former colonial powers – when Britain obtains funding or a political gesture for Sierra Leone, France will expect a similar concession on Côte d'Ivoire.[9] The only exceptions to this rule are those cases where the EU has been running CSDP missions – the DRC, Sudan, Chad and the Central African Republic and Guinea-Bissau. For these missions, the largest member state permanent representations in Brussels have staff members in charge of thematic portfolios such as crisis management or civil operations,[10] i.e. people who certainly possess the necessary technical military and security knowledge but may know very little about African political affairs and are not in a position to contribute to longer-term conflict prevention in the fields of intervention.

The EU's diplomatic limits are not only due to this serious imbalance between the member states' African diplomacies and their European inter-governmental and community counterparts, however. The competition and often unclear division of labour between the Council and the Commission is certainly also partly responsible. Both are in charge of parts of the EU's foreign policy. It now seems clear and accepted by both parties that the Commission is in charge of the European development agenda and the Council of the European Union's security policies, although the division of labour in the latter field, especially when it comes to civilian missions, could certainly be made clearer (Bagayoko and Gibert 2009: 802–4). The purely political dimension – the diplomatic part – of the EU's relations with third states, on the other hand, is in an area whose location and limits remain extremely blurred, to say the least. This is certainly in the interest of the member states themselves, which jealously protect their monopoly on what remains one of the principal attributes of national sovereignty, i.e. foreign policy-making. This last observation on the unclear location of the EU's foreign policy and the aforementioned comments on its missing diplomatic competency in West Africa in turn raise the question of the exact nature of the EU's policy in Africa.

Defining the nature of the EU's policy in Africa

After the end of the Cold War, the EC was faced with new challenges. New members from the former Eastern bloc were to be integrated, while Europe quickly understood that it would need to increasingly provide for its own security since the end of the superpower competition would most probably mean at least a partial American disengagement from the continent. The European regional organization would therefore have to go a step further on the path of integration. The creation of the CFSP and that of the CSDP in the 1990s were clear signs of this realization and of European member states' willingness to achieve more integration in the fields of external affairs and security, notably through the EU's emergent conflict prevention and crisis management policies. Meanwhile, Africa, which had already been an ideal experimentation field for the first EC delegations, could be relied upon to play that role again, as was made clear in the Commission's communication on conflict prevention in Africa (European Commission 1996) and with the first extra-European ESDP mission, Operation Artemis, in 2003 (Bayart 2004).

As underlined in the introduction to this volume, the foundation of the CFSP and CSDP gave way to a wealth of academic literature that tries to best define the new European foreign and security policies. Describing it as 'civilian', 'soft' or 'normative', accounts of Europe's international identity and power do not always agree on their exact nature but would seem to share two characteristics. They insist, first, on the originality of the EU's international identity and foreign policy, at times opposing them – implicitly at least – to that of traditional Westphalian states and their 'hard power' diplomacies. Second, they often underline the obvious links between the nature of the EU's foreign policy and the regional organization's own identity, history and achievements (Manners 2002; Nicolaïdis and Howse 2002; Diez 2005). The EU is indeed often said to embody a set of principles. First and foremost among these are generally peace or security community, democracy, liberal economy and respect for human rights (Nicolaïdis and Howse 2002; Diez 2005; Farrell 2005). The EU's capacity to maintain peace between France and Germany, and to subsequently extend this peace, as well as democracy and economic prosperity, to its Southern and Eastern borders through membership, both define and justify this list. Simultaneously, the association of the EU's identity with these principles has generated outside expectations that have further reinforced the EU's focus on these issues, first and foremost among them political stability and conflict prevention (Youngs 2004: 417).

The EU has moreover moved a step further in actively embodying this set of principles and attempting to export it beyond Europe through what Stephan Keukeleire calls its 'structural foreign policy':

> The policy aims at the transferral – in varying degrees – of various ideo-
> logical and governing principles that characterize the political, social, eco-
> nomic, and interstate system of the EU: democracy and good government,
> human rights, the various OSCE principles (such as the peaceful solution of
> conflicts), regional political and economic cooperation and integration, free
> market principles, and so on.
>
> (Keukeleire 2003: 47).

This rather ambitious and comprehensive list of principles – understood as inter-
dependent – the use of the term 'ideological' and the notion of 'transferral' would
tend to seriously question the earlier quoted descriptions of the EU's foreign policy
as 'soft' or even benign, and suggests that 'normative power Europe' may indeed
be more coercive than is generally thought.

Interestingly, Stephan Keukeleire's definition may be described as a softer
version of the US administration's definition of its own foreign policy in fragile
states, i.e. to the definition of what US Secretary of State Condoleezza Rice calls
'transformational diplomacy':

> I would define the objective of transformational diplomacy this way: To work
> with our many partners around the world to build and sustain democratic,
> well-governed states that will respond to the needs of their people – and con-
> duct themselves responsibly in the international system [. . .] Transforma-
> tional diplomacy is rooted in partnership, not paternalism – in doing things
> *with* other people, not *for* them. We seek to use America's diplomatic power to
> help foreign citizens to better their *own* lives, and to build their *own* nations,
> and to transform their *own* future.
>
> (Rice 2006, emphasis on the website of the
> State Department's website).

The term 'transformational diplomacy' has the advantage, over that of 'structural
foreign policy', of clearly identifying the aims of the policies – transforming other
states to the advantage of their peoples and the international system – and the
instruments necessary for its achievement – a diplomatic body. We have already
noted earlier that the EU lacks a diplomatic body and tools in West Africa. Let us
here look at the aims of the EU's policies in the region. Transforming states is certainly an ambitious task, but one that is not unknown to Europe nor to its regional
organization. In spite of Condoleeza Rice's and the EU's insistence on the term
'partnership'[11] and while one should be wary of easy accusations of neo-colonialism, the idea of states transforming other states is evidently highly reminiscent
of Europe's colonial project in Africa and its very disputed results in terms of
state-building. The EU, on the other hand, is often credited for having largely contributed to the democratic transitions and consolidations of its Southern and, more
recently, Eastern member states. The perspective of membership, and the demand-
ing requirements for its achievement, certainly were essential – if not infallible,
as the Balkans have shown – 'carrots and sticks' in these countries' transition

processes. In their absence, however, one may wonder whether the EU disposes of enough leverage and influence to export its 'good governance, security and development' formula. A precedent has yet to be set.

This first and natural move of scepticism set aside, it must be underlined that the EU has at its disposal effective means of influence and pressure to convince its African partners of the validity of its model and of the necessity to emulate it. In spite of the recurrence of the term 'partnership' in all EU policy documents, the relationship between the EU and Africa is clearly not one of equals. The EU has been better able to embody the continuity of the Euro-African colonial imbalance than to break with it. The EU's increasing involvement in the domestic affairs of sovereign African states further underlines this inequality, while the increasing technicalization of its programmes, which I hinted at in the first part of this chapter and will analyse in greater detail in the following and last part, clearly seeks to hide this interference.

Beyond this question of leverage, the EU's conflict prevention and crisis management approach itself seriously hinders any perspective of EU diplomacy in Africa. The term 'transformational diplomacy', as defined by Condoleeza Rice, describes the EU's foreign policy in Africa as well as it does the US's, and is an obvious contradiction in terms. Let us here define diplomacy as the art of negotiation conducted between sovereign states in order to reconcile their duties, rights and interests. Implicit here is the notion of equality between the negotiating parties. Indeed, African states, according to international law, have an equal status to that of European states. The notion of 'transformation', however, underlines the limits of international law and the obvious reality. Even when this is done in the name of their people's prosperity and security, what sort of sovereignty do African states enjoy if their American and European partners can intervene in their domestic affairs and most sovereign attributes – such as the security sector – and decide to 'transform' these according to their own priorities and perceptions of international relations? Although the aforementioned definition suggests that there may be a natural complementarity between 'the needs of [fragile states'] people' and those of the international system, this is far from obvious and there are numerous examples of interventions in fragile states driven by international interests in direct contradiction with local needs (Woodward 2005).

Rather than 'diplomacy', therefore, it would seem fair to use the term 'development policy', more appropriate to define the unequal relationship between donor and recipient, and to describe the EU's policy in Africa as a 'structural' or 'transformational' development policy. The EU's conflict prevention and crisis management policies in Africa clearly fall in this field of transformational development policy, where Africa's insecurity and instability are thought to be best solved through a set of technical reforms aiming at improving the state's capacity to drive development, govern democratically and prevent rising insecurity. And there is little hope this will change soon since, as was already underlined, current international trends favour the incorporation of political elements into development programmes – if necessary, under the guise of technical reforms, rather than the politicization of relations with Africa's fragile states. Taking a close look at the technicalization of the EU's role in Africa, however, enables us to underline the highly political and, at times, coercive character of the EU's reform programmes in Africa.

The EU's Africa policy: unacknowledgedly political and intrusive?

The conceptualization of the different stages of state reform – the EU has defined its own concepts of rule of law and civilian administration in 2003, of security sector reform in 2005 and of disarmament, demobilization and reintegration in 2006 – underlines the very technical character now taken on by the EU's development and conflict prevention programmes (see Council of the European Union 2006c and 2006e). The EU is translating its set of normative preferences – or of structural stability, as Stephan Keukeleire puts it – into technical handbooks, and its 'mission civilisatrice' (Nicolaïdis and Howse 2002: 782) – a term there again reminiscent of Europe's, more specifically France's, colonial past in Africa – is in effect becoming an x-steps lesson in state-building. Good governance can be achieved through the establishment of an independent electoral commission, the liberalization of the media, the organization of free, transparent and democratic elections, decentralization, and so on.[12] In a similar fashion, the security sector should undergo a set of reforms that encompasses all of its elements, from the traditional security forces – including intelligence – to the institutions in charge of controlling them – ministries and Parliament – to those necessary for their good working order – the judiciary system (Leboeuf 2005: 66). And both good governance and security sector reforms, along with a number of other democratization and security reforms, are in turn meant to jointly contribute to the prevention of future political conflicts and crises and to economic development.

Numerous critiques have underlined this new 'technicalizing' tendency.[13] Some attribute it to the end of the Cold War. By removing political categories and classificatory devices, the end of the ideological superpower conflict led to an 'exaggeration of the criminal aspects of recent civil wars and a concomitant neglect of their manifold political aspects' (Kalyvas 2001: 117), thus privileging more technical understandings and responses. Another part of the explanation certainly lies in the nature of these outside interventions. Donors' involvement in the reconstruction of a post-conflict state is generally characterized by its short duration and very targeted nature, the aim being to ensure that a new regime is in place and that no new intervention will be necessary in the future (Paris 2003: 462). There is, finally, an ethical side to this attitude. Outside actors cannot easily justify an intervention in the internal affairs of a sovereign state. The technical disguise of the current reform packages helps to ensure that there can be no suspicion of unjustified interference.[14]

This explanation of donors' focus on technical reforms also hints at their obvious limits. The necessity of achieving quick, inexpensive and tangible results often leads reformers to neglect endogenous processes. The same reform packages are applied in all cases, independent of local realities (Caplan and Pouligny 2005: 135). Let us here consider a specific reform currently supported by the EU in Sierra Leone, namely decentralization. Decentralization in Sierra Leone, it is hoped, will establish a link between the state and local communities, reduce the overcentralization tendencies of the former, improve services to the rural poor, and introduce more transparency and democracy into local government.[15] Recent academic analyses have underlined that some of the root causes of the conflict in Sierra Leone were to be found in abuses associated with rural custom and a resulting feeling of exclusion among rural young people (Richards 2005). Decentralization was thus a major element in Sierra Leone's peace agreement and many felt it should be implemented as soon as possible, so as to give a clear sign of democratic change to local communities.[16] The success of the decentralization programme, however, will depend on a number of issues that seemed to have been little considered when the programme was launched and local elections were organized in 2004. A crucial point, in particular, is the relations between local and central government, on the one hand, and between the elected local councils and the customary chiefs, on the other hand. The Local Government Act of 2004, however, does little to define these relations and the responsibilities of the different actors (Jackson 2007: 104). Observers have underlined the high potential for tensions between them (Fanthorpe 2006; Jackson 2007) and the risk that confusion at local government level could isolate further the rural poor who still feel very strong bonds with their customary chiefs.[17] It has also been noted that the focus on the abuses committed in the name of customary law had overshadowed the limits of the formal justice system at local level, which is generally considered inefficient and unfair by rural Sierra Leoneans (Sawyer 2008: 399). Attempts at reforming local courts have so far had limited success,[18] thus casting doubt on their ability to replace customary chiefs in the delivery of land justice, which is so central to rural societies and economies. Critical voices have noted that a decentralization programme is premature in Sierra Leone, where the central state is still very fragile and that the reform is, like many others, rushed in, with the destabilizing effects this can entail in a country with a long history of warlords and state fragility (Fanthorpe 2006).[19] It also seems that donors – the EU among them – pushed for and engaged in the decentralization programme without quite having measured the many other reforms and capacity-building programmes – and funds – that would be needed to ensure its success.

This failure to consider local perceptions and the importance of internalization certainly accounts for some of the hurdles the international community and the EU come up against in Africa, namely the absence of sustainable results and the continuing instability and fragility of many African states (Keukeleire 2004: 160). It may also explain why imported reform programmes are often resented as unsuited to local realities and intrinsically coercive. The international agenda in so-called 'fragile' states is indeed – possibly, at times, unconsciously – eminently political and ideological. The example of the decentralization programme in Sierra Leone underlines that, under the guise of an essentially technical reform, stabilization and conflict prevention measures deal with sensitive political and social matters, without ever addressing them directly.[20] Observers note that the main objective of these programmes is to transform the targeted political systems so as to reinforce their legitimacy in the eyes of the international community, rather than in those of their citizens (Woodward 2005). Here lies, in a nutshell, the ambiguity of the EU's engagement in favour of conflict prevention in West Africa. While it does not devote any particular means – human, institutional or financial – to the political analysis of the states or local political systems in which it intervenes and seems to understand its involvement as an essentially technical and politically-neutral one, its policies intervene in highly political fields. While the denial, or neglect, of this aspect enables the EU to carry on its relations with West Africa as before, it also means that the effects of its policies, in terms of conflict prevention, may be more short-term than expected.

Conclusion

As was shown in the first part of this chapter, it is true that the EU has become increasingly involved in programmes meant to resolve and prevent conflicts in Africa. It is equally true, as was underlined in part four, that this involvement, under the guise of technical and ideologically neutral reforms, is taking on an increasingly political character. It would therefore seem logical to conclude that the EU is strengthening its capacity to deal with external political affairs and slowly developing a diplomatic culture. A close look at the EU's foreign policy in Africa, however, shows that this last evolution has yet to occur. The EU remains an essentially developmental actor in Africa, tying political reforms to development programmes rather than creating a diplomatic body able to analyse political events and systems, negotiate with conflicting parties and prevent political crises. The priority, it seems, is to transform these – however sovereign – states into 'strong states' more legitimate in the eyes of the international community, i.e. into states that better fit the current international – if not legal – definition of what makes a state.

While they have certainly contributed to expanding the EU's development agenda, conflict prevention policies have failed to qualitatively transform the EU's relations with the region and, in particular, to add a measure of EU political engagement – political analysis and preventive diplomacy – to these relations. There are many reasons for this, some of which have already been briefly mentioned. The institutional argument, often put forward to account for the limited visibility and efficiency of the EU's foreign policies, is of course highly relevant. The European institutions – and this seems to be in the particular interest of those member states involved in Africa – lack the means and tools necessary to 'politicize' their involvement. Moreover, the institutional rivalry between the Commission and Council has more naturally led to a quantitative expansion of their respective, traditional fields of intervention – development on the one hand and security on the other – than to the emergence of a new, more political, foreign policy. Beyond these institutional explanations, African states themselves seem unwilling to see the EU become involved in other activities than traditional developmental ones, such as the financing of infrastructure building, where the EU, thanks to its considerable financial means, enjoys a comparative advantage.[21] The

EU's 'transformational development policy', finally, also forms part of a historical European tendency to consider Africa as a politically virgin field that does not require any political or diplomatic involvement and can be dealt with through essentially technical, transformative policies – hence the fact, for example, that the EU's Africa policy is in the remit of the Commission's Directorate-General Development (DG Dev) only, and not in that of its DG External Relations (DG Relex) like the EU's other external policies. Whatever its root causes – and these would deserve to be explored further– it seems doubtful that the EU can realistically claim to contribute effectively to the prevention of conflicts in Africa as long as it cannot – or will not – actively engage with Africa's politics.

Notes

1 On the historical interactions between the EU's development and conflict prevention policies, please also refer to Chapter 3 in this volume.

2 These arrangements have been regularly renewed, expanded and modified and took the names of the African cities where they were successively signed: Yaoundé I and II (1963–75), Lomé I – which made provision for Britain's former colonies in Africa, the Caribbean and the Pacific – to IV bis (1975–2000), and Cotonou since 2000.

3 'Good governance is the transparent and accountable management of human, natural, economic and financial resources for the purposes of equitable and sustainable development. It entails clear decision-making procedures at the level of public authorities, transparent and accountable institutions, the primacy of law in the management and distribution of resources and capacity building for elaborating and implementing measures aiming in particular at preventing and combating corruption.' (Cotonou Agreement, Council of the European Union 2000 and 2005, art. 9.3).

4 The EU is currently running two security sector reform missions in the DRC. EUPOL DR Congo (launched in June 2007) succeeded a previous CSDP mission in the capital city, EUPOL Kinshasa, and focuses particularly on the police and its relations with the judiciary. EUSEC DR Congo (launched in June 2005) provides advice and assistance to the Congolese authorities in charge of security. The only CSDP mission in West Africa, EUSSR Guinea-Bissau (launched in June 2008), provides advice and assistance on reform of the security sector in Guinea Bissau in order to contribute to creating the conditions for the implementation of the country's National Security Sector Reform Strategy.

5 Interview with a staff member of the Directorate-General Development (DG Dev), European Commission, in Brussels, October 2008.

6 According to Youngs (2006: 345), 'Sierra Leone is cited as a clear case where some additional problems have arisen due to deconcentration, the latter making it difficult for diplomats planning overall strategy in Brussels to get information on what work the delegation had been supporting in situ.'

7 At the time of fieldwork (2005–2006), this was the case in the EC delegations located in Conakry (Guinea) and Dakar (Senegal), apparently much less so in the ones in Freetown (Sierra Leone) and Bissau (Guinea-Bissau). A member of the EC delegation's staff in Bissau was also asked to contribute and monitor the government's progress towards state reform. The importance of this human dimension – from the political sensitivity of chiefs of delegations to personal and informal relations between delegation staffs in one region – seems highly underestimated by the EU, which does not have any clear human resources policy in this regard. Interviews with EC delegation staff in Guinea (November 2005), Sierra Leone (November-December 2005) and Guinea-Bissau (March 2006).

8 This is not likely to change anytime soon. A clear sign of this is some member states' – and especially former colonial powers' – determination to continue sending Africa regional directors from their capital cities to attend the Council's Africa working group rather than have a Brussels Africa person who would do so. This obviously limits the input of smaller EU member states, which do not always have the means to send out an Africa expert to every Africa working group meeting, and maintains much of the initiative in a small number of member state capitals. Interviews with staff from the UK and French permanent representations to the EU in Brussels, July 2007.

9 Interview with a staff member of the British Foreign and Commonwealth Office in London, July 2005.

10 Interview with a member of staff from the French permanent representation to the EU in Brussels, June 2006.

11 The term is repeatedly used in EU policy papers concerning Africa, including the Cotonou Agreement with the ACP states (Cotonou Agreement 2000 and 2005) and, of course, the EU-Africa Strategic Partnership (Council of the European Union 2005a).

12 For a detailed overview of the good governance reforms supported by the EU in the Mano River region of West Africa, see Gibert (2007).

13 See, in particular, Merlingen with Ostrauskaite (2006) on the EU's policing missions in the Balkans.

14 For an interesting discussion of this ethical debate, see Châtaigner (2004).

15 Interviews with Sierra Leonean consultants in charge of the implementation of the decentralization programme and staff members of the EC delegation in Freetown (Sierra Leone), December 2005.

16 Interview with a member of the EC delegation in Freetown (Sierra Leone), December 2005.

17 The recent parliamentary and presidential elections (August-September 2007) in Sierra Leone, however, suggest an increasing autonomy of rural dwellers *vis-à-vis* their local chiefs. The All People's Congress (APC), in the opposition since the end of the civil war, won both elections although the governing Sierra Leone People's Party was said to have the support of local chiefs.

18 Interview with staff from the British Department for International Development, London, July 2008.

19 Interviews with NGO staff in Freetown, Sierra Leone, December 2005. Staff at the EC delegation also admitted that decentralization may be premature, but the feeling was that the government of Sierra Leone – and the international community – were obliged to rapidly deliver on post-conflict promises of reform, whether or not the reforms were effective or timely. Interview with a member of the EC delegation in Freetown (Sierra Leone), December 2005.

20 Observers of development aid in Africa have already underlined the problematic gap between developmentalists' claim to technical expertise – or even omniscience – and non-interference in political affairs, on the one hand, and the deep political and social consequences – or simple absence of effective results, in some cases – of their development programmes, on the other hand (Ferguson 1990; Mitchell 2002).

21 Interviews with DG Dev staff in Brussels, September 2005.

8 The EU in Afghanistan

Crisis management in a transatlantic setting

Eva Gross

Introduction

Afghanistan represents one of the most complex conflict settings the EU has engaged in through its Common Security and Defense Policy (CSDP), but also through its range of political and economic instruments. In addition to fighting a growing insurgency, international engagement also focuses on good governance, institution building, and economic development in a country that is poor, ethnically diverse and marked by decades of conflict. After the fall of the Taliban in 2001, Afghanistan and the international community faced the challenge of building sustainable state structures and institutions. The 2001 Bonn Agreement subsequently set out a process for drafting a new constitution and for holding presidential and parliamentary elections. Hamid Karzai was elected President in 2004, and the parliamentary elections of 2005 formally concluded the Bonn Process. A UN-mandated peacekeeping force, the International Security Assistance Force (ISAF), initially tasked with providing stability in Kabul was brought under NATO command in 2004 and since 2006 has operated throughout the country. Despite international efforts of the past decade, however, internal instability persists and the security situation in the country has deteriorated significantly since the start of international engagement in the country's reconstruction. The increasing focus on instability in Pakistan and its link to the conflict in Afghanistan further illustrates the complexity of the political and security situation in the country and its immediate neighborhood. Beyond operating in a complex local but also regional conflict setting, the EU's engagement in Afghanistan is also taking place under an overall military and political lead of the United States (US). An analysis of the EU's evolving range of activities and policies in the country, therefore, raises two separate yet interrelated issues: the manner and extent to which EU activities in Afghanistan contribute to the country's reconstruction; and the EU's position as a political and security actor in a US-led setting. This chapter analyzes the evolution of EU engagement in Afghanistan since the fall of the Taliban. It evaluates EU policies in Afghanistan from the standpoints of impact and effectiveness in terms of the actual conflict setting, but also the EU's global role. While the EU has applied a number of its conflict prevention and crisis management instruments, this chapter argues that while EU policies in Afghanistan have had an impact, this impact has been restricted on account of the conflict setting but also the EU's international political standing and its representation in Brussels as well as in the field. Limitations arise from the scale of commitments, lacking political leverage and strategy, but also from EU member states prioritizing their transatlantic rather than European commitments. This further fragments EU presence and negatively affects the EU's impact. Operating in a US-led intervention thus raises questions not just over the EU as an actor in crisis management but also the EU's position in the broader transatlantic security relationship alongside NATO and individual member states. The chapter argues that in Afghanistan, the EU has fallen victim to unrealistic expectations. This shows that the EU is some way away from representing a coherent actor in this particular conflict setting – nor can it expect to reach equal footing with the US in the transatlantic political and security space.

The evolution of EU activities in Afghanistan

The EU bases its current engagement on the Afghanistan Compact that was forged at the 2006 London Conference, which was to follow on from the Bonn process. The Afghanistan Compact seeks 'to continue in the spirit of the Bonn, Tokyo and Berlin conferences, to work toward a stable and prosperous Afghanistan, with good governance and human rights protection for all under the rule of law' (Afghanistan Compact 2006). Based on the Afghanistan Compact, the EU has developed formalized bilateral cooperation and commitments. The EU currently employs a range of political, civilian, and economic instruments that contribute to international reconstruction and institution-building efforts. Although the EU has not assumed a role in the military aspect of crisis management – member states contribute individually to ISAF – the EU has carved out a potentially significant political and economic role both in terms of its financial contributions and its international profile. Following the fall of the Taliban in 2001, EU activities focused on immediate humanitarian and institution-building needs. The European Commission made use of its conflict prevention instruments by drawing €4.93 million from its Rapid Reaction Mechanism (RRM) to help finance and legitimize the political transition begun with the Bonn Conference in 2001 (European Commission 2003b). Apart from humanitarian aid and establishing government institutions and public services, Community programmes also focused on building infrastructure. For the 2007–13 funding period, the European Commission has identified rural development, governance and health as priority sectors (European Commission 2007). With €1.1 billion in economic contributions between 2002 and 2006, coupled with €2.6 billion from the member states, the EU is also the second largest donor to Afghanistan after the US.

The EU also raised its political visibility through the appointment of an EU Special Representative (EUSR) in 2001. Initially at least, this appointment was to signal the EU's interest in claiming a political profile and to play a united role in Afghanistan (Klaiber 2002), especially in light of member states' apparent prioritization of national or transatlantic interests following the attacks of 11 September (Hill 2002). The position has since developed into an information and coordination role. The EUSR liaises with Afghan stakeholders and regularly reports on Afghanistan to the Political and Security Committee (PSC) in Brussels. An emphasis on coordination of EU institutions but also that of individual EU member states engaged in the country is to improve coherence as well as the impact of EU instruments. Initially at least, EU activities in Afghanistan focused on political and economic contributions rather than on civilian or military crisis management operations through CSDP. The option of launching a CSDP mission, or of coordinating European activities in ISAF, was dismissed immediately following the fall of the Taliban. Given member states' transatlantic priorities when it came to military peacekeeping and post-conflict reconstruction, the EU seemed relegated to a 'soft' security actor (see Gross 2006).

Despite the initial rejection of the CSDP format for military crisis management, debates over launching a civilian CSDP operation did take place, and in June 2007 the EU launched EUPOL Afghanistan, a civilian police mission. Launching a civilian crisis mission had been discussed for a while and was formally decided during the German Presidency during the first half of 2007. Prior to that, a joint EU assessment report in 2006 had recommended to 'consider contributing further to support the police sector through a police mission' (European Council 2007), and a fact finding mission was dispatched to Afghanistan in late 2006; and the Council approved the Crisis Management Concept (CMC) in February 2007. EUPOL Afghanistan is to 'significantly contribute to the establishment under Afghan ownership of suitable and effective civilian policing arrangements' (European Council 2007). Initial tasks set for the mission included working on strategy development, supporting the government of Afghanistan in implementing their strategy, improving coordination among international actors, and supporting linkages between the police and the wider rule of law. EUPOL Afghanistan is a non-executive mission, which means that it carries out its tasks through monitoring, mentoring, advising and training. Authorized at 400 personnel, EUPOL staff is to be deployed at central, regional and provincial levels: Kabul, the five regional commands, and in the provinces through Provincial Reconstruction Teams (PRTs). In Brussels, the Civilian Planning and Conduct Capability (CPPC) exercises the operational command of the mission and EUPOL Afghanistan receives strategic direction from the Political and Security Committee (PSC). The EUSR in Kabul is to provide 'local political guidance', but is not part of the official chain of command.

The launch of EUPOL Afghanistan signalled an increasing focus on the rule of law on the part of the EU, but also on broader issues of good governance. Consequently, strengthening the rule of law and structures of government at the provincial and the district level has become a priority in Commission programming, with EUR 200 million devoted to that particular sector (European Commission 2008a). The Commission became involved in this area after the 2006 London Conference that tasked the EU with justice reform. In preparation for an EC justice programme, and financed by the Instrument for Stability (IfS), the follow-on instrument from the RRM, a judiciary expert team was set up in 2007 to support programme definition, management reform, and to suggest models of legal aid for the Ministry of Justice (European Commission 2008a). The

Commission has since developed a justice programme that focuses on a number of priority areas, including technical assistance, the UNDP's 'access to justice' project, and the multilateral Afghanistan Reconstruction Trust Fund (ARTF) justice project (European Commission 2008a).

Most recently, the EU has also sent an EU Election Observation Mission (EOM) to monitor the conduct of the 2009 Presidential Election in Afghanistan. The mission's mandate was to conduct a comprehensive assessment of the electoral process and to observe the extent to which the election complied with international standards for elections as well as domestic law (EU Election Observation Mission 2009). The mission's assessment, however, illustrates the extent to which reconstruction in Afghanistan is marred by a political system that lacks accountability and transparency, and that is mired by corruption and warlordism (see Ayub and Kouvo 2008; Hodes and Sedra 2007). Noting that the 'Presidential and Provincial Council Elections took place in an exceptionally challenging environment', the report went on to state that

> since the internationally organized elections in 2004 and 2005 missed opportunities to reinforce key institutions, strengthen the rule of law and control corruption have contributed to a degree of impunity and insecurity which has severely damaged faith in the credibility and effectiveness of democratic governance.
>
> (EU Election Observation Mission 2009: 3)

Despite international reconstruction efforts over the past decade, therefore, the success of EU conflict prevention and crisis management policies in Afghanistan remains curtailed by a challenging political and security context – and the lack of accountable, democratic structures.

The EU in the context of international engagement in Afghanistan

Beyond the specific conflict setting in which they are placed, the evaluation of EU policies in Afghanistan must take into account the place these policies occupy within the broader structure of international efforts. Here, a number of factors stand out – among them the fragmentation of international efforts, lack of leadership or political direction by the assigned coordination bodies and lead institutions, and a de facto US political and military lead. The fragmentation and lack of international leadership to a large extent was the result of the international community adopting a 'light footprint' approach towards post-conflict reconstruction after the fall of the Taliban. The light footprint approach emphasized a quick devolution to Afghan ownership after the establishment of democratic government structures. A similar decision was taken with respect to the provision of security: rather than sending a large peacekeeping force in addition to large-scale international engagement in post-conflict reconstruction, ISAF's geographical mandate was initially restricted to Kabul. Reluctant to engage in military, let alone civilian, peacekeeping or to involve NATO, the US instead preferred to rely on local warlords for the provision of security until national security forces could be trained (see Dobbins 2008). Outside Kabul, PRTs that consisted of military as well as civilian staff were set up to aid in the reconstruction process beyond Afghanistan's capital. It was not until 2004 that Washington – in light of increasing instability in the country and the need for a stronger military engagement – amended its approach and consented to NATO involvement but also a larger overall military presence in Afghanistan.

The lack of overall investment in Afghanistan, coupled with an increasingly fragmented international presence, also affected other actors engaged in the country's reconstruction. The UN Assistance Mission to Afghanistan (UNAMA) was tasked with taking the lead in overseeing the implementation of the Bonn Agreement in 2001. UNAMA in principle at least was also given a coordinating role – a role, however, that it was unable to fulfill in practice (International Crisis Group 2008). Limited resources and a resulting limited visibility, particularly in light of the overlay of the US and NATO who tend to set the overall political tone and direction, have not made the UN sufficiently strong to assume the coordinating mandate originally assigned to it.[1] Instead, contributing nations to Afghanistan's reconstruction pursued individual – and largely independent – reform programmes. Coordination mechanisms, although they were introduced, were institutionalized retroactively and their performance has varied.

This applied in particular to Security Sector Reform (SSR), an activity where the EU has become increasingly involved through EUPOL Afghanistan and the Commission's rule of law programme. Following a SSR conference hosted by the UN in 2002, the G8 adopted a lead nation approach to individual areas of post-conflict reconstruction. The tasks of reforming the army, police and the justice sector were taken over by the US, Germany and Italy, respectively. The UK took the lead in counter narcotics, and Japan provided support for Disarmament, Demobilization and Reintegration (DDR). This approach further reinforced fragmentation in what are essentially interrelated policy areas: for SSR to be effective, police reform for instance needs to go hand in hand with reforms in other parts of the security sector, such as the courts, the prison system and border management (see Buxton 2008). More fundamentally, the rule of law lies at the heart of government stability and legitimacy. The fact that individual lead nations' contributions varied not only in size but also in approach did not help matters: Germany spent up to €12 million per year, a number increased to €36 million after 2008 (Federal Foreign Office 2007); whereas the Italian Justice Office (IJO) consisted of 4–5 Kabul-based staff. In contrast, the US Department of Defense in 2007 allocated $2.5 billion to police training (New York Times 2007).

In the wake of an increasing focus on the coherence of international efforts as well as on the police as a security institution, the reform of the police and the justice sectors have become key tasks in Afghanistan's reconstruction. The low starting point for reform efforts in 2001, but also the trajectory of both police and justice reform have significantly complicated the EU's task. The Bonn Agreement provided for the creation of a Ministry of the Interior responsible for police and correction. As for the justice sector, the Ministry of Justice oversees the oversight of the prison service. The Attorney General's office has authority over the investigation of crimes and includes 2,500 prosecutors. While the primary source of law is the Constitution, Afghanistan's legal system is based on mixed civil and Sharia law and Afghanistan has not accepted jurisdiction of the International Criminal Court. Beyond the need for constructing formal institutions, an additional challenge facing the international community was that a national civilian police force did not exist in Afghanistan. Rather, the police was perceived as a quasi-military force, and a coercive instrument of the state (International Crisis Group 2007). In addition, the estimated 50,000 men working as police at the start of international intervention were untrained, ill-equipped, and largely illiterate. They also owed their allegiance to local militia commanders or warlords rather than to the central government (International Crisis Group 2007). In addition to having to establish formal state structures, the training of police officers emerged as key challenges. When it comes to the justice sector, none of the judicial institutions at present have the resources to deliver an effective system of justice. In many cases, judges may not have access to legal texts, may not have been trained properly, and simply apply their version of Sharia law to many disputes (see Thier 2004).

Germany as the key partner nation in charge of coordinating the reform of the Afghan National Police (ANP) took on the task through the German Police Project Office (GPPO). Working in Kabul as well as in field offices in Mazar-e-Sharif, Kunduz and Feyzabad, GPPO projects included building the Police Academy in Kabul and the organization of training programmes for police officers from across the country. German training efforts focused on long-term training, including three-year and nine-month courses to build up a backbone of the police force. The long-term approach of 'training the trainers', however, did not do justice to the need for basic training of large numbers of police officers.

Given the increasingly precarious security situation in the country the overall emphasis on a civilian police force, long-term institutional change, but also a focus on human rights and citizen outreach moved into the background. Instead, the police became increasingly regarded as a front line in the fight against insurgency. The US, which became increasingly involved in police reform as of 2003, focused on rapid training rather than long-term institutional change. US efforts were carried out through the Focused District Development (FDD) programme, which trained district police over a period of eight weeks, under the Combined Security Transition Command Afghanistan (CSTC-A). German and American training programmes were carried out simultaneously and increasingly overlapped but also contradicted one another on account of their different approaches to policing. Given insufficient resources extended on the part of Germany as the lead nation for police reform alongside increasing US political and financial resources allocated to police reform, discussions over increasing European engagement in police reform through ESDP gained currency.

The political process leading to the launch of EUPOL Afghanistan reflected a coming of age for the EU in one key respect. Rather than merely a result of an internal debate among member states over the value of better coordinating individual national police reform efforts, EUPOL Afghanistan came about in no small part on account of external pressures, mainly from the US. This indicates transatlantic pressures acting on EU member states – as well as on EU institutions, as US officials also had talks with Javier Solana over launching an ESDP mission in Afghanistan.[2] More broadly, it also indicated a shift in the EU-NATO relationship and division of labor. Rather than emphasizing European contributions through NATO, the US recognized the EU as an individual and potentially beneficial security actor. While EU member states continue to operate with strong bi-lateral transatlantic reflexes in Afghanistan, the creation of EUPOL Afghanistan and the political processes that led to its creation, indicate a shift towards EU-US political and security relations, thereby broadening the transatlantic space. As later sections in this chapter show, however, the EU has fallen short of transatlantic expectations.

In addition to increasing the overall European contribution to police reform in Afghanistan, the added advantage of EUPOL Afghanistan was that it subsumed police reform activities of individual EU member states as well as third states active in police reform. This could potentially improve coordination through exchange of information and more targeted programme design. Initially, EUPOL Afghanistan was to contribute to the formulation of an overall international police strategy, to mentor staff in the Ministry of Interior, and to support the linkages between the police and the wider rule of law. While not including large-scale training, these tasks were to complement US training that focuses on short-term rather than long-term structural training and mentoring (see Gross 2009a).

In addition to a late arrival in a crowded and overly politicized international environment, EUPOL from the beginning suffered from a mismatch between its intended role and capacities. A complex international context that included fragmentation of international efforts; a multitude of actors engaging in police reform; different emphases in training and views on the role of police; and insufficient coordination mechanisms coupled with ongoing shortages in resources and personnel have made EUPOL Afghanistan a heavily criticized ESDP missions (see International Herald Tribune 2008). Problems experienced in other civilian ESDP missions affected EUPOL as well, but were compounded by the security situation on the ground, frequent changes in the Head of Mission, and inter-institutional disputes between EU and NATO over the provision of security for EUPOL personnel in PRTs. Delays in procurement, staffing, administration and security concerns, furthermore, prohibited the running of the operation. Lastly, member states' enduring reluctance to equip the mission with sufficient numbers of staff negatively affected EUPOL's ability to carry out its mandate: rather than the 400 authorized, mission strength at the end of 2009 was 277 internationals (EUPOL 2009).

The inability of EUPOL to carry out its mandate as a result of limited personnel and ultimately also the low political profile of the mission refers in particular to the initial aim of coordinating and working on an overall international strategy towards reforming the ANP. The EU through EUPOL assumed the main coordinating role of the International Police Coordination Board (IPCB), a body set up in 2006 to coordinate international police reform efforts and ensure coherence among actors – in close cooperation with the Afghan Minister of the Interior, who heads the Board. However, the relatively low importance attached to the IPCB on the part of EUPOL but also US officials weakened the IPCB's coordination function.[3] The task of strategy development moved into the background – the mission simply did not possess the required political, financial and personnel strength to assume the strategic and coordination roles initially foreseen for the mission. Given EUPOL's approved (and actual) size, and the lack of member states' support, this was an unrealistic proposition. The IPCB has since been reformed to improve coordination and to work on formulating strategic goals rather than training outcomes.

The challenge of EU coordination with other international institutions in post-conflict reconstruction activities, however, goes beyond EUPOL and has negatively affected other areas of EU engagement. The EU Election Observation Mission similarly noted in its final report that

> constraints, in addition to the general security limitations [. . .] that seriously affected the EU EOM observers' access to the polling stations, included the recurring lack of willingness by important interlocutors such as the Independent Election Commission (IEC) and the UNDP ELECT to facilitate access to information required for effective observation.
>
> (EU Election Observation Mission 2009: 3)

The missions' difficulty in productively interacting with agencies and institutions already on the ground underlines the EU's difficulty in assuming an operational but also a political function in a crowded environment. While the EU is a key actor in Afghanistan in financial and political terms, and while it is the only, or the most suited, actor to assume certain functions – those that involve coordinating European contributions in certain fields such as police reform, or those that require an additional 'neutral' actor in the case of the 2009 Presidential election[4] – the EU has not managed to exert political influence that is commensurate with its contributions.

While the creation of unrealistic expectations over EUPOL's broader goals have caused the mission to fall short of its initially declared goals, the EU's broader presence also suffers from institutional overlap and difficulties in coordination with other actors involved in aspects of SSR but also the broader reconstruction agenda. This has negatively affected the coordination with other actors in the field. While the EU has continuously adjusted its programmes and its political representation to the changing political priorities but also the changing security dynamics on the ground, the example of EUPOL Afghanistan in particular shows the enduring difficulties the EU faces in Afghanistan – despite efforts to fine-tune the mission and its mandate.

Responding to mission challenges: EUPOL's changing focus

Given the very real and enduring limitations facing the mission, EUPOL has had to significantly amend its approach since its launch in June 2007. To a certain extent this demonstrates the EU's flexibility and its ability to find and occupy a niche for itself. On the other hand, many of EUPOL's shortfalls are home-made. Still, the deteriorating security situation, and a focus on counterinsurgency on the part of the US that includes the training of the security forces so that Afghan authorities themselves can take on security functions (see ISAF 2009), mean that the role of the police is seen in a security and counter-insurgency context. The ANP has increasingly turned into a counter-insurgency force, with high mortality rates and a high level of attrition. Attracting, training and maintaining a working police force, therefore, represents a serious challenge. When it comes to training, high illiteracy rates, and unclear alliances among the recruits represent additional challenges. In this context, EUPOL's overall aim – of creating or of at least working towards a civilian police force – is currently not a priority in light of the state of security in the country but also the role currently played by the police. This means, however, that the EU as a crisis manager cannot play to its strengths by applying a mission model of mentoring, advising and training that has produced results in other theatres.

Despite its initial and enduring growing pains, EUPOL has found a niche for its approach. EU and US police reform activities are much more closely coordinated than they were in the past. Whereas US – and, since 2009, also NATO – efforts continue to focus on training, EUPOL provides strategic advice and focuses on specific goals and priority areas. Specifically, EUPOL is currently focused on six objectives, three in the rule of law (anti-corruption strategy; links with prosecutors; human right and gender) and three in police (PC3, intelligence-led policing, and the city police project in Kabul). Essentially, EUPOL staff view the role of the mission as aimed at the future: beyond the establishment of security EUPOL is to build a professional civilian force for once after security has been established.[5] Within this broad remit, EUPOL activities do support CSTC-A and the NATO Training Mission Afghanistan (NTM-A). In addition or perhaps as a result of EUPOL's changed objectives, cooperation with CSTC-A and NATO has improved.[6]

EUPOL has also had an impact in the sense that Afghan authorities have recognized the mission as an important tool for institutional reform. This has further helped EUPOL define its operational mandate. Upon his appointment in 2008, then Minister of the Interior Hanif Atmar formulated a number of priority areas that EUPOL was to address. These included implementing a comprehensive anti-corruption strategy, reinforcing intelligence and investigative capacity in the fight against organized crime; completing and expanding the police *tashkeel* (recruiting system); improving security in principal cities and ensuring security during the 2009 elections (see Peral 2009). This shows that from the perspective of the security consumer – in this case the Afghan government, rather than the Afghan public – EUPOL is regarded as providing added value; and that the Afghan Ministry of Interior is proactive in utilizing EUPOL as well as other international institutions for the reform of parts of the administration. Beyond fine-tuning its approach, and beyond the establishment of a constructive relationship with the Afghan government, however, the balance sheet for EUPOL remains mixed. Member states remain reluctant to deploy beyond their national areas, EUPOL remains under-staffed, and mission staff are still not deployed throughout the entire country. The problem of effectiveness and impact is magnified if one places EUPOL in the broader framework of EU policies in Afghanistan: here, the lack of coordination and of an overall political strategy further diminishes the EU's role in post-conflict reconstruction.

Enduring challenges

Coordinating EU instruments in the field, but also managing the link between Kabul and Brussels, has proven an enduring challenge. With EUPOL, the office of the EUSR and the Commission Delegation, the EU is represented in Afghanistan through three separate offices that pursue separate, yet essentially, interrelated activities. This has not only affected the EU's ability to influence the Afghan government but also its ability to project a united political profile among the international actors operating in Afghanistan. In addition to informing the PSC on political developments in Afghanistan, the EUSR also fulfills a coordinating function. At the same time, communicating and making visible the EU's contributions has been exceedingly difficult – as has the application of political pressure on the Afghan government. The office of the EUSR, despite its political function, does not have financial instruments at its disposal and this weakens the political influence the position could potentially exert. Similarly, neither the Commission nor EUPOL have a political mandate. The difficult process of intra-EU coordination in the absence of formal mechanism has further affected the EU's coherence in the field. Despite the introduction of regular meetings among the key EU actors in the field, the EU's presence on the ground remained divided. Suggestions of double-hatting the post of EUSR and Head of Delegation, although repeatedly discussed, were rejected by the Commission – and it was not until after the ratification of the Lisbon Treaty that a decision was taken to appoint former Lithuanian foreign minister Vygaudas Usackas as EUSR and Head of the EU Delegation in Kabul (European Voice 2010).[7]

The lack of coordination and coherence but also the number of actors representing different aspects of EU policy in the field has negatively affected EU visibility in Afghanistan. It has also affected the EU's ability to exert political pressure on the Afghan government. As far as visibility and unity of purpose in Afghanistan is concerned, the set-up of EU activities in Afghanistan has made exerting conditionality difficult – after all, until very recently the financial and political EU instruments were wielded separately. In addition, the European Commission's financial contributions are either paid into UN-administered trust funds, such as the Law and Order Trust Fund Afghanistan (LOTFA) that, among other things, pays police salaries. Given that the Afghan state is not self-sustaining, these expenses are non-negotiable – and the EU and the larger international community do not have much bargaining leverage.[8]

With respect to the EU's standing vis-à-vis other international actors, this lack of coherence has negatively affected the EU's political weight. While the US was initially supportive of EUPOL Afghanistan, for instance, the enduring shortfalls in personnel have made many US officials doubt the EU's willingness but also its ability to provide a significant civilian presence in Afghanistan.[9] The deteriorating security conditions in Afghanistan has further sidelined the visibility and impact of the EU's contribution in favor of increasing US and NATO involvement – both in terms of military counter-insurgency operations but also in aspects of SSR, mainly the training of the ANA and ANP. The de facto US lead in police reform, but also NATO's growing involvement in this area, threaten to further sideline the EU. Both US and NATO efforts focus on basic training of large number of police recruits. Models of police reform differ from that advocated by the EU, which focuses on civilian policing and European standards – and which deploys police experts rather than military trainers. Furthermore, EU involvement as it concerns ESDP but also the broader area of rule of law administered by the Commission, was essentially reactive and in response to increasing US pressures. As a result, the EU as a whole but also its component parts – the Commission, the Council and the member states – did not formulate an overall political strategy towards the country, and this has negatively affected the political leverage the EU had vis-à-vis its international partners.

The problematic EU-NATO relationship has negatively affected the EU's ability to deploy throughout the country, and contributed to delays in the mission's overall deployment. EUPOL is not a Berlin plus operation and, therefore, the relationship between EUPOL and NATO falls outside formal EU-NATO arrangements that would permit coordination and cooperation between the two organizations. Due to Turkish opposition, a formal agreement between EUPOL and ISAF could not be arrived at, and EUPOL had to draw up bilateral technical agreements with respective lead nations of EU-member state-led PRTs on the provision of security for EUPOL staff through ISAF. Significantly, agreements with US-led and Turkish-led PRTs have not been concluded, which limits the overall reach of EUPOL Afghanistan.

What do the EU's activities in Afghanistan say about its capacity, its effectiveness, its impact?

The evaluation of the impact of the EU's activities in Afghanistan entails the analysis of the overall EU contributions as well as its constitutive parts – the EUSR, Commission, EUPOL, but also member states' coordination and alignment with the EU – and their collective impact on institution-building and post-conflict reconstruction. In general, it can be said that while individual EU activities have had an impact, individual EU actors have faced an uphill battle in adjusting their activities to the conflict setting, but also to their capabilities – and to match the rhetoric to the available resources and capabilities. The case of EUPOL Afghanistan illustrates this most clearly – despite the fact that the mission came into existence mainly on account of NATO and US prodding, and despite the fact that member states and the EU proclaimed as an operational goal of the mission strategy formulation, the mission from the start was conceived too small, and not equipped with the necessary resources to fulfill its mission.

Generally speaking the application of conflict prevention instruments that the EU has at its disposal, while crucial for the long-term post-conflict reconstruction goals do not lend the EU political capital, or weight in an environment where emphasis remains on military intervention and counterinsurgency. The EU may have all instruments that enable a 'comprehensive approach' at its disposal (see Gross 2008), but in Afghanistan cannot combine them for political leverage – for one, because the EU does not deploy military instruments that would complete its range of activities. The EU also lacks political leverage, however, because it has so far been unable to combine the various instruments it deploys to a political effect. This is mainly due to the lack of inter- and intra-EU coordination, and divergent priorities of the EU and its member states that have been analyzed earlier in this chapter.

If one breaks EU engagement into individual parts and analyzes each separately, it becomes clear that each instrument has had impact to a varying degree on the conflict setting, the EU's interaction with the Afghan government, but also on the EU's ability to exert itself vis-à-vis other international actors. The levels and the nature of impact have, however, varied over time. To begin with, the post of EUSR proved effective initially to make the EU a visible actor in Afghanistan and to increase its range of activities beyond the financial instruments of the European Commission. The lengthy country-specific Afghanistan expertise of the second appointment to the post – Ambassador Francesc Vendrell, who had previously served with the UN in Afghanistan – proved beneficial in terms of access and personal influence. Over time, the position of the EUSR developed into an important coordinating actor, and in transmitting information between the field and Brussels. Where the post of EUSR fell short in impact, however, was its lack of financial resources and of political weight at its disposal.

The European Commission, on the other hand, enjoys a generally good reputation for its programming on the ground.[10] It also cooperates with member states in the implementation of programmes; its portfolio of 'EU wide' programmes with member states included, for instance, the Kabul-Jalalabad-Torkham road project in cooperation with Sweden and the electricity rehabilitation of Kabul in cooperation with Germany (European Commission 2003b). The Commission's financial contributions to various trust funds, including LOTFA, are vital to the functioning of state structures, including the payment of salaries for civil service personnel. The impact of programmes, therefore, can be measured both in financial terms, but also in the completion of specific infrastructure projects. However, the lack of political leverage without the political weight of the Council or EU member states have rendered the EU Commission a purely financial actor in conflict prevention and crisis management, without the power to exert political influence on either international allies or its Afghan interlocutors.

When it comes to EUPOL Afghanistan, the mission amply illustrates the limitations of CSDP when member states do not honor their commitments to send sufficient personnel, and when a mission enters a contested political space. While EUPOL can look to some impact, especially given its civilian training activities and its focus on advising the Ministry of Interior on fighting corruption, its broader international impact has suffered. Beyond the immediate setting of Afghanistan, this CSDP mission was deployed also in the service but also in support of transatlantic relations – on which it has not had an altogether positive impact. While US attitudes initially were rather positive towards EUPOL Afghanistan, and supportive of its launch, mission but also member state conduct has revealed difficulties over burden sharing beyond NATO, and has led to significant disillusionment on the part of the US with EU civilian capabilities in Afghanistan.[11] With EUPOL, the EU essentially was caught in the cross-fire between member state interests, adverse security conditions on the ground, and US interests that determined the political and operational direction of police reform. While the US has recognized the Commission as a financial partner, the US has not necessarily been keen on the overall EU decision-making structure. The EU did improve infrastructure, did train police and implement programmes, and aimed for the introduction of civilian policing tradition – however, a vast lead on the part of the US left the EU in a subordinate role. The EU in Afghanistan is perceived as an important actor, but it is one that has not been able to fully translate its commitments into political visibility.

Conclusion

European engagement in Afghanistan suffers from 'many Europeans, not enough EU'. This lack of 'Europeanized' engagement is partly due to member states commitment through a number of institutional venues, most importantly NATO for their military contributions to ISAF; and partly due to an overall US lead. For the last decade this has meant that member states orient themselves on their transatlantic rather than their European commitments. For the EUPOL mission, which has suffered from member state reluctance to provide the necessary personnel, this has meant not only political but also operational neglect – EUPOL to date has not been able to perform all tasks assigned to it, and to do so throughout the country. This means that, although the EU has made progress in defining its role, and in adjusting its policies to contribute to the overall international engagement, its impact in international terms has been limited. Rather than setting political priorities together with other key international players in Afghanistan, the EU has adopted a reactive approach. This, together with individual EU member states pursuing bilateral policies in Afghanistan has meant that the EU's impact on the international scene has not been decisive: rather, the EU – in particular through its EUPOL mission – has raised expectations that it in the end could not fulfill.

Despite its limited impact on the international scene, however, the EU makes a potentially important contribution to conflict management as well as post-conflict reconstruction. This applies in particular to the European Commission, which is regarded as a partner in reconstruction also in transatlantic terms. The EU's long-term structural as well as its short-term impact suffer, however, from the lack of political and strategic weight and representation due to its de-centralized presence on the ground. The EUSR and EUPOL operating without financial instruments to exert political pressure and induce compliance have impacted their efforts; as does the European Commission's lack of conditionality mechanisms. Beyond a doubt, double-hatting the post of Head of Delegation with the EUSR in the wake of the ratification of the Treaty of Lisbon will improve coordination , as it brings the financial and the political instruments the EU has at its disposal under one institutional roof. As long as EUPOL suffers from shortages in personnel and limited coordination with other international actors, the EU's presence on the ground and its international political prestige will continue to suffer. The particular conflict setting in Afghanistan has crystallized the tensions inherent in member states' transatlantic versus European commitments. It has also demonstrated the pitfalls of insufficient resources extended.

Notes

1 Interview, December 2008.
2 Interview with US official, December 2008.
3 Interview with EU official, December 2008.
4 Interview, November 2009.
5 Interview, September 2009.
6 Interview, October 2009.
7 Research on this chapter was completed prior to the entry into force of the Treaty of Lisbon in December 2009. In light of further institutional changes through the European External Action Service (EEAS), it is too soon to draw conclusions over improved coherence between EU instruments in Afghanistan. The physical merger of the office of the EUSR and the Delegation has had positive results when it comes to the coordination of activities, however, and this bodes well for future improvements.
8 Interview with EU official, September 2009.
9 Interview, September 2009.
10 Interview, November 2008.
11 Interview with member state official, December 2008.

9   The EU in Georgia

Towards a coherent crisis management strategy?

Giselle Bosse

There is a lot that the European Union can do [. . .] What is changing in practice are the resources and the instruments that the European Union has at its disposal. When the European Neighbourhood Policy starts to take effect [. . .] in 2007, there will be considerable resources available for various activities, not least those related to conflict resolution and support for the development and rehabilitation of the conflict areas.

(Semneby 2006)

The war in Georgia divided the EU instead of uniting it.

(Valasek 2008: 1)

Introduction

Georgia is one of the keenest 'new' neighbours of the European Union (EU). It has long stated its interest in joining the EU and has, compared to other partners in the European Neighbourhood Policy (ENP), made significant progress in undertaking political and economic reforms. Georgia itself is, however, involved in two frozen conflicts on its own territory. Ever since Georgia gained independence in 1998, the regions of Abkhazia and South Ossetia have become contested territory between Georgia as a former republic of the Soviet Union, and the Russian Federation. The continued presence of armed Russian military personnel in the regions – once the industrial heartland of the South Caucasus – has impacted significantly on the political and economic stability of Georgia and therefore hampered the reform process. For the EU, the region has become more and more interesting in recent years following successive energy 'crises' between Russia and Ukraine in 2007 and 2009, and the recognition among Western European governments of the urgency to diversify their energy supplies. Despite Georgia's strategic importance as a transit country for gas from Central Asia, the Union has hitherto lacked a coherent policy towards Georgia and was very reluctant to become involved in the settlement of the frozen conflicts.[1] In 2005, however, the EU's heads of state and government decided to include Georgia, alongside Azerbaijan and Armenia, into its new European Neighbourhood Policy in recognition of the need to build a stronger partnership with the South Caucasus. The provisions of the ENP originally aimed at political and economic reform in the EU's neighbourhood. Following the inclusion of the South Caucasus into the policy, however, new security provisions were added to the ENP, including crisis management and conflict resolution.

This chapter examines the role and impact of the EU's conflict prevention and crisis management efforts in Georgia and evaluates to what extent the ENP has contributed to the consistency of EU policies towards the country. The existing literature has predominantly focused either on the unrealistic conflict prevention/crisis management provisions in the ENP in general or the potential of the ENP to streamline the EU's efforts in future conflicts (e.g. Cameron and Balfour 2006). Less attention is given on the evolution of these policies in the ENP over time and its concrete impact in actual crisis situations.

Georgia is a formidable 'test-case' for the role and impact of the ENP on conflict prevention and crisis management. In August 2008, the frozen conflict in South Ossetia escalated into an open and large-scale conflict with the Russian Federation, which many commentators already view as a crucial landmark for the EU's strategy. Some concluded that the August war shook the 'foundations of the post-Cold War security order' and 'constituted an impetus for more soul-searching among the main European security actors' (Popescu 2009: 1). On a less positive note, others concluded that: 'for years, the EU has neglected the region and there is no overarching strategy for it [. . .] It only paid attention after the war had broken out, prompting French President Sarkozy, on behalf of the EU presidency, to embark on a frantic shuttle mission.' (Vogel 2009: 2). Even the EU's own Independent International Fact-Finding Mission on the Conflict in Georgia (IIFFMCG) in its report on the Russian-Georgian war recently concluded that the EU's engagement was 'cooperative but cautious on contentious political issues and, except for some bilateral support from very few EU members, mostly distanced in terms of military support and sensitive security issues' (IIFFMCG 2009: 16). In other words, the general perceptions of the EU's efforts during the August war suggest that the ENP has contributed very little to improve the consistency of EU conflict prevention and crisis management. Given the emphasis in the ENP on 'adding value' to existing efforts in these areas, it seems of utmost importance to carefully evaluate the policy's impact on conflict prevention and crisis management in Georgia in light of these (broadly negative) perceptions.

The precise meaning and constituent elements of consistency in the context of EU foreign policy tend to differ in the scholarly literature (e.g. Portela and Raube 2009; Gauttier 2004; Vanhoonacker 2008). I will therefore focus on consistency in a broader sense, such as the process of drafting and implementing conflict prevention and crisis management measures at the EU level, including multiple actors (institutional and vertical consistency) as well as competing policy paradigms (horizontal consistency).

In this chapter, I will analyse (i) the evolution and role of conflict prevention and crisis management in the EU's policy towards Georgia following the introduction of the ENP, (ii) the role and impact of the EU's efforts during the Russia-Georgia war in August 2008 and (iii) the prospects for EU conflict prevention and crisis management within the framework of the Eastern Partnership (EaP), following the 2008 war. In order to evaluate the contribution of the ENP to the consistency of these policies, I first introduce the notions of 'vertical' and 'horizontal' consistency. I argue that in practice, the ENP has not improved the consistency of EU conflict prevention and crisis management. Instead, the Union's reaction to conflict remains firmly in the hands of the member states and thus the consistency of these policies continues to depend on their political will and engagement.

Defining 'consistency' in EU conflict prevention and crisis management policies

Institutional consistency is primarily concerned with the interplay between EU institutions, such as intergovernmental and the EC's bureaucratic apparatuses and pillars, or constitutional responsibilities and competences across bureaucratic boundaries (Nuttall 2001: 6–8). In the context of EU foreign policy, this generally includes 'infighting' or 'turf-wars' between the European Commission, the Council, the High Representative (HR), between different Directorate General in the Commission and/or the European Parliament (Rummel and Wiedemann 1998: 54–59). Institutional consistency also roots in concrete manpower, such as the ability (time, knowledge) of EU officials to 'weave together an increasingly complicated network of institutions across pillars' (Duke 2002: xix–xx). Vertical consistency refers to the congruence between policy positions and actions of the member states with EU foreign policy statements and implementation of policy (Nuttall 2001: 8–10). Congruence between the EU and member states also depends on the 'rhetoric-resources gap', the willingness of the member states to contribute appropriate resources to 'match' common EU foreign policy aims (Duke 2002: 192). Institutional and vertical consistency are particularly useful to examine conflict prevention and crisis management provisions under the ENP, which were initially developed by the Commission, but in practice draw heavily on policy instruments within the remit of the Council and the member states.

Horizontal consistency is linked to the degree to which EU policies, including different policy areas, measures, implementation actions and policy paradigms of each pillar, mutually reinforce one another (Duke 2002: 192). This type of consistency, for example, refers to the continuum between conflict prevention, civilian crisis management and/or the development or use of military instruments within this policy area, but also the links between 'soft' security (democratization and economic development) and 'hard' security issues (conflict management) (Duke 2002: 162).

A sea-change in EU-Georgia relations? The European Neighbourhood Policy

Following the end of the Cold War, the Union's involvement in the South Caucasus has not been led by a clear conflict prevention or crisis management strategy. The actions of the EU were decided in an *ad hoc* manner and primarily led by

events. Actions in the region ranged from humanitarian support, to capacity building and economic cooperation but most programmes and operations did not run
with much success (International Crisis Group 2006). Apart from the lack of an
overall EU strategy, EU assistance was not effective because of ongoing conflicts
in the region. The Commission gradually recognized the importance of conflict
settlement for EC external financial assistance to be effective but the member
states insisted that the framework of the Partnership and Cooperation Agreement
(PCA) offered the optimal framework for the support of Georgia's transformation
(Lynch 2006: 61).

Initially, the ENP, too, did not include the Southern Caucasus. The policy in
general lacked considerable detail and engagement with specific conflicts or
indeed crisis management and conflict resolution. In March 2003, the Commission
published its first *Communication of Wider Europe-New Neighbourhood: A New
Framework for relations with our Eastern and Southern Neighbours* (European
Commission 2003a). The Communication identified political stability, economic
development and the reduction of poverty and social divisions as key objectives
in its enhanced relations with neighbouring states. The achievement of these aims
would, however, require the 'whole range' of the Union's policies, including foreign and security policy. Under the three key headings of 'Proximity, Prosperity
and Poverty', the Communication placed emphasis on fighting trans-border mutual
security threats, defined in terms of illegal immigration, trafficking, organized
crime, terrorist networks and communicable diseases; the need to tackle poverty,
social exclusion and slow economic growth; and the importance of democracy
and the rule of law. The effects of political conflict on economic and political
development were highlighted with reference to the Western Sahara, the Pal-
estinian Territories and Transdnistria (European Commission 2003a: 9). It is
clear, however, that the Commission intended to resolve these conflicts with the
traditional instruments at the disposal of the European Community. The Commission wanted to 'reduce poverty and create an area of shared prosperity and values
based on deeper economic integration, intensified political and cultural relations, [and] enhanced cross-border cooperation.' (European Commission 2003a:
9). These measures are traditionally associated with conflict prevention through
political and economic reforms rather than the direct management or resolution
of conflicts.

The ENP in theory: towards 'hard' security and crisis management in the South Caucasus

The priorities within the official documents on the ENP began to change towards
a greater emphasis on 'hard' security issues between December 2003 and spring
2004. That initial shift can be explained by the decision to expand the ENP to
include the three states in the Southern Caucasus (Georgia, Armenia, and Azerbaijan), and the need to address the 'frozen' conflicts in the region (Abkhazia, South
Ossetia, Nagorno-Karabach) in order to create more stable political and economic
conditions for cooperation with the EU (i.e. on energy). The development of the

European Security Strategy (ESS) was another important factor in the (rhetorical) shift within the ENP. The ESS listed 'Building Security in our Neighbourhood' as one out of three key challenges for the Union's external relations in the coming decades (Council of the European Union 2003d). In this document, violent conflict around its borders was seen as one of the key problems for Europe. Apart from extending economic and political cooperation, the ESS stressed the resolution of the Arab/Israeli conflict as a strategic priority and highlighted continued engagement with the Mediterranean partners through more effective economic, security and cultural cooperation under the Barcelona Process. The conflicts in the South Caucasus were, however, not explicitly mentioned in the ESS.

The Commission Strategy Paper of May 2004 confirmed the initial 'soft-security' paradigm of the ENP, but placed a much greater emphasis on the Common Foreign and Security Policy (CSFP) and Common Security and Defence Policy (CSDP):

> The European Neighbourhood Policy will reinforce existing forms of regional and sub-regional cooperation and provide a framework for their further development. The ENP will reinforce stability and security and contribute to efforts at conflict resolution. [. . .] It will reinforce efforts to meet the objectives of the European Security Strategy.
>
> (European Commission 2004a: 4)

The Action Plans (implementation tools of the ENP) would include provisions related to CFSP and political cooperation. The settlement of conflicts was now highlighted in particular in respect to the Southern Caucasus where 'increased efforts' were emphasized but not further explained (European Commission 2004a: 11). Political dialogue on foreign and security issues was to be strengthened in respect to regional and international issues (crisis management and participation in EU-led crisis management operations, common security threats such as terrorism, etc.). The provisions on conflict resolution were, however, kept very vague. In terms of 'linking the existing instruments to the policy', only Commission-led policy was mentioned (MEDA, TACIS, EIB and EIDHR) (European Commission 2004a: 24). There was no mention in this context of existing conflict resolution efforts in the South Caucasus. In other words, the principal ENP framework documents were not mapping a consistent approach to show the continuum between conflict prevention and crisis management.

Nevertheless, the EU took some encouraging, albeit general, steps towards civilian crisis management in Georgia. In July 2003, the Council appointed the Finnish diplomat Heikki Talvitie as first Special Representative (EUSR) for the South Caucasus. One year later, in July 2004, the EU Rule of Law mission (EUJUST THEMIS) was launched. It aimed at reforming the criminal justice sector and legislative reform in the country. A team comprising thirteen EU experts from various member states (Finland, Italy, Greece, Latvia, Lithuania, Sweden, Germany, the Netherlands, Poland, Slovakia and Germany) and from Georgia, was tasked to implement these reforms.

Back to reality: ENP Country Reports and Action Plans

The 2005 ENP Country report for Georgia made numerous positive references to the EUJUST THEMIS rule of law mission (European Commission 2005). The settlement of internal conflicts was given priority and the role of the EUSR (working closely with the Commission) was highlighted. Yet, the report made only vague references to the conflicts in South Ossetia and Abkhazia. Already well before the conclusion of the negotiations, the Action Plans were perceived by Tbilisi as highly inconsistent with earlier promises made by the EU in respect to conflict resolution efforts.[2] The negotiations of the Action Plan with Georgia (concluded in November 2006) were seriously delayed because, among other reasons, the Georgian delegation was pressing the EU to become more actively involved in conflict resolution efforts in South Ossetia and Abkhazia. This was originally partly supported by the Commission and the EUSR, but quickly discarded by a number of representatives from the member states who communicated through the Presidency during the negotiations of the Action Plans.[3]

Although two out of five chapters of the Action Plan focused on the EU's role in conflict resolution in the region, the main emphasis was placed on economic and political change, i.e. soft security issues. Once again the Georgian political elites expressed frustration that the EU was unwilling to incorporate more conflict resolution commitments in the text, in particular instruments from the ESDP to promote regional stability and crisis management (International Crisis Group 2006: 10–11). The EU, however, proposed a rather soft approach to conflict resolution, such as the provision of further economic assistance subject to progress with the settlement of disputes, and was generally more interested in supporting existing UN and OSCE negotiation efforts and formats in the region (International Crisis Group 2006: 10–11).

The content of the ENP Country report and the Action Plan for Georgia clearly demonstrated the limits of implementing the ambitious conflict resolution agenda developed in the framework documents of the ENP. At the same time, the late decision to include the South Caucasus into the ENP confirmed a continuation of the *ad hoc* nature of EU engagement with Georgia and the region more generally. In other words, the ENP did not immediately aid the development of a more consistent strategy for the region as a whole.

A number of factors contributed to this *ad hoc* approach, which made it virtually impossible for the EU to draw up a consistent strategy for conflict resolution in Georgia. First, the Union hardly raised the conflicts in high level discussions with its partners. This was evident in particular in EU-Russian relations. Already in 2005, the majority of member states had rejected the EU's involvement in the continuation of an OSCE Border Monitoring operation in Georgia which could not be prolonged because of a Russian veto to extend the mandate of the OSCE (Lynch 2006: 55). At the time, the French government was among those who fiercely opposed the EU's engagement. The EU therefore also paid little attention to a number of 'minor' incidents, such as the Russian attack of a radar station in Georgia in 2007. Member states did not change their preferences of prioritizing relations with Russia over and above the need for conflict resolution in Georgia. The 'hard security' rhetoric of the ENP could do little to change this. As one commentator put it: '[t]hough Tbilisi is keen on greater engagement, it may not have understood how reluctant Brussels is to take on a greater role with regard to conflict resolution – especially with regard to Russia.' (International Crisis Group 2006: 10).

Second, the EU did not speak with one voice, which undermined vertical consistency of its efforts in Georgia. The member states kept tight control over the EUSR. His mandate and room for action derive directly from the member states, which were rarely able to find agreement on a clear mandate (Council of the European Union 2006a: 15). There were, however, signs that the EUSR tried to create more room for independent action. This raised questions about the level of effective communication between the Council and the EUSR and thus institutional consistency. One commentator observed that 'he is largely dependent on the good offices of the EU Presidency embassy to prepare his agenda [. . .] although [there are] complaints by member states that the EUSR does not share sufficient information' (International Crisis Group 2006: 23). At the same time, Commission officials also admitted that instead of contacting the EUSR when facing political obstacles on the ground, they turned to the OSCE or the UN who they saw as more connected and influential (International Crisis Group 2006: 23). In other words, there were clear signs of a continuous lack not just in vertical but also institutional consistency, despite the introduction of the ENP.

Third, the Commission still lacked sufficient expertise on the South Caucasus. Although the Commission was very involved in implementing programmes in Georgia, the number of personnel responsible for the region in the Commission was insufficient and constantly changing. Only a handful of officials in DG external relations were working on proposals for the ENP Action Plan for Georgia, for example. One official joined half-way into the negotiation process and was asked to enter into negotiations with the Georgian delegation straight away.[4]

Fourth and finally, although EU financial allocations to Georgia increased significantly (for example, an extra € 4.6 million under the Rapid Reaction Mechanism to stabilize the country) following the Rose Revolution in 2003, the European Neighbourhood Policy Instrument (ENPI) did not prioritize traditional conflict resolution measures. The ENPI was designed in 2003 and 2004, before the inclusion of the South Caucasus into the ENP. As a result, the EU mainly provided humanitarian and rehabilitation aid to Abkhazia and South Ossetia, but did little to bring civil society from the regions together with Georgians. Neither the rule of law nor security sector reform featured in the National Indicative Programme for 2007–10. Post-conflict rehabilitation measures in the ENPI therefore continued to be programmed in separation from conflict prevention and conflict management, thereby contributing little to increase horizontal consistency. Moreover, the EU's financial and political engagement with Georgia under the new ENPI envelope (€ 120 Million from 2007–10) remained minimal compared to that of the US, the UN or the OSCE (International Crisis Group 2006: 5–6).

In conclusion, the role of EU conflict prevention and crisis management provisions in the early ENP was sketched in very vague terms and few linkages were created between traditional EC instruments and CFSP/CSDP measures to deal with the conflicts in South Ossetia and Abkhazia. Apart from lacking horizontal consistency in theory, the EU's efforts in practice lacked vertical and institutional consistency, and were severely limited in reach because of the reluctance of the member states to commit to a resolution of the conflicts. The following section analyses to what extend the escalation of the frozen conflict in South Ossetia in August 2008 brought about any change for the coherence of conflict prevention and crisis management policies under the ENP.

Coherent crisis management or 'frantic shuttle mission'? The EU's response to the war between Georgia and Russia in August 2008

During the night from 7 to 8 August 2008, heavy fighting was reported from the South Ossetian town Tskhinvali between Georgian and Russian armed forces. The fights quickly spread to other parts of Georgia and lasted for five days. According to the report published by the EU's Fact-Finding Mission on the Conflict in Georgia, about 850 persons were killed in the fighting, including over 200 civilians, and 1747 persons were left wounded. 100,000 civilians fled their homes, of whom 35,000 still have not been able to return (IIFFMCG 2009: 5).

The initial response by the EU 27 to the break-out of the conflict was diverse and divided. At the heart of the disagreement lay the question of relations with the Russian Federation. On the one end of the spectrum, the British government argued for the necessity of the EU to impose major sanctions on Russia, such as its temporary exclusion from the G8. In the words of Prime Minister Gordon Brown, 'the EU should review – root and branch – our relationship with Russia' (Brown, quoted in The Guardian 2008). Similar views were expressed by the governments of the new EU member states in Central and Eastern Europe, as well as the Baltic states. The French, German and Italian governments, on the other end of the spectrum, did not favour any form of tough sanctions by the EU27 which, they argued, would only further provoke the Russian government and further escalate the conflict. The High Representative, Javier Solana, the French EU presidency and the Commission each issued separate statements each in the response to the escalation of the situation in South Ossetia on 7 and 8 August, respectively. These first reactions demonstrated that the ENP did not immediately offer a new platform for coherent conflict management. Instead, the lack of a unified EU response to the escalation of the conflict in South Ossetia disclosed the incongruence between the positions of the member states.

The French government then used its role as EU Presidency to cover up these inconsistencies and to react to the crisis. The first to travel to Tbilisi and Moscow was Bernard Kouchner, the French Minister for Foreign and European Affairs, together with Finnish Minister for Foreign Affairs and Chairman-in-Office of the OSCE. Under the leadership of the French President Nicolas Sarkozy, a six-point cease-fire agreement was signed on 12 August 2008.

At the end of August, however, the Russian government announced that it would recognize the independence of the break-away republics of Abkhazia and South Ossetia. Prime Minister Vladimir Putin, for example, commented on the reaction of Europeans stating that:

> If any of the European countries wants to serve someone's narrow political interests, then go ahead. We cannot stop them. But we think, as they say in such cases, 'You have to look out for number one'.
>
> (Putin, quoted in The Guardian 2008)

President Sarkozy, still acting though the EU Presidency, then entered into a new round of negotiations with Moscow and, on 8 September, agreement was reached on the 'Sarkozy-Medvedev Plan', which set out a concrete timeframe (one month) for the withdrawal of Russian troops from the undisputed territories and provided grounds for the deployment of EU monitors in the conflict zones around South Ossetia and Abkhazia.

Sarkozy then convened an Extraordinary European Council meeting in Brussels on 1 September to discuss the crisis in Georgia and the course of action that the EU would take in terms of aid to Georgia and its future relations with Russia. Despite the very different views of the member states on the relationship with Russia, the conclusions of the Council sent a relatively clear message, condemning 'the disproportionate reaction of Russia' and insisting on the full application of the six-point agreement:

> To that end, the President of the European Council will go to Moscow on 8 September, accompanied by the President of the Commission and the High Representative. Until troops have withdrawn to the positions held prior to 7 August, meetings on the negotiation of the Partnership Agreement will be postponed.
>
> (Presidency of the EU 2008)

The French Presidency had successfully engineered a consensus among the member states to condemn the reaction of Russia to the conflict. Nevertheless, the increase in vertical consistency among member state positions is clearly not the result of the provisions contained in the ENP, but rather the outcome of a strong (and at times uncompromising) member state holding the EU Presidency.

On 15 September, the General Affairs and External Relations Council decided to dispatch 200 observers – a civilian crisis management operation under the ESDP – to the conflict region, ready to be employed by 1 October 2008. In addition, the Council endorsed the Commission proposal to mobilize financial aid for Georgia over €500 million over the period 2005–10, and to strengthening the EU's relations with Georgia by 'expediting the preparatory work on the facilitation of visas and on readmission, as well as on free trade' (GAERC 2008).

The EU's crisis management bureaucracy, comprised of the Council Secretariat and the new Civilian Planning and Conduct Capability (CPCC) also functioned remarkably smoothly, which at first sight, suggested improvements to vertical consistency in the EU's response to the conflict in South Ossetia. Within only a few days, the necessary staff were gathered and arrangements made to borrow vehicles and equipment from the member states, and a contact centre/headquarters were created in Tbilisi. The mission was launched on schedule on 1 October. Solana concluded that 'this has been the fasted deployment that the EU has ever undertaken. States made a tremendous effort [. . .] in this short period of time. The EU has shown its capacity to act with determination and speed' (Solana 2008: 1–2). The unprecedented speed of the deployment of the EU Monitoring Mission (EUMM) has brought the EU much praise and led some commentators to state that 'EUMM could become quite a milestone in the development of Europe's crisis management' (Korski 2008: 1). At first sight, the mission was also considerably successful. Within two weeks of its employment, Russian forces seemed to have withdrawn from those zones around Abkhazia and South Ossetia. The GAERC concluded that 'Russian troops have withdrawn from the zones adjacent to South Ossetia and Abkhazia as an essential additional step in the implementation of the agreements of 12 August and 8 September' (GAERC 2008). Nevertheless, the supply of equipment depended entirely on the goodwill of a number of member states. Without their immediate support, the crisis management bureaucracy could have done very little, regardless of its outstanding management capabilities.

The EU's immediate response to the war between Georgia and Russia was thus predominantly led by the member states, and most prominently the French President Sarkozy. On the one hand, the support of a number of member states enabled the speedy deployment of the monitoring mission. Yet, on the other hand, the member states were no guarantors for consistency of crisis management in the long run.

Despite the early success, the EU's engagement with Georgia quickly became caught in vertical and institutional inconsistencies once again. In its conclusions, the European Council in Brussels in mid-October 2008 tasked the Commission and the Council to 'continue a in-depth evaluation of EU-Russia relations' (European Council 2008: 9). Subsequently, the member states which had been in favour of 'engagement' with Russia began to put pressure on the EU to resume negotiations on the PCA. And indeed, at the EU-Russia summit in Nice in November 2009, the EU did no longer mention the Russian intervention in Georgia. The only critique was voiced by Lithuania's Deputy Minister of Foreign Affairs Pavilionis, reminding the member states that

> we are questioning the timing and we are questioning this U-turn of our [EU] positions [. . .] is it the right signal to send to Kiev, to Moldova, to Belarus, even to the Baltic States today, that by military force you can change borders?
> (Pavilionis 2008, quoted in Mikhelidze 2009: 17)

On the ground, too, the EU mission had to face serious challenges. At the end of August, after the Russian government had recognized the independence of Abkhazia and South Ossetia, EU monitors were no longer allowed to enter both regions.

In addition, the Russian government did interpret the terms of the 6-point ceasefire – as laid out in the agreement between Sarkozy and Medvedev – rather creatively, and failed to provide the EU mission with any information about the withdrawal of their troops.

Meanwhile, the Commission continued to increase its broader support for Georgia within the framework of the ENP. By the end of September 2008, the Commission had drafted a mandate in view of the negotiation of a Community visa-facilitation agreement with Georgia, providing facilitations for Georgian citizens equivalent to those granted to Russian citizens. The Commission also gained approval from the Council for its € 500 million comprehensive assistance package, drawing on programmed funds under the ENPI envelope as well as crisis instruments (Instrument for Stability, ECHO and grants for Macro-Financial Assistance). For 2008, the package foresaw a total of € 181.9 million to target *inter alia* the needs of internally displaced persons, recovery of the Georgian economy, dept reduction and ongoing assistance (education and economic rehabilitation of conflict regions, democracy, non-state actors) (European Union 2008). The Commission therefore continued its approach of providing post-conflict humanitarian and rehabilitation aid to Georgia and the conflict regions, rather than the 'hard security' tools of conflict resolution. Overall, the Commission had little involvement in the planning and execution of the monitoring mission, despite its competences in the area of civilian crisis management. This suggests a decrease, rather than an increase, in institutional consistency between the Council and the Commission in this area, regardless of the highly efficient crisis management of the Council Secretariat.

At the time of writing, it is still too early to judge the impact of the comprehensive assistance package. The process of project selection for EU external assistance funds like the ENPI or the EIDH is notoriously long, and no single project under the ENPI envelope had been concluded by November 2009. It appears that a handful of projects bring together civil society actors from Georgia and South Ossetia and Abkhazia respectively, but most of that information is not available publicly.[5] The 2009 ENP Progress Report issued by the Commission does not focus on the effectiveness of the EU's crisis management efforts back in 2008. It recognizes that 'the year 2008 was marked by a number of extraordinary events and a slow-down of the implementation of the ENP Action Plan', but explicitly states that the report is 'not a general review of the political and economic situation in Georgia' (European Commission 2009: 2). In the first half of 2008, the EU had agreed with Georgia to further implement the confidence-building measures between Georgia and South Ossetia to revive the peace talks under the Joint Control Commission on South Ossetia. The Progress Report concludes that 'in the light of the August 2008 events, they [the new measures] had to be temporarily put on hold.' (European Commission 2009: 7).

In conclusion, the EU's response to the August war in Georgia was marked by greater consistency among member state short-term commitment and coordination in the area of crisis management, but also institutional inconsistency between the involved EU institutions overall. Neither the Commission nor the

ENP provided a ready-made template for crisis response and it was the Council Secretariat which by and large managed the EU's crisis response and capabilities. The member states' were divided over their reaction vis-à-vis Moscow and therefore prevented the EU from formulating an integrated and long-term crisis management and post-conflict rehabilitation strategy. Has the EU learned from the 2008 war between Russia and Georgia? In the next section, I will briefly discuss the extent to which the new Eastern Partnership promises to address the consistency of conflict prevention and crisis management policies vis-à-vis Georgia.

A new promise for the consistency in EU conflict prevention and crisis management? The Eastern Partnership with Georgia

> Despite the current ceasefire between both sides, all the ingredients for another military conflict are still in place.
>
> (Valasek 2008)

In May 2009, the EU had launched the Eastern Partnership (EaP), a new policy to enhance its relations with Eastern Europe, including Ukraine, Moldova and Belarus, in addition to Georgia, Azerbaijan and Armenia in the South Caucasus. In its Communication of December 2008, the Commission had highlighted the need to further engage with the EU's Eastern neighbours, and the recognition of the Council to respond to 'the need for a clearer signal of EU commitment following the conflict in Georgia and its broader repercussions' (European Commission 2008b: 2). The EaP introduces a number of new thematic platforms to enhance regional cooperation, although support is mainly geared towards democratization, economic reform and 'soft security' issues, such as transport, energy, borders or the environment. Under the first thematic platform 'Democracy, good governance and stability', a vague reference is made to cooperation on CFSP/CSDP, through 'political dialogue in fields of common interest and cover specific CFSP and CSDP issues, including the participation of partner countries in CSDP missions and exercises.' And that 'early-warning arrangements should be enhanced, with particular focus on conflict areas' (European Commission 2008b: 11). Eventually, the EaP should, amongst other indicators, lead to a 'reduced level of internal conflict', although that point is nowhere explained further in the Commission's Communication (European Commission 2008b: 20).

In their Joint Declaration of the Prague Eastern Partnership Summit, the heads of state and government from the EU and of their Eastern partners concluded that

> The Eastern Partnership should further promote stability and multilateral confidence building. Conflicts impede cooperation activities. Therefore the participants of the Prague summit emphasize the need for their earliest peaceful settlement on the basis of principles and norms of international law and the decisions and documents approved in this framework.
>
> (Council of the European Union 2009: 6)

Overall, the framework documents on the EaP have very little to say on conflict prevention and crisis management, including the linkages between the two. Concrete conflicts, like the one in South Ossetia, are not mentioned explicitly, and questions raised about the vertical and institutional consistency of these policies in the context of the conflict in Georgia are not addressed.

In practice, Russian forces remain in South Ossetia and Abkhazia. They still occupy Georgian territory which they entered during the Georgia-Russia war, which is de facto a violation of the Russia-EU agreement that Sarkozy and Medvedev signed in August 2008. In addition, Russian forces are still not informing the EU mission of their deployment of troops and continue to bar observers entering Abkhazia or South Ossetia.

The EU's 220 member strong Monitoring Mission is now the only international presence left to monitor the situation in the break-away provinces of Abkhazia and South Ossetia. Both UNOMIG, a UN mission observing the 1994 ceasefire between Russia-backed separatists and Georgia in Abkhazia (130 staff), as well as the OECD, which has monitored the 1992 ceasefire in South Ossetia (20 staff), had to leave Georgia. Russia, who is a member of both organizations, vetoed the extension of their monitoring mandates in June 2009 (Vogel 2009: 2). Therefore, the Union's heads of state and government in the Council agreed on extending the mandate of the existing EU Monitoring Mission until mid-September 2010.

Yet despite the *ad hoc* agreement on the prolongation of the mission, the member states remain divided over the future EU strategy vis-à-vis Georgia. In July 2009, the Georgian government asked the US to take part in the EU monitoring mission. Once again, the EU's response was divided. Some governments, including France, Italy and Belgium, view US participation as an unnecessary irritant for Russia which would further reduce the chances of the EU mission being allowed to enter the break-away regions. Yet others, such as the UK, Finland, Lithuania and Estonia, see US involvement as a chance to make the Union's mission more effective overall (Knigge 2009: 3; Rettman 2009). This development appears to confirm that the consistency of EU conflict prevention and crisis management in Georgia continues to depend on the political will of the member states, and in particular their relationship with the Russian Federation.

The lack of vertical consistency among member state positions on Russia also affects the effective involvement of Georgia into the regional dimension of the EaP. Many regional projects, for example in the areas of transport and energy infrastructures, depend on the cooperation with Russia. The Commission has recognized the need to further involve Russia into the EaP, but this has already attracted much criticism from a number of member states, including the UK and many of the new member states from Central and Eastern Europe, as well as the European Parliament.[6] In other words, the disagreement on Russia between the member states and between EU institutions threatens to undermine not just the consistency of the crisis management efforts in Georgia, but also the consistency in the Union's indirect conflict prevention and post-conflict resolution policies, such as economic and political cooperation and reform under the umbrella of the EaP.

Conclusion

This chapter has shown that, although the EU has managed to respond surprisingly swiftly to the outbreak of the war between Georgian and Russian forces in August 2008, the overall approach of the EU towards Georgia and its conflicts remains hostage to a number of inconsistencies rooted in its institutional structure. The early framework documents of the ENP, designed predominantly by the Commission, made little references to conflict prevention and crisis management, although that quickly changed after the inclusion of the South Caucasus into the policy and in light of the European Security Strategy. Nevertheless, in practice, efforts in this area were not coordinated between the instruments available to the Commission and the CFSP/CSDP. The EU's response to the war was led by the member states and the French Presidency in particular, and executed by the new Civilian Planning and Conduct Capability in the Council Secretariat. Yet a comprehensive strategy, integrating traditional conflict prevention and the crisis management tools of Commission and CFSP/CSDP, does still not exist.

Does the EaP potentially add to the consistency of EU conflict prevention and crisis management in Georgia? The policy framework documents issued by the Commission and the Council hardly engage with crisis management, and conflict prevention as such does not feature prominently. In practice, the member states have stuck to their commitment to monitor the situation in and around the conflicts in Abkhazia and South Ossetia, but there is already a new disagreement among them about the future of the mission beyond September 2010. The lack of a coherent strategy vis-à-vis Russia currently prevents a consistent and long-term commitment of the member states to conflict management and also limits the potential of the EaP to contribute to conflict prevention through regional cooperation for political dialogue and economic development.

The EU's fact-finding mission warned in its 2000 report that 'there is yet no adequate replacement for the dismantled international presence [. . .] and while EUMM should continue its duties, further efforts should be made to provide for an independent, neutral and effective international presence for the purpose of peacekeeping in conflict areas' and that 'the risk of a new confrontation remains serious' (IIFFMCG 2009: 35 and 37).

Without a clear and consistent strategy, the EU will still depend on the *ad hoc* commitment of the member states to extend the EU's Monitoring Mission beyond 2010, as well as the future developments in the EU's relations with Russia, which will also in large parts be determined by the member states. It therefore remains to be seen if the EU can effectively help reduce the risk of a new confrontation among the conflict parties in Abkhazia and South Ossetia. In the absence of other international presence on the ground, the resolution of the conflicts in Georgia is certainly one of the toughest challenges facing EU conflict prevention and crisis management efforts in the near future.

Notes

1 In 2004, for example, the Russian Federation vetoed the extension of the mandate of the OSCE Border Monitoring Mission in Georgia. The Georgian government had then asked the EU to take over that mission. France, Spain, Italy, Greece and Germany cautioned against such an EU involvement and the mission was discontinued.
2 Interview, Commission Official, Brussels, 8 June 2006.
3 Ibid.
4 Ibid.
5 Interview Commission Official, Brussels, 3 December 2009.
6 Interview, Commission Official, Brussels, 13 January 2010.

10 Conclusions and outlook

Eva Gross and Ana E. Juncos

This concluding chapter discusses some of the strategic, institutional but also the implementation challenges highlighted in the individual contributions to this book. In the process it also offers some avenues for further exploration. The chapter is structured around a set of common themes that have been raised more or less explicitly by the contributing authors so as to facilitate the assessment of the evolution but also the likely future trajectory of EU conflict prevention and crisis management policies. The development of these policies over the past decade has been rapid, but their success, and the quality of policy implementation uneven. Although the EU can claim by virtue of the geographic spread of its policies to be a global actor in the management of conflicts, its performance in the field has been impacted by institutional, but also political constraints. Emanating from EU member states but also the EU's partners, these constraints suggest a number of conceptual but also empirical avenues for future research, both within EU studies as well as International Relations and the fields of conflict and peace studies.

Contributions to this volume particularly those considering the evolving role of the EU in conflict prevention and crisis management, point towards a fast development and improvement of institutional structures. However, they also reveal enduring limitations in the formulation of policy and its implementation in the field. The development of the EU as a security actor, operating alongside the US, but also the UN and NATO, continues to raise questions over the existence of a European strategy and the emergence of a putative European strategic and security culture (see also Biscop and Andersson, 2008). The institutional evolution that culminated with the ratification of the Lisbon Treaty in 2009 suggests that EU conflict prevention and crisis management has reached a period of consolidation. Furthermore, the impending institutional changes, most notably the European External Action Service (EEAS), are bound to lead to further improvements even if, at least in the short term, they are likely to exacerbate tensions already apparent in the EU's decision-making processes (see Missiroli, 2010).

Conceptually, the challenge remains one of how to best capture and analyze the formulation and implementation of EU conflict prevention and crisis management policies. The evidence gathered in the chapters of this volume indicates that the EU remains a *sui generis* actor and unit of analysis. While member states continue to have an impact on EU policies and on the EU's role in the world, their influence is increasingly mediated by the EU's institutional setting. The *sui generis* nature of the EU as well as the multi-level nature of the EU policy-making process (and policy output) mean that approaching the topic of EU conflict prevention and crisis management from a theoretical perspective continues to represent a challenge in terms of the explanatory value of individual theoretical approaches and in terms of placing the subject matter in the broader general literature(s) on international relations and/or conflict management.

Coherence, effectiveness – and impact

Among the most frequently stated challenges for the Common Security and Defence Policy (CSDP) – as ESDP is now called after the Lisbon Treaty – has been that of coherence. Whereas before the creation of CFSP and later ESDP this applied mainly to the relationship between member states' foreign policies and an emerging Brussels-based decision-making framework, the growing institutional framework after Maastricht, and the pillar-structure it created, turned the Council and Commission into common, yet also distinct, EU foreign policy actors. Decision-making and organizational structures have been expanded, reorganized and fine-tuned in response to learning from past experiences, the growing demand for ESDP missions, and the need for greater coordination between different agencies and bureaucracies. Still, there exists an enduring coordination challenge. Recognized as an obstacle, formal and informal institutional reforms have sought to deal with this problem.

The latest reform, as laid out in the Lisbon Treaty, has at least the potential to improve the coherence of EU conflict prevention and crisis management with the establishment of a double-hatted High Representative for Foreign Affairs and Security Policy, a European External Action Service (EEAS) as well as allowing for Permanent Structured Cooperation in military matters (cf. Whitman and Juncos 2009). For instance, the fact that new position of High Representative can finally utilize both the diplomatic weight of the High Representative and the economic clout of the EU, with the organizational support of the of the EEAS, constitutes a significant upgrade from the previous situation. The fact that the foreign policy provisions in the Lisbon Treaty were not a bone of contention also signals that member states are in principle in support of a stronger, more coherent, European foreign policy.

Yet, it remains a question to what extent the new structures will facilitate, further or exhibit unity of effort, purpose, and political direction. Negotiations about the precise configuration of the EU's external machinery were still ongoing at the time of writing but have exposed differences between the Commission, Council and the member states. This is a concern because coherence refers not only to the lack of contradictions between different objectives, policies and/or institutional actors. It also goes beyond achieving coordination in conveying political messages on behalf of the EU, or jointly implementing EU policies. Fundamentally, coherence requires a joint formulation, with policies pursuing a common purpose, and strong synergies between the policies that make up the whole spectrum of EU conflict prevention and crisis management, ranging from development, democratization and security policies.

Similarly, work on a 'culture of coordination' as part of efforts to institutionalize a comprehensive approach suitably called Civil-Military Coordination (CMCO) can be expected to remain a challenge as both member states and EU institutions must find ways to work together more coherently. For instance, the chapter by Nadia Klein in this volume illustrates how bureaucratic politics between the European Commission and the Council Secretariat were a recurring problem in Brussels due to overlapping mandates. Future research, also in light of growing crisis management tasks undertaken by the EU, will need to assess to what extent coordination between civilian and military, first and second pillar, EU and member state instruments has been improved as a result of the establishment of the new double-hatted High Representative and the External Action Service.

As the chapters in Part III demonstrate, the EU's performance has also been negatively affected by *ad hocism* in policy development and implementation. Rather than pursuing a set of strategic goals and political interests towards West Africa, Afghanistan or South Caucasus that would take into account the place of a specific conflict and region in the EU's overall priorities, policy goals have largely been defined on account of external demands and then not pursued coherently. Reactive rather than proactive policy-making holds true even for the Western Balkans, a region where two overarching policy objectives (security and eventual EU accession) often appear in conflict on account of political contingencies. Often, as the example of the Caucasus but also West Africa demonstrates, conflict prevention and crisis management aspects have been superimposed on existing policies. At the worst of times, this has resulted in the various EU actors implementing policy working at cross-purposes rather than in pursuit of a shared goal. The coordination problems between EUFOR and EUPM in Bosnia are a case in point here. In the best of times, the EU's international presence has been marked by a cacophony of voices and actors that at least tried to convey a similar message, and that over time have worked towards coordinating their individual presences in the field. Despite these efforts, EU activity in the world does not add up to a single voice, or single policy implementation. Often, various policy strands are only vaguely connected, verbal statements on the part of EU officials notwithstanding.

The question of coherence in turn raises the question of what makes for a successful or effective policy – in other words, of the impact of EU policies. Implicitly, coherence is often conflated with effectiveness – yet in practice increasing coherence has not necessarily increased the EU's impact in the field. This may be because the link between Brussels and the field is often tenuous or contentious, as the examples of Afghanistan or Bosnia demonstrate. Despite this, CSDP has come increasingly in demand, so clearly it has had an impact on how the added value of an EU CSDP mission is perceived by other international actors (such as the US in the case of Afghanistan), but also on the way recipient countries have viewed the benefits of an EU security presence (such as Georgian elites).

A discussion about impact, effectiveness and policy success first requires a distinction between different standards or definitions. If impact is defined as establishing the EU as an international security actor, the conclusion must be that the EU has had an impact through its conflict prevention and crisis management policies (see also Ginsberg 2001). On the downside, the EU has not been able to assume a 'diplomatic' or key role in many of the areas in which it intervenes as the analysis of EU policies in West Africa demonstrates. This suggests that the EU lacks political weight – but also a set of clearly defined policy and strategic objectives. On the other hand, if one takes a minimalist approach to effectiveness defined as achievement of intended goals, i.e. fulfilling a mission's mandate, one might conclude that the EU has been effective (see for a similar assessment Dobbins *et al.* 2008). All the EU's civilian and military operations completed to date have achieved their end goals and have officially been branded as 'successful'. This might have a lot to do with a lack of appetite for self-criticism, but also with the modest scope and lack of ambitions of the EU's undertakings (Menon 2009) and the fact that the EU has often deployed its missions in relatively benign security environments such as in the case of EUFOR in Bosnia. In the same vein, if one considers the operations launched in the first ten years of the CSDP to be a test of the EU's resolve then the assessment of its effectiveness must be a positive one too (Dobbins *et al.* 2008: xxviii).

However, if one defines impact and effectiveness as having an influence on conflict cycles, brokering peace agreements or contributing to long-term conflict resolution based on clearly formulated strategic goals and objectives, the EU's track record looks less promising. In Afghanistan, the EU is playing a supporting role in police reform, a coordinating role in political terms, and a developmental role in the fields of health and rural development. However, the EU has not left a political mark in the international approach to the conflict that is commensurate with its financial, political and civilian contribution. The EU's policies in West Africa also show that the EU's rhetorical ambitions of becoming a diplomatic actor have been hampered by political and institutional constraints. Closer to home, in Georgia, the EU is constrained by member states' priorities over Russia. Preventing the unqualified success of EU conflict prevention and crisis management policies, therefore, is more than just a lack of coherence, or institutionalization of decision-making structures and processes. This problem appears more pronounced in regions far away from the EU's borders, specifically those that have a strong US-overlay, such as Afghanistan or the Middle East. But it is also the case closer to home, as the case of Georgia demonstrates. Beyond the Balkans where an ultimate end state – that of eventual EU accession – exists and where there have been some successes in crisis management, the EU's record in terms of effectiveness, impact and success is thus mixed.

In sum, the impact and effectiveness of EU policies, particularly its ability to bridge security and development functions, will continue to be of analytical interest in the future. In this respect it will be interesting to see whether the EU will be able to move beyond Marie Gibert's assessment of the EU's performance in Western Africa as one of rhetorical ambitions; and whether it will be able to set the political agenda alongside implementing rule of law and development policies in Afghanistan, as Eva Gross has argued it should.

The role of institutions in the making – or constraining – of policies

The discussion of coherence and effectiveness is closely linked to a general question of the role of institutions in the formulation of policy and their implementation. The ratification of the Treaty of Lisbon has launched a new phase of implementation and consolidation different from the phase of expansion that marked the first decade of CSDP. Foreign and security policy in this sense has turned from an outward-looking activity towards an inward-looking process of consolidation and institutional re-structuring. In the period of re-adjustment, as the competences of the EEAS and its relationship to the Council, the Commission, the member states but also the European Parliament have to be negotiated, the EU is likely to be less exploratory. The newly acquired agenda-setting powers of the High Representative will also contribute to consolidate, rather than increase the EU's geographical scope, as was often the case during the Solana era. At the same time, this consolidation may also mark a more explicit conceptualization of geographic and conflict-type priorities in the EU's overall foreign policy agenda.

It is still too early to tell, of course, but if the past is anything to go by, rather than a 'big bang' event one can expect gradual changes in terms of policy practices and member state priorities (see chapter by Petrov). The creation of foreign policy institutions has enabled the EU to act in international politics, but has not transformed the EU into a crisis manager across the board (Gross 2009b): too often in times of international crises, member states have decided on a different institutional format for crisis response whether in the form of a UN operation, NATO intervention or coalition of the willing. Reactions to the 2008 war Georgia were an exception – although it is too soon to tell whether this marks a turning point in the way member states privilege (or downplay) the EU in their crisis response.

The role of institutions in shaping EU crisis management and conflict prevention policies as well as their implementation should not be underestimated. As the chapters of Part II have aptly demonstrated, institutional actors (the Commission, the Council Secretariat, as well as implementing agents on the ground) have been able to deviate from the original goals set by their principals in the implementation of EU foreign policy. Second, existing institutions in Brussels have changed decision-making practices, facilitating consensus building and a coordination reflex and have led to socialization of national diplomats – even if they have not yet led to a significant increase in common norms (Juncos and Pomorska 2006; Meyer 2006). The EEAS and the creation of the new position of the High Representative for Foreign and Security Policy might yet increase the possibilities for agents to influence not only the implementation, but also the substance of EU conflict prevention and crisis management (crucially, the Lisbon Treaty foresees a right of initiative for the High Representative). In the post-Lisbon era, it is also not inconceivable that the reach of the EU will yet broaden and consolidate, and that its structural diplomacy (Keukeleire 2003) will gradually extend to the foreign and security policy arena. But how much the EU will be able to move beyond structural policy towards crisis management understood as military intervention remains to be seen. The growing institutionalization of EU crisis management policies has also revealed the need for internal restructuring – but also the likelihood of internal turf wars and organizational overlaps, procedures and conflicts. With growing maturity, therefore, EU foreign policy has also grown more constrained as a result.

Policy competences increasingly rest with EU institutions themselves, but the formulation and implementation of policies also necessitates political will, strategic thinking, and the formulation of political and strategic interests – on behalf of both EU and its member states. One can expect that the role of the member states will remain crucial in EU conflict prevention and crisis management. However, the chapters in this volume also show that the locus of analysis has moved to the EU institutions themselves. Debates over definitions of EU foreign policy, therefore, no longer start exclusively with the member states. To be sure, member states remain an important and in many ways essential component in EU conflict prevention and crisis management policies. However, much of the implementation as well as the external signalling rest with the EU and its institutions. The EU label, in other words, has gained in visibility – and this has also resulted in external demands, and challenges to the EU's international credibility. Although, working with others in the pursuit of 'effective multilateralism' has been a professed goal of the EU as stated in the European Security Strategy (ESS), in terms of conflict prevention and crisis management the EU also has had to establish its place in the European and, increasingly also, global security architecture.

The EU, a team player? Working with others

When it comes to 'effective multilateralism' and more generally the EU's place in the global security architecture, the first item to note is the link between, or mutual effect of, the pursuit of effective multilateralism with inter-institutional competition. As discussed in Chapter 3, this applies most starkly to EU relations with NATO, where the two institutions considerably overlap; but to a lesser extent also to the OSCE, which saw the EU move into an area of activity previously reserved for itself. Beyond the question of the reason for creating CSDP, while constituting an valid empirical puzzle (Hofmann 2004), overlap between the two institutions have resulted in inter-institutional competition and, at least up to present, less than impressive working relationship (Toje 2008). While recognition of the need for improvement, along with two successive US administrations less hostile to CSDP, has resulted in a more constructive climate, the problem rests in the capitals and affects the formal channels of EU-NATO communication. This also constitutes a reminder of the continuing relevance of member states in the analysis of policy formulation and of the institutional evolution of the EU and NATO, particularly when it comes to military crisis management. As for the UN, although priority has been given to this inter-institutional relationship when it comes to implementing 'effective multilateralism', gaps exist even here (see Laatikainen and Smith 2006).

The relationship with the EU's most natural partner – the US – has intensified, but has not led to a change in institutional links. The Obama administration poses new challenges for the EU if only because it will be more difficult for the EU to carve a global role for itself – during the Bush era, and particularly after the war in Iraq, this happened by default rather than design. What one can expect to observe in the coming years is that the EU's relationship with the US will be recalibrated in light of EU capabilities and commitments to transatlantic burden sharing. It remains to be seen however whether discussions between EU member states and the Obama administration will be defined by reluctant European engagement in Afghanistan and elsewhere, or whether they will be defined by the EU increasingly taking over near exclusive security functions not just in the Balkans, but also the Middle East as well as the Caucasus.

The questions of impact and coherence, therefore, also pose themselves with respect to the EU's external coordination efforts. Despite verbal commitments, acting with others has revealed itself a challenge; perhaps because these commitments are an end in itself rather than in pursuit of clearly defined interests.

The question of strategy

From the previous discussion it can be concluded that, improvements in decision-making structure and implementation practices notwithstanding, the operational code underlying the EU's external activities also needs consideration. The question of a strategic roadmap that guides policy choices, institutional structures but also the evolving role of the EU – and the trade-offs between crisis management and conflict prevention activities – poses itself particularly in light of the inconsistencies identified by the individual chapters in this volume. A grand strategy could also bring some clarity as to what kind of division of labor might emerge between the EU, NATO and the UN (see Biscop 2009). The role of the EU as a strategic actor is also particularly important in view of the EU's strategic partnerships with new emerging powers such as Brazil, Russia, India or China for the pursuit of effective multilateralism.

A clear strategy could also provide the missing link between short term crisis management and medium-long term conflict prevention by setting a list of purposive goals directing EU action. Since the launch of the CSDP in 1998, the focus has tended towards the short term (crisis management) and not enough attention has been paid to how these short term activities fitted within longer term, structural efforts to peace building – a problem highlighted by Stewart in her chapter. In general, and despite the official rhetoric, the EU has failed to develop a 'culture of prevention'. Another added problem that has compounded strategic action has been the increase in EU activities to include not only traditional economic assistance and civilian and military crisis management, but also statebuilding through conditionality, disarmament, demobilization, and reintegration, security sector reform and transitional justice.

However, the ESS and its review exercise in 2008 have not brought clarity as to any emerging grand strategy; rather, it has focused on implementation over the past five years. Given the foreign policy acquis, development of strategic concept of role in the world, and purpose of foreign policy tools, including the military ones, have not resulted in a reliable roadmap. Rather they have resulted in constructive ambiguity. As experience has shown, and as several chapters demonstrate, this ambiguity reaches its limits in light of different agencies and organizations defining their task differently, or with different leads in mind; in light of external demands on the EU that it reacts to but is then only partially able to fulfill. The quest for a strategy continues – but is also affected by the current process of consolidation rather than innovation as a result of the Lisbon Treaty and its implementation. Whether or not the EU can design and implement a grand strategy will certainly affect the nature and quality of the EU's conflict prevention and crisis management policies.

Conceptual and theoretical challenges

Given the growing range of EU activities, including their institutionalization and concurrent moves from conflict prevention towards crisis management, the question of how to conceptualize the EU's security activities poses itself anew. But, rather than bringing with it new definitions over EU foreign policy, the growth of the EU as an international actor and as a crisis manager has broadened the scope of theoretical approaches to explain policy formulation, policy input and output. This volume shows that the study of EU crisis management has moved from one mostly concerned with gathering empirical evidence and describing the institutional and operational changes since the 1990s to more theoretically sophisticated accounts, including those drawing on role theory, institutionalist approaches and Europeanization research.

While traditional concepts in the EU literature such as civilian and military power are still frequently used, a focus on the EU's global role provides a much better tool to explore the complex development of the EU as an international actor, how it perceives itself and how it is perceived by others. Future research still needs to explore in more detail why some roles (and not others) might become embedded in the EU's discourse and practice and what kind of impact roles have on actors' behavior.

The focus on institutions is hardly surprising given the remarkable institutional development that has taken place at the EU level. Institutionalist approaches provide a well-needed counterbalance to intergovernmentalist approaches that have dominated the field – and, interestingly can offer very different yet complementary perspectives on EU conflict prevention and crisis management policies. While the member states have been, and still continue to be, key actors in decision-making processes and policy implementation, a more nuanced approach based on institutionalist perspectives emphasizes the role of institutional actors (rationalist institutionalism), unintended consequences and path dependency (historical institutionalism) and norms and socialization processes (sociological institutionalism). The chapters in Part II also suggest that a more careful examination of the everyday implementation of EU conflict prevention and crisis management, where arguably the control of the member states is mitigated by information asymmetries and the complexity of joint action, can also shed new light on the importance of institutional factors. Despite their different emphases on different factors, a tentative division of labor could also be sketched with historical institutionalism looking at the development of this policy over time, rational choice being particularly helpful in explaining the creation of institutions and principal-agent relations and sociological institutionalism examining the impact of institutions on actors' preferences and identities and the independent dynamics affecting institutions that sometimes make them rather ineffective.

However, the chapters also showed that the role of the member states will continue to be crucial in EU conflict prevention and crisis management. Here the question is not so much whether or not the member states have an impact on EU foreign policy, but what kind of impact and in what areas (Larsen 2009). Furthermore, another issue that it is closely linked to the previous point, but that it is only implicitly dealt with in this volume, refers to how the development of the EU conflict prevention and crisis management policies might shape member states policies, not only in the form of adaptation to EU impacts, but also policy projection. Here Europeanization research might prove particularly useful (Gross 2009b).

Future research also needs to investigate the impact of the EU on the conflict cycle itself, incorporating more insights from the wider literature on conflict resolution and peace research. In particular, research on EU conflict prevention and crisis management ought to examine whether EU operations contribute to preventing or resolving conflict. To paraphrase Ramsbotham *et al.* (2005: 317) the final criterion to determine whether EU conflict prevention and crisis management has been successful or not is 'the verdict of those affected by it'. Only a focus on the recipient end of EU conflict prevention and crisis management will help avoid charges of (neo-)imperialism which would certainly have a negative impact on the EU's international image and credibility.

Conclusion

The points made in the previous sections suggest that there are significant practical, political and theoretical challenges surrounding EU conflict prevention and crisis management. Challenges of coherence and effectiveness will likely continue to affect the EU's performance in its neighborhood and beyond – despite the institutional reforms introduced by the Lisbon Treaty. The influence of institutional actors will continue to depend on their control over the day-to-day policy-making process. Effective multilateralism will also be put to a test in the coming years, not only through the implementation of the EU's partnership with NATO and the UN, but also in its relations with the US and, even more importantly, with the emerging powers such as China and India. And in relation to these challenges, the formulation of a grand strategy could provide a framework of the possible.

While the last decade has been one of intense institution-building and operational testing, we might expect that as the EU enters a post-Lisbon phase, more attention will be paid to lesson learning and consolidation of existing instruments and institutions. In the same vein, scholars in this field will seek to consolidate the conceptual and theoretical foundations of research on EU conflict prevention and crisis management. The chapters in this volume can provide a starting point by bringing academic reflection to bear on the current consolidation and this potential turning point in EU foreign policy.

References

Ackermann, A. (2003) 'The Idea and Practice of Conflict Prevention', *Journal of Peace Research*, 40(3): 339–47.

Afghanistan Compact (2006) '*Building on Success: The London Conference on Afghanistan*'. London, 31 January – 1 February 2006, online, available at: http://www.nato.int/isaf/docu/epub/pdf/afghanistan_compact.pdf (accessed 18 August 2010).

Aggestam, L. (2004a) *A European Foreign Policy? Role Conceptions and the Politics of Identity in Britain, France and Germany*, Stockholm: Stockholm University, Department of Political Science.

—— (2004b) 'Role Identity and the Europeanization of Foreign Policy: a Political-Cultural Approach', in Tonra, B. and Christiansen, T. (eds) *Rethinking EU Foreign Policy*, Manchester: Manchester University Press, 81–98.

—— (2006) 'Role Theory and European Foreign Policy: A Framework of Analysis', in Smith, M. and Elgström, O. (eds) *The European Union's Roles in International Politics: Concepts and Analysis*, London: Routledge, 11–29.

Albright, M. (1998) 'The Right Balance Will Secure NATO's Future', *Financial Times*, 7 December.

Allen, D. (1998) 'Who Speaks for Europe? The Search for an Effective and Coherent External Policy', in Peterson, J. and Sjursen, H. (eds) *A Common Foreign Policy for Europe? Competing Visions of the CFSP*, London: Routledge.

Allen, D. and Smith, M. (1990) 'Western Europe's Presence in the Contemporary International Arena', *Review of International Studies*, 16(1): 19–37.

Allison, G. T. and Halperin, M. H. (1972) 'Bureaucratic Politics: A Paradigm and Some Policy Implications', *World Politics*, 24 (Supplement): 40–79.

Allison, G. T. and Zelikow, P. (1999) *Essence of Decision: Explaining the Cuban Missile Crisis*, 2nd edn, New York: Addison Wesley Longman.

Anderson, S. (2008) *Crafting EU Security Policy*, Boulder: Lynne Rienner.

Anderson, S. and Seitz, T. (2009) '"Your Choice is Peace": Testing the EU Model in the New Global Insecurity Environment', EUSA Review 22(3): 13–17.

Andréani, G., Bertram, C. and Grant, C. (2001) *Europe's Military Revolution*, London: Centre for European Reform.

Annan, K. (2005) In Larger Freedom: Towards Development, Security and Human Rights for All. Report of the Secretary-General, A/59/2005, online, available at: http://www.un.org/largerfreedom/contents.htm (accessed 18 August 2010).

Armstrong, K. and Bulmer, S. (1998) *The Governance of the Single European Market*, Manchester: Manchester University Press.

Aspinwall, M. D. and Schneider, G. (2000) 'Same Menu, Different Tables: The

Institutionalist Turn in Political Science and the Study of European Integration', *European Journal of Political Research*, 38(1): 1–36.

Ayub, F. and Sari K. (2008) 'Afghanistan: Intervention and the War on Terror', *International Affairs*, 84 (4): 641–58.

Bagayoko, N. and Gibert, M. V. (2009) 'The Linkage Between Security, Governance and Development: The European Union in Africa', *Journal of Development Studies*, 45(5): 789–814.

Bailes, A. J. K, Haine, J.Y and Lachowski, Z. (2008) 'Reflections on the OSCE-EU Relationship', *OSCE Yearbook 2008*, Baden-Baden: Nomos Verlag.

Barbé, E. and Johansson, E. (2001) 'EU and Conflict Prevention', *Working Paper of the CFSP Observatory*, Barcelona: Universidad Autonoma de Barcelona.

Bayart, J.-F. (2004) 'Commentary: Towards a New Start for Africa and Europe', *African Affairs*, 103(412): 453–58.

Beatty, A. (2006) 'EU's Growing Role in the Middle East', *European Voice*, 21 September.

Bereskoetter, F. (2005) 'Mapping the Mind Gap: A Comparison of US and European Security Strategies', *Security Dialogue*, 36(1): 71–92.

Bertin, T. (2007) 'The EU Military Operation in Bosnia', in Merlingen, M. and Ostrauskaite, R. (eds) *The European Security and Defence Policy: An Implementation Perspective*, London: Routledge, 61–77.

Bildt, C. (2000) 'Force and Diplomacy', *Survival*, 42(1): 141–48.

Biscop, S. (ed.) (2009) *The Value Of Power, the Power Of Values: A Call for an EU Grand Strategy*. Egmont Paper 33. Brussels, Egmont – The Royal Institute for International Relations, October.

Biscop, S. and Andersson, J. (eds) (2008) *The EU and the European Security Strategy*, Abingdon, Routledge.

Björkdahl, A. (2002) *From Idea to Norm. Promoting Conflict Prevention*, Lund: Department of Political Science, published PhD Thesis, Lund University.

Björkdahl, A. and Strömvik, M. (2008) *EU Crisis Management Operations. ESDP Bodies and Decision-Making Procedures*, Danish Institute for International Studies (DIIS), Copenhagen.

Blockmans, S. (ed.) (2008) *The European Union and Crisis Management: Policy and Legal Aspects*, The Hague: TMC Asser Press.

Boin, R. A., Ekengren, M. and Rhinard, M. (2006) 'The Commission and Crisis Management', in Spence, D. (ed.) *The European Commission*, 3rd ed, London: John Harper.

Bono, G. (2002) *European Security and Defence Policy: Theoretical Approaches, the Nice Summit and Hot Issues*, Bradford: Bradford University.

—— (2004) 'The EU's Military Doctrine: An Assessment', *International Peacekeeping*, 11(3): 439–56.

Bretherton, C. and Vogler, J. (2006) *The European Union as a Global Actor*, 2nd ed, London: Routledge.

Brown, M. E. and Rosecrance, R. N. (eds) (1999) *The Costs of Conflict: Prevention and Cure in the Global Arena*, New York: Carnegie Commission on Preventing Deadly Conflict/ Rowman & Littlefield.

Brunsson, N. and Olsen, J. P. (1998) 'Organization Theory: Thirty Years of Dismantling and then . . .?' in Brunsson, N. and Olsen, J. P. (eds) *Organizing Organizations*, Bergen: Fagbokforlaget, 13–43.

Bull, H. (1982) 'Civilian Power Europe: A Contradiction in Terms?', *Journal of Common Market Studies*, 21(2): 149–64.

Bulmer, S. (1994) 'The Governance of the European Union: A New Institutionalist Approach', *Journal of Public Policy*, 13(4): 351–80.

—— (1998) 'New Institutionalism and the Governance of the Single European Market', *Journal of Public Policy*, 5(3): 365–86.

Bulmer, S. and Burch, M. (1998) 'The Europeanisation of Central Government: the UK and Germany in Historical Institutionalist Perspective', *EPRU Series*, Manchester: Manchester University Press.

Burch, M., Hogwood, P., Bulmer, S., Carter, C., Gomez, R. and Scott, A. (2003) 'Charting Routine and Radical Change: A Discussion Paper', *Manchester Papers in Politics, Devolution and European Policy Making Series*, 6. Online, available at: http://www. socialsciences.manchester.ac.uk/disciplines/politics/publications/workingpapers/ (accessed 18 August 2010).

Butler, M. (2009*) International Conflict Management*, London: Routledge.

Buxton, I. (2008) 'The European Community Perspective on SSR: the Development of a Comprehensive EU Approach', in Spence, D. and Flurri, P. (eds) *The European Union and Security Sector Reform*, London, John Harper Publishing.

Buzan, B. and Little, R. (2000) *International Systems in World History: Remaking the Study of International Relations*, Oxford and New York: Oxford University Press.

Cameron, F. (2007) *An Introduction to European Foreign Policy*, London/New York: Routledge.

Cameron, F. and Balfour, R. (2006) 'The European Neighbourhood Policy as a Conflict Prevention Tool', *EPC Issue Paper*, No.47, European Policy Centre, Brussels, June.

Caplan, R. and Pouligny, B. (2005) 'Histoire et contradictions du state building', *Critique internationale*, 28, July-September: 123–38.

Carment, D. and Schnabel, A. (eds) (2003) *Conflict Prevention: Path to Peace or Grand Illusion?* Tokyo: United Nations University Press.

Carnegie Commission on Preventing Deadly Conflict (1997) *Preventing Deadly Conflict: Final Report*, Washington DC: Carnegie Corporation.

Chandler, D. (2006) *Empire in Denial: The Politics of State-Building*, London: Pluto Press.

Châtaigner, J.-M. (2004) 'Aide publique au développement et réformes des systèmes de sécurité: l'improbable rencontre du Dr Jekyll et de Mr Hyde', *Afrique Contemporaine*, 209: 23–49.

Checkel, J. (2001) 'Why Comply? Social Learning and European Identity Change', *International Organization*, 55(3): 553–88.

—— (2005) 'International Institutions and Socialization in Europe: Introduction and Framework', *International Organization*, 59(4): 801–26.

Chinkin, Ch. (2004) 'European Security Strategy: an International Law Framework with Respect to International Peace and Security'. *Background Paper for the Barcelona Group*, London: The Centre for the Study of Global Governance.

Chotard, J.-R. (1997) 'Articulating the New International Role of the United States During Previous Transitions, 1916–19, 1943–47', in Le Prestre, P. (ed.) *Role Quests in the Post-Cold War: Foreign Policies in Transition*, Montréal: McGill-Queens University Press, 40–64.

Christiansen, T. (1997) 'Tensions of European Governance: Politized Bureaucracy and Multiple Accountability in the European Commission', *Journal of European Public Policy*, 4(1): 73–90.

—— (2001) 'Intra-institutional Politics and Inter-institutional Relations in the EU: Towards Coherent Governance?', *Journal of European Public Policy*, 8(5): 747–69.

Christiansen, T. and Vanhoonacker, S. (2008) 'At a Critical Juncture? Change and Continuity in the Institutional Development of the Council Secretariat', *West European Politics*, 31(4): 751–70.

Clement, S. (1997) 'Conflict Prevention in the Balkans: Case Studies of Kosovo and the FYR of Macedonia', *Chaillot Paper* No. 30, Paris: WEU Institute for Security Studies.

Collier, R. B. and Collier, D. (1991) *Shaping the Political Arena: Critical Junctures, the Labor Movement and Regime Dynamics in Latin America*, Princeton: Princeton University Press.

Cooper, R. (2003) *The Breaking of Nations. Order and Chaos in the 21st Century*, London: Atlantic Books.

Coppieters, B. (ed.) (2004) *Europeanization and Conflict Resolution: Case Studies from the European Periphery*, Gent: Academia Press.

Cosgrove, C. A. and Twitchett, K. J. (eds) (1970) *The New International Actors: The UN and the EEC*, London: Macmillan.

Cotonou Agreement (2000 and 2005) Partnership Agreement Between the Members of the African, Caribbean and Pacific Group of States of the One Part, and the European Community, of the Other Part, signed in Cotonou on 23 June 2000, and the revised version of this agreement, June 2005. European Commission, DE-132, September 2006, online, available at: http://ec.europa.eu/development/icenter/repository/Cotonou_EN_2006_en.pdf (accessed 18 August 2010).

Cottey, A. (1998) 'NATO Transformed: the Atlantic Alliance in a New Era' in Park, W. and Rees, W. (eds) *Rethinking Security in Post-Cold War Europe*, Harlow and New York: Addison Wesley Longman, 43–67.

Council of the European Union (2001) Council Regulation (EC) No 381/2001 of 26 February 2001 Creating a Rapid-Reaction Mechanism, Doc. 381/2001, OJ L 57/5–9, 27 Feburary, http://eur-lex.europa.eu/LexUriServ/LexUriServ.do?uri=OJ:L:2001:057:0005:0009:EN:PDF (accessed 23 August 2010).

—— (2002) Follow-Up to the Action Plan for Further Strengthening of Civil-Military Co-ordination in EU Crisis Management: Participation of the Comission [sic!] in EUMC Meetings, Doc. 12307/02, Brussels, 24 September.

—— (2003a) Interoperability of Integrated Police Units and Police Headquarters, Doc. 8009/03, Brussels, 2 April.

—— (2003b) Suggestions for Procedures for Coherent, Comprehensive EU Crisis Management, Doc. 11127/03, Brussels, 3 July.

—— (2003c) Joint Declaration on UN-EU Co-operation in Crisis Management, Brussels, 19 September, http://www.consilium.europa.eu/uedocs/cmsUpload/st12730.en03.pdf (accessed 20 August 2010).

—— (2003d) A Secure Europe in a Better World: European Security Strategy, 12 December, http://www.consilium.europa.eu/uedocs/cmsUpload/78367.pdf (accessed 19 August 2010).

—— (2004a) Council Joint Action 2004/570/CFSP of 12 July 2004 on the European Union Military Operation in Bosnia and Herzegovina, Official Journal, L252, 28 July, 10–14.

—— (2004b) Civilian Headline Goal 2008. 15863/04. Brussels, 7 December, http://register.consilium.eu.int/pdf/en/04/st15/st15863.en04.pdf (accessed 20 August 2010).

—— (2005a) The EU and Africa: Towards a Strategic Partnership, 19 December, http://www.unhcr.org/refworld/category,POLICY,EU,,,43e1fde04,0.html (accessed 20 August 2010).

—— (2005b) Draft EU Concept for Comprehensive Planning, Doc. 13983/05, Brussels, 3 November, http://register.consilium.europa.eu/pdf/en/05/st13/st13983.en05.pdf (accessed 23 August 2010).

—— (2006a) Joint Action, 2006/121/CFSP, Brussels, 21 February, http://www.consilium. europa.eu/uedocs/cmsUpload/l_04920060221en00140016.pdf (accessed 23 August 2010).

—— (2006b) Civil-Military Co-ordination: Framework Paper of Possible Solutions for the Management of EU Crisis Management Operations, Doc. 8926/06, Brussels, 2 May.

—— (2006c) Council Conclusions on a Policy Framework for Security Sector Reform, 12 June, http://www.initiativeforpeacebuilding.eu/resources/Council_Conclusions_on_ a_Policy_framework_for_SSR.pdf (accessed 20 August 2010).

—— (2006d) Possible Solutions for the Management of EU Crisis Management Operations – Improving Information Sharing in Support of EU Crisis Management Operations, Doc. 13218/5/06 REV 5, Brussels, 31 October, http://www.europarl.europa.eu/meetdocs/2009_ 2014/documents/sede/dv/sede260410cmcoinformationsharing_/sede260410cmcoinfor- mationsharing_en.pdf (accessed 23 August 2010).

—— (2006e) EU Concept for Support to Disarmament, Demobilisation and Reintegration, 11 December, http://www.eplo.org/documents/EU_Joint_concept_DDR.pdf (accessed 20 August 2010).

—— (2007a) Presidency Report on ESDP, Doc. 10910/07, Brussels, 18 June, ://register. consilium.europa.eu/pdf/en/07/st10/st10910.en07.pdf (accessed 20 August 2010).

—— (2007b) Council Joint Action 2007/677/CFSP of 15 October 2007 on the European Union Military Operation in the Republic of Chad and in the Central African Republic, Doc. 2007/677/CFSP, OJ L 279/21–24, 23 September, http://eur-lex.europa.eu/ LexUriServ/LexUriServ.do?uri=OJ:L:2007:279:0021:0024:EN:PDF (accessed 20 August 2010).

—— (2008) Council Decision 2008/298/CFSP of 7 April 2008 Amending Decision 2001/80/ CFSP on the Establishment of the Military Staff of the European Union, Doc. 2008/298/ CFSP, OJ L 102/25–33, 12 April, http://eur-lex.europa.eu/LexUriServ/LexUriServ. do?uri=OJ:L:2008:102:0025:0033:EN:PDF (accessed 20 August 2010).

—— (2009) Joint Declaration of the Prague Eastern Partnership Summit, 8435/09, Prague, 7 May, http://www.consilium.europa.eu/uedocs/cms_data/docs/pressdata/en/er/107589. pdf (accessed 20 August 2010).

—— (2010) European Security and Defence Policy (ESDP): EU Operations, online, avail- able at: http://www.consilium.europa.eu/showPage.aspx?id = 268&lang = EN (accessed 31 January 2010).

Council Secretariat (2007) Factsheet EU Special Representatives (EUSRs). Representing the EU Around the World in Key Policy Areas, Brussels, April 2007, http://www. consilium.europa.eu/uedocs/cmsUpload/070426-Factsheet.pdf (accessed 31 August 2009).

Cram, L. (1994) 'The European Commission as a Multi-Organization: Social Policy and IT Policy in the EU', *Journal of European Public Policy*, 1(2): 195–217.

—— (1997) *Policy-Making in the European Union. Conceptual Lenses and the Integration Process*, London/New York: Routledge.

Davis Cross, M. K. (2008) 'Which Epistemic Communities Matter? The Case of EU Security Integration', paper presented at the *2008 International Studies Association Conference*, March 26–29.

Dehousse, R. (2008) 'Delegation of Powers in the European Union: The Need for a Multi- principals Model', *West European Politics*, 31(4): 789–805.

Diez, T. (2005) 'Constructing the Self and Changing Others: Reconsidering "Normative Power Europe"', *Millennium*, 33(3): 613–36.

Dijkstra, H. (2008) 'The Council Secretariat's Role in the Common Foreign and Security Policy', *European Foreign Affairs Review*, 13 (2): Conflict Prevention and Crisis Management 149–66.

DiMaggio, P. and Powell, W. (1983) 'The Iron Cage Revisited: Institutional Isomorphism and Collective Rationality in Organizational Fields', *American Sociological Review*, 48: 147–60.

—— (1991) 'Introduction', in DiMaggio, P. and Powell, W. *The New Institutionalism in Organizational Analysis*, Chicago and London: The University of Chicago Press, 1–40.

Dobbins, J. (2008) *After the Taliban: Nation-Building in Afghanistan*, Washington, DC, Potomac Books.

Dobbins, J., McGinn, J.,Crane, K., Jones, S., Lal, R., Rathmell, A., Swanger, R., Timilsina, A. (2003) *America's Role in Nation-Building: From Germany to Iraq*, Santa Monica: Rand Corporation.

—— (2008) *Europe's Role in Nation-Building: From the Balkans to Congo*, Santa Monica: Rand Corporation.

Dorman, A. M. and Treacher, A. (1995) *European Security: An Introduction to Security Issues in Post-Cold War Europe*, Aldershot: Dartmouth Publishing Company Ltd.

Downs, A. (1967) *Inside Bureaucracy*, Boston: Little, Brown and Company.

Doyle, D. (2002) 'EU and OSCE, Natural Born Partners?' *European Security Review* No. 14, September. Brussels: ISIS Europe.

Drieskens, E. (2007) *EU Representation in the UN Security Council: A Principal-Agent Perspective*, EU-CONSENT Wider Europe, Deeper Integration? Constructing Europe Network, www.eu-consent.net/library/phd/Award-winner2_2007.pdf (accessed 21 January 2008).

Duchêne, F. (1972) 'Europe's Role in World Peace', in Mayne, R. (ed.) *Europe Tomorrow: Sixteen Europeans Look Ahead*, London: Fontana, 32–47.

Duke, S. (2000) *The Elusive Quest for European Security. From EDC to CFSP*, Basingstoke, Palgrave Macmillan.

—— (2001) 'CESDP: Nice's Overtrumped Success?', *European Foreign Affairs Review*, 6(2): 155–75.

—— (2002) '*The EU and Crisis Management: Development and Prospects*', European Institute of Public Administration, Brussels.

—— (2005) *The Linchpin COPS. Assessing the Workings and Institutional Relations of the Political and Security Committee*, European Institute of Public Administration, Maastricht, http://www.eipa.nl (accessed 21 January 2008).

Elgström, O. and Smith, M. (eds) (2006) *The European Union's Roles in International Politics: Concepts and Analysis*, Abingdon, Routledge.

Epstein, D. and O'Halloran, S. (1999) *Delegating Powers. A Transaction Cost Politics Approach to Policy Making under Separate Powers*, Cambridge: Cambridge University Press.

EU Election Observation Mission (2009) *EU Election Observation Mission to the Islamic Republic of Afghanistan, Final Report on the Presidential and Provincial Council Elections*. Brussels, 20 August.

EUPOL (2009) *EUPOL-Serving Afghanistan*. Online bi-weekly Newsletter 26–09. 16 December, p. 9.

European Commission (1996) Communication from the Commission to the Council: The European Union and the Issue of Conflicts in Africa: Peace-Building, Conflict Prevention and Beyond, 6 March.

—— (2001a) Communication from the Commission on Conflict Prevention, COM (2001) 211 final, 11 April, http://eur-lex.europa.eu/LexUriServ/LexUriServ.do?uri=COM: 2001:0211:FIN:EN:PDF (accessed 20 August 2010).

—— (2001b) Communication from the Commission to the Council and the European

Parliament. Financing of Civilian Crisis Management Operations, Doc. COM(2001) 647 final, Brussels, 28 November, http://ec.europa.eu/external_relations/peace_security/docs/com01_647_en.pdf (accessed 23 August 2010).

—— (2003a) Wider Europe-Neighbourhood. A New Framework for Relations with our Eastern and Southern Neighbours, COM(2003) 104 final, Brussels, 11 March, http://ec.europa.eu/world/enp/pdf/com03_104_en.pdf (accessed 23 August 2010).

—— (2003b). Rapid Reaction Mechanism End of Program Report Afghanistan. Conflict Prevention and Crisis Management Unit. Brussels, December.

—— (2004a) Communication, European Neighbourhood Policy – Strategy Paper. COM(2004) 373 final, Brussels, 12 May, http://ec.europa.eu/world/enp/pdf/strategy/strategy_paper_en.pdf (accessed 20 August 2010).

—— (2004b) Communication from the Commission to the Council and the European Parliament. On the Instruments for External Assistance under the Future Financial Perspective 2007–13, Doc. COM(2004) 626 final, Brussels, 29 September, http://ec.europa.eu/development/icenter/repository/Thematic_pogrammes_COM2006_en.pdf (accessed 20 August 2010).

—— (2005) Commission Staff Working Paper, Country Report Georgia, Brussels, SEC(2005) 288/3, 2 March, http://ec.europa.eu/world/enp/pdf/country/georgia_country_report_2005_en.pdf (accessed 20 August 2010).

—— (2006) European Neighbourhood and Partnership Instrument, Georgia, National Indicative Programme 2007–10, online, available at: http://ec.europa.eu/world/enp/documents_en.htm (accessed 22 December 2009).

—— (2007) Country Strategy Paper, Islamic Republic of Afghanistan 2007–13. Brussels. http://www.delafg.ec.europa.eu/en/downloadable_documents/report/plans/CSP-07-13-FINAL.pdf (accessed 15 February 2010).

—— (2008a) State of Play: Major Milestones towards Reconstruction and Peace Building in Afghanistan. Brussels, 30 June, online, available at: http://ec.europa.eu/europeaid/where/asia/documents/state_of_play_afghanistan_june_2008_en.pdf (accessed 15 February 2010).

—— (2008b) Communication, Eastern Partnership, COM(2008) 823 final, Brussels, 3 December 2008, http://eeas.europa.eu/eastern/docs/com08_823_en.pdf (accessed 20 August 2010).

—— (2009) ENP Progress Report Georgia (2009), Commission Staff Working Document, SEC(2009) 513/2, http://ec.europa.eu/world/enp/pdf/progress2009/sec09_513_en.pdf (accessed 20 August 2010).

European Council (1999a) European Council Cologne, 3 and 4 June 1999. Presidency Conclusions, Doc. Press Release 150/99, Brussels, 4 June, http://www.consilium.europa.eu/uedocs/cms_data/docs/pressdata/en/ec/57886.pdf (accessed 19 August 2010).

—— (1999b) European Council Helsinki, 10 and 11 December 1999. Presidency Conclusions, Doc. Press Release 00300/1/99, Brussels, 11 December, http://www.consilium.europa.eu/uedocs/cms_data/docs/pressdata/en/ec/ACFA4C.htm (accessed 19 August 2010).

—— (2000a) European Council Lisbon, 23 and 24 March 2000. Presidency Conclusions, Doc. Press Release 100/1/00, Brussels, 24 March, http://www.consilium.europa.eu/uedocs/cms_data/docs/pressdata/en/ec/00100-r1.en0.htm (accessed on 19 August 2010).

—— (2000b) European Council Nice, 7 to 9 December 2000. Presidency Conclusions, Doc. Press Release 400/1/00, Brussels, 8 December, http://www.consilium.europa.eu/uedocs/cms_data/docs/pressdata/en/ec/00400-r1.%20ann.en0.htm [last accessed on 19 August 2010].

—— (2000c) European Council Santa Maria da Feira, 19 and 20 June 2000. Presidency Conclusions, Doc. Press Release 200/1/00, Brussels, 20 June, http://www.consilium. europa.eu/uedocs/cms_data/docs/pressdata/en/ec/00200-r1.en0.htm (accessed 19 August 2010).

—— (2001) EU Program for the Prevention of Violent Conflicts, Gothenburg European Council, 15–16 June, http://ec.europa.eu/governance/impact/background/docs/gote-borg_concl_en.pdf (accessed 19 August 2010).

—— (2002) Copenhagen European Council. Presidency Conclusions. Copenhagen, 12–13 December.

—— (2003) A Secure Europe in a Better World: European Security Strategy. Brussels, 12 December. http://www.consilium.europa.eu/uedocs/cmsUpload/78367.pdf (accessed 19 August 2010).

—— (2007) Council Joint Action 2007/369/CFSP of 30 May 2007 on establishment of the European Union Police Mission in Afghanistan (EUPOL AFGHANISTAN) OJ L 139/33. Brussels, http://eur-lex.europa.eu/LexUriServ/site/en/oj/2007/l_139/l_13920070531en00330038.pdf (accessed 19 August 2010).

—— (2008) Council Conclusions on Georgia/Russia, Luxembourg, 13 October, www.con-silium.europa.eu/ueDocs/cms_Data/docs/pressData/en/gena/103435.pdf (accessed 19 August 2010).

European Parliament and Council of the European Union (2006) Regulation (EC) No 1717/2006 of the European Parliament and of the Council of 15 November 2006 Estab-lishing an Instrument for Stability, Doc. 1717/2006, OJ L 327/1–11, 24.11.2006.

European Union (2003a) 'EU and NATO Concerted Approach for the Western Balkans', (11605/03 (Presse 218)), Brussels, 29 July 2003.

—— (2003b) Draft Council Conclusions on EU-OSCE Cooperation in Conflict Prevention, Crisis Management and Post-Conflict Rehabilitation, (14512/03), Brussels, 10 November 2003.

—— (2008) EU Assistance Fact Sheet: Georgia (2008), MEMO/08/645, Brussels, 22 October 2008.

European Voice (2010) *Lithuanian Appointed EUSR to Afghanistan*. Brussels, 25 February, p. 7.

Evans, P., Rueschemeyer, D. and Skocpol, T. (eds) (1985) *Bringing the State Back In*, Cambridge: Cambridge University Press.

Everts, S. (2002) 'Shaping a Credible EU Foreign Policy?', *CER Pamphlet*, London: Centre for European Reform.

Fanthorpe, R. (2006) 'On the Limits of Liberal Peace. Chiefs and Democratic Decentralization in Post-War Sierra Leone', *African Affairs*, 105(418): 27–49.

Farrell, M. (2005) 'EU External Relations: Exporting the EU Model of Governance?', *European Foreign Affairs Review*, 10(4): 451–62.

Federal Foreign Office (2007) *Funding for Police Assistance in Afghanistan Tripled*. Berlin, 18 November.

Ferguson, J. (1990) *The Anti-Politics Machine: 'Development', Depoliticization, and Bureaucratic Power in Lesotho*, Cambridge: Cambridge University Press.

Finnemore, M. and Sikkink, K. (1998), 'International Norm Dynamics and Political Change', *International Organization*, 52(4): 887–917.

Fursdon, E. (1980) *The European Defence Community: A History*, London, Macmillan Press.

GAERC (2008) Council Conclusions on Georgia, Brussels, 15–16 September 2008.

Galtung, J. (1973) *The European Community: A Superpower in the Making*, London: George Allen & Unwin.

Gates, R. (2009) 'A Balanced Strategy: Reprogramming the Pentagon for a New Age', *Foreign Affairs*, 88(1): 28–40.

Gauttier, P. (2004) 'Horizontal Coherence and the External Competencies of the European Union', *European Law Journal*, 10: 23–41.

Gibert, M.V. (2007) *Monitoring a Region in Crisis: the European Union in West Africa*, Chaillot Paper No. 96, Paris: European Union Institute for Security Studies.

Giegerich, B., Pushkina, D. and Mount, A. (2006) 'Towards a Strategic Partnership? The US and Russian Response to the European Security and Defence Policy', *Security Dialogue* 37(3): 385–407.

Ginsberg, R. H. (2001) *The European Union in International Politics. Baptism by Fire*. Oxford: Rowman & Littlefield Publishers.

Gomez, R. and Peterson, J. (2001) 'The EU's Impossibly Busy Foreign Ministers: 'No One is in Control', *European Foreign Affairs Review*, 6(1): 53–74.

Gordon, P.H. (1997/1998) 'Europe's Uncommon Foreign Policy', *International Security*, 22(3): 74–100.

Gordon, S. (2006) 'Exploring the Civil-Military Interface and Its Impact on European Strategic and Operational Personalities: "Civilianisation" and Limiting Military Roles in Stabilisation Operations?', *European Security*, 15(3): 339–61.

Gorges, M. (2001) 'New Institutionalist Explanations of Institutional Change: A Note of Caution', *Politics*, 21(2): 137–45.

Gourlay, C. (2006) *Community Instruments for Civilian Crisis Management*, Institute for Security Studies (ISS), Paris, http://www.iss.europa.eu/uploads/media/cp090.pdf (accessed 18 August 2010).

Grant, C. (1999) *European Defence Post-Kosovo?* CER Working Paper, London: Centre for European Reform.

Grevi, G. (2007) *Pioneering Foreign Policy. The EU Special Representatives*, Paris: EU Institute for Security Studies, November 2007.

Gross, E. (2006) 'The EU in Afghanistan: What Role for EU Conflict Prevention and Crisis Management Policies?' *CFSP Forum*, 4(4), 11–14.

—— (2008) *EU and the Comprehensive Approach*. DIIS Report 2008:13. Copenhagen, Danish Institute for International Studies.

—— (2009a) 'Security Sector Reform in Afghanistan: the EU's Contribution'. *Occasional Paper* 78. Paris, EU Institute for Security Studies, April.

—— (2009b) *The Europeanization of National Foreign Policy: Continuity and Change in European Crisis Management*, Basingstoke: Palgrave Macmillan.

Guéhenno, J. (2005) 'Foreword', in Ortega, M. (ed.) '*The EU and the UN – Partners in Effective Multilateralism*', Chaillot Paper 78, Paris: EUISS, 7–12.

Haas, E. B. (1990) *When Knowledge is Power: Three Models of Change in International Organisations*, Berkeley, University of California Press.

Haass, R. N. (2006) 'How to Avoid Iraq Syndrome', *Times Magazine*, 10 December.

Hall, P. and Taylor, R. C. (1996) 'Political Science and the Three New Institutionalisms', *Political Studies*, 44(5): 936–57.

Halperin, M.H. (1974) *Bureaucratic Politics and Foreign Policy*, Washington, DC: The Brookings Institutions.

Hawkins, D. G. and Jacoby, W. (2006) 'How Agents Matter', in Hawkins, D. G., Lake, D. A., Nielson, D. L. and Tierney, M. J. (eds) *Delegation and Agency in International Organizations*, Cambridge: Cambridge University Press.

Hawkins, D. G., Lake, D. A., Nielson, D. L. and Tierney, M. J. (2006) 'Delegation Under Anarchy: States, International Organizations, and Principal-Agent Theory', in Hawkins,

D. G., Lake, D. A., Nielson, D. L. and Tierney, M. J. (eds) *Delegation and Agency in International Organizations*, Cambridge: Cambridge University Press.

Hewitt, A. (1989) 'ACP and the Developing World', in Lodge, J. (ed.) *The European Community and the Challenge of the Future*, London: Pinter, 285–300.

Hill, C. (1990) 'European Foreign Policy: Power Bloc, Civilian Model – or Flop?' in Rummel, R. (ed.) *The Evolution of an International Actor. Europe's New Assertiveness*, Boulder, San Francisco, Oxford: Westview Press, 31–55.

—— (1993) 'The Capability-Expectations Gap, or Conceptualising Europe's Foreign Policy', *Journal of Common Market Studies*, 31(3): 305–28.

—— (2001) 'The EU's Capacity for Conflict Prevention', *European Foreign Affairs Review*, 6(3): 315–33.

—— (2002) 'EU Foreign Policy since 11 September 2001: Renationalising or Regrouping?' *EFPU Working Paper 2002/4*, First annual guest lecture in the 'Europe in the World' Centre series, University of Liverpool, 24 October.

—— (2003) *The Changing Politics of Foreign Policy*, Houndmills, Basingstoke/New York: Palgrave Macmillan.

Hodes, C. and Sedra, M. (2007). *The Search for Security in Post-Taliban Afghanistan.* Adelphi Paper 391. London: International Institute for Strategic Studies.

Hoffmann, S. (2000) 'Towards a Common European Foreign and Security Policy', *Journal of Common Market Studies*, 38(2): 189–98.

Hofmann, S. C. (2004) 'Why Am I? That Is the Question. Norm Contestation, Reinforcement and Coexistence and the Creation of CFSP', *Cahiers européens de Sciences Po*, online, available at: http://www.cee.sciences-po.fr/en/publications/les-cahiers-europeens.html (accessed 18 August 2010).

Holsti, K. (1970) 'National role conceptions in the study of foreign policy', *International Studies Quarterly*, 14(3): 233–309.

Howorth, J. (2000a) 'European Integration and Defence: The Ultimate Challenge', *Chaillot Papers* 43, Paris: WEU Institute for Security Studies.

—— (2000b) 'Britain, France and the European Defence Initiative', *Survival*, 42(2): 33–55.

—— (2001) 'European Defence and the Changing Politics of the European Union: Hanging Together or Hanging Separately', *Journal of Common Market Studies*, 39(4): 765–89.

—— (2004) 'Discourse, Ideas and Epistemic Communities in European Security and Defence Policy', *West European Politics*, 27(2): 211–34.

—— (2007a) *Security and Defence Policy in the European Union*, New York: Palgrave Macmillan.

—— (2007b) 'The Political and Security Committee and the Emergence of a European Security Identity', *IntUne Papers,* No.EX-07-02, October 2007, online, available at: www.intune.it/file_download/120/DP (accessed 17 August 2009).

House of Lords Minutes of Evidence (2004) Evidence taken before the Select Committee on the EU Sub-Committee C, The European Union Security Strategy, Tuesday 6 July 2004, Mr Javier Solana, online, available at: http://www.publications.parliament.uk/pa/ld200304/ldselect/ldeucom/180/180.pdf (accessed 18 August 2010).

—— (2006) '"Normative" Power Europe: A Realist Critique', *Journal of European Public Policy*, 13(2): 217–34.

IIFFMCG (2009) *Report of the Independent International Fact-Finding Mission on the Conflict in Georgia*, September 2009, online, available at: http://www.ceiig.ch (accessed 18 November 2009).

International Crisis Group (2001) *EU Crisis Response Capability: Institutions and Processes for Conflict Prevention and Management*, ICG Issues Report N° 2, Brussels.

—— (2006) '*Conflict Resolution in the South Caucasus: The EU's Role*', Europe Report, No. 173, 20 March.

—— (2007) *Reforming Afghanistan's Police*. Asia Report no.138. Kabul/Brussels, 30 August.

—— (2008) *Afghanistan: The Need for International Resolve*. Asia Report no. 145. Kabul/Brussels, 6 February.

International Herald Tribune (2008) *Europe Lagging in Effort to Train Afghan Police*. New York, 28 May.

Ioannides, I. (2006) 'EU Police Mission Proxima: Testing the "European" Approach to Building Peace', in Nowak, A. (ed.) *Civilian Crisis Management: the European Way*, Chaillot Paper, No. 90, Institute for Security Studies (EU-ISS), Paris, online, available at http://www.iss.europa.eu/uploads/media/cp090.pdf (accessed 18 August 2010).

ISAF (2009) *Commander's Initial Assessment*. NATO International Security Assistance Force, Afghanistan, 30 August.

Jackson, P. (2007) 'Reshuffling an Old Deck of Cards? The Politics of Local Government Reform in Sierra Leone', *African Affairs*, 106(422): 95–111.

Jackson, R. H. (1993) *Quasi-States: Sovereignty, International Relations, and the Third World*, Cambridge: Cambridge University Press.

Jäger, T. and Oppermann, K. (2006) 'Bürokratie-und organisationstheoretische Analysen der Sicherheitspolitik: Vom 11. September bis zum Irakkrieg', in Siedschlag, A. (ed.) *Methoden der sicherheitspolitischen Analyse. Eine Einführung*. Wiesbaden: Verlag für Sozialwissenschaften.

Johnston, A. I. (2001) 'Treating International Institutions as Social Environments', *International Studies Quarterly*, 45(4): 487–515.

Jorgensen, K. E. (2002) 'Making the CFSP Work', in Peterson, J. and Shackleton, M. (eds) *The Institutions of the European Union*, Oxford: Oxford University Press, 210–32.

Juncos, A.E. and Pomorska, K. (2006) 'Playing the Brussels Game: Strategic Socialisation in the CFSP Council Working Groups', *European Integration Online Papers*, Vol. 10(11).

Juncos, A. E. and Reynolds, C. (2007) 'The Political and Security Committee: Governing in the Shadow', *European Foreign Affairs Review*, 12(2): 127–47.

Kagan, R. (2004) *Of Paradise and Power. America and Europe in the New World Order*, London: Vintage Books.

Kalyvas, S. (2001) '"New" and "Old" Civil Wars: A Valid Distinction?', *World Politics*, 54(1): 99–118.

Kassim, H. and Menon, A. (2003) 'The Principal-Agent Approach and the Study of the European Union: Promise Unfulfilled?', *Journal of European Public Policy*, 10(1): 121–39.

Kaufman, B. (1982) *Trade and Aid: Eisenhower's Foreign Economic Policy 1953–61*, Baltimore, MD: Johns Hopkins University Press.

Keohane, D. (2009) 'ESDP and NATO', in Grevi, G., Helly, D. and Keohane, D. (eds) *European Security and Defence Policy. The First Ten Years (1999–2009)*, Paris: EU Institute for Security Studies.

Keohane, R., Nye, J. and Hoffmann, S. (eds) (1993) *After the Cold War: International Institutions and State Strategies in Europe, 1989–1991*, Cambridge, Mass.; London: Harvard University Press.

Keukeleire, S. (2003) 'The European Union as a Diplomatic Actor: Internal, Traditional, and Structural Diplomacy', *Diplomacy and Statecraft*, 14(3): 31–56.

—— (2004) 'EU Structural Foreign Policy and Structural Conflict Prevention', in Kronenberger, V. and Wouters, J. (eds) *The European Union and Conflict Prevention: Policy and Legal Aspects*, The Hague: T.M.C. Asser Press, 151–72.

Keukeleire, S. and MacNaughtan, J. (2008) *The Foreign Policy of the European Union*, Houndmills/New York: Palgrave Macmillan.

Khol, R. (2006) *Civil-Military Co-ordination in EU Crisis Management*, Institute for Security Studies (ISS), Paris, http://www.iss.europa.eu/uploads/media/cp090.pdf (accessed 18 August 2010).

Klaiber, K. (2002). *The European Union in Afghanistan: Impressions of My Term as Special Representative*. National Europe Centre Paper No. 44. Canberra, Australian National University. http://dspace.anu.edu.au/bitstream/1885/41711/3/klaiber.pdf (accessed 19 August 2010).

Klein, N. (2010) *European Agents Out of Control? Delegation and Agency in the Civil-Military Crisis Management of the European Union 1999–2008*, Baden-Baden: Nomos.

Knigge, M. (2009) '*Praise for the EU Mission in Georgia, But Questions Over US Role Remain*', Deutsche Welle, 6 August 2008, online, available at: http://dw-world.de (accessed 18 November 2009).

Korski, D. (2008) '*Learning from the EU's Georgia Success*', European Council for Foreign Relations, 10 October.

Kratochwil, F. V. (2006) 'The Genealogy of Multilateralism: Reflections on an Organizational Form and Its Crisis', in Newman, E., Thakur, R. and Tirman, J. (eds) *Multilateralism under Challenge? Power, International Order, and Structural Change*, Tokio, New York and London: United Nations University Press, 139–59.

Kronenberger, V. and Wouters, J. (eds) (2004) *The European Union and Conflict Prevention: Policy and Legal Aspects*, The Hague: TMC Asser Press.

Kurowska, X. (2008) 'The Role of Missions in the ESDP', in Merlingen, M. and Ostrauskaite, R. (eds) *The European Security and Defence Policy: Implementation and Impact*, London and New York: Routledge, 25–42.

—— (2009) '"Solana Milieu" – Framing Security Policy', *Perspectives on European Politics and Society*, 10(4): 523 – 540.

Kurowska, X. and Tallis, B. (2009) 'EU Border Assistance Mission to Moldova and Ukraine – Beyond Border Monitoring?', *European Foreign Affairs Review*, 14(1): 47–64.

Laatikainen, K. and Smith, K. (eds) (2006) *The European Union at the United Nations: Intersecting Multilateralisms*, Basingstoke: Palgrave.

Laffan, B. (1997) 'From Policy Entrepreneur to Policy Manager: the Challenge Facing the European Commission', *Journal of European Public Policy*, 4(3): 422–38.

Larsen, H. (2002) 'The EU: a Global Military Actor?', *Cooperation and Conflict*, 37(3): 283–302.

—— (2009) 'A Distinct FPA for Europe? Towards a Comprehensive Framework for Analysing the Foreign Policy of EU Member States', *European Journal of International Relations*, 15(3): 537–66.

Leakey, D. (2006) 'ESDP and Civil/Military Cooperation: Bosnia and Herzegovina, 2005', in Deighton, A. (ed.) with Mauer, V., *Securing Europe? Implementing the European Security Strategy*, Zürcher Beiträge zur Sicherheitspolitik, 77, 59–68.

Leboeuf, A. (2005) 'La réforme britannique du secteur de la sécurité en Sierra Leone: vers un nouveau paradigme?', *Politique africaine*, 98: 63–78.

Le Prestre, P. (1997) (ed.) *Role Quests in the Post-Cold War: Foreign Policies in Transition*, Montréal: McGill-Queens University Press.

Lewis, J. (2005) 'The Janus Face of Brussels: Socialisation and Everyday Decision Making in the European Union', *International Organization*, 59(4): 937–71.

—— (2006) 'Where Informal Rules Rule: The Council General Secretariat and Presidency in Everyday EU Decision Making', paper presented at the *2006 International Studies Association Conference*, San Diego, 22–25 March.

Lindley-French, J. (2002) 'In the Shade of Locarno? Why European Defence is Failing', *International Affairs*, 78(4), 789–811.

—— (2003) 'The Ties that Bind', *NATO Review* No. 3 (Autumn).

Link, W. (2001) Die Entwicklungstendenzen der Europäischen Integration (EG/EU) und die neorealistische Theorie, *Zeitschrift für Politik*, 48302–21.

Lomé IV Agreement (1989) Fourth ACP-EEC Convention, signed in Lomé on 15 December 1989, online, available at: http://ec.europa.eu/development/policies/legislation/general-leg_int2_en.cfm (accessed 18 August 2010).

Lomé IVbis Agreement (1995) Agreement Amending the Fourth ACP-EC Convention of Lomé, signed in Mauritius on 4 November 1995, online, available at: http://www.acpsec.org/en/conventions/lome4_e.htm (accessed 18 August 2010).

Lord, C. (2005) 'Accountable and Legitimate? The EU's International Role', in Hill, C. and Smith, M. (eds) *International Relations and the European Union*, Oxford and New York: Oxford University Press, 113–33.

Lowndes, V. (2002), 'Institutionalism', in Marsh, D. and Stoker, G. (eds) *Theory and Methods in Political Science*, London: Palgrave Macmillan, 2nd ed, 90–108.

Lupia, A. and McCubbins, M. D. (1994) 'Learning From Oversight: Fire Alarms and Police Patrols Reconstructed', *The Journal of Law, Economics and Organization*, 10(1): 96–125.

Lynch, D. (2006) 'Why Georgia Matters', *Chaillot Paper*, No 86, Institute for Security Studies, Paris.

—— (2009) 'ESDP and the OSCE', in Grevi, G., Helly, D. and Keohane, D. (eds) *European Security and Defence Policy. The First Ten Years (1999–2009)*, Paris: EU Institute for Security Studies.

Lyne, M. M., Nielson, D. L. and Tierney, M. J. (2006) 'Who Delegates? Alternative Models of Principals in Development Aid', in Hawkins, D. G., Lake, D. A., Nielson, D. L. and Tierney, M. J. (eds) *Delegation and Agency in International Organizations*, Cambridge: Cambridge University Press.

Manners, I. (2002) 'Normative Power Europe: A Contradiction in Terms?' *Journal of Common Market Studies*, 40(2): 235–58.

Manners, I. and Whitman, R. (2000) 'Introduction', in ibid. (eds) *The Foreign Policies of European Union Member States*, Manchester: Manchester University Press, 1–18.

March, J. G. (1991) 'Exploration and Exploitation in Organizational Learning', *Organization Science*, 2(1): 71–87.

March, J. G. and Olsen, J. P. (1984) 'The New Institutionalism: Organizational Factors in Political Life', *American Political Science Review*, 78(3), 734–49.

—— (1989) *Rediscovering Institutions: The Organizational Basis of Politics*, New York: Free Press.

—— (1996) 'Institutional Perspectives on Political Institutions', *Governance*, 9(3): 247–64.

—— (1998) 'The Institutional Dynamics of International Political Orders', *International Organization*, 52(4): 943–69.

Mawdsley, J. and Quille, G. (2004) '*The EU Security Strategy: A New Framework for ESDP and Equipping the EU Rapid Reaction Force*', International Security Information Service (ISIS) Europe/ Bonn International Centre for Conversion (BICC) Brussels.

McCubbins, M.D. and Schwartz, T. (1984) 'Congressional Oversight Overlooked: Police Patrols versus Fire Alarms', *American Journal of Political Science*, 28(1): 165–79.

Menon, A. (2009) 'Empowering Paradise? The ESDP at Ten', *International Affairs*, 85(2): 227–46.

Mérand, F. (2006) 'Social Representations in the European Security and Defence Policy', *Cooperation and Conflict*, 41(2): 131–52.

Merlingen, M. and Ostrauskaite, R. (2006) *European Union Peacebuilding and Policing. Governance and the ESDP*, London and New York: Routledge.

—— (2008) *European Security and Defence Policy: An Implementation Perspective*, London: Routledge.

Meyer, C.O. (2006) *The Quest for a European Strategic Culture: Changing Norms on Security and Defence in the European Union*, London: Palgrave Macmillan.

Migdal, J. S. (1988) *Strong Societies and Weak States: State-Society Relations and State Capabilities in the Third World*, Princeton and Chichester: Princeton University Press.

Mikhelidze, N. (2009) '*After the 2008 Russia-Georgia War: Implications for the Wider Caucasus and Prospects for Western Involvement in Conflict Resolution*', background paper for the conference on 'The Caucasus and Black Sea region: European Neighbourhood Policy (ENP) and beyond', Rome, 6–7 February.

Missiroli, A. (ed.) (2001) 'Coherence for Security Policy: Debates – Cases – Assessments', *Occasional Paper* No 27, Paris: WEU-ISS.

—— (2004) 'ESDP – How it works', in Gnesotto, N. (ed.) *EU Security and Defence Policy. The First Five Years (1999–2004)*, Paris: EU Institute for Security Studies, 55–73.

—— (2010) Implementing the Lisbon Treaty: The External Policy Dimension. *Bruges Political Research Papers* No. 14. Bruges, College of Europe, May.

Mitchell, T. (2002) *Rule of Experts: Egypt, Techno-Politics, Modernity*, Berkeley: University of California Press.

Modified Brussels Treaty (1954), online, available at: http://www.weu.int/index.html (accessed 20 August 2009).

Moravcsik, A. (1993) 'Preferences and Power in the European Community: A Liberal Intergovernmentalist Approach', *Journal of Common Market Studies*, 31(4): 473–524.

Müller-Brandeck-Bocquet, G. (2002) 'The New CFSP and ESDP Decision-Making System of the European Union', *European Foreign Affairs Review*, 7(3): 257–82.

Munuera, G. (1994) 'Preventing Violent Conflict in Europe: Lessons from Recent Experience', *Chaillot Paper* No. 15/16. Paris: WEU Institute for Security Studies.

NATO (2000) *NATO Civil–Military Cooperation (CIMIC) Doctrine*, Provisional Final Draft, doc. AJP-9 2000, online, available at: http://www.nato.int/ims/docu/ajp-9.pdf (accessed 18 August 2010).

—— (2001) *NATO Handbook*, online, available at: http:// www.nato.int (accessed 17 August 2009).

—— (2002) *EU-NATO Declaration on ESDP*, (Press Release 142), Brussels, 16 December.

New York Times (2007) 'Pentagon Spending $2.5 Billion to Revamp Afghan Police'. New York, 18 October.

Nicolaïdis, K. and Howse, R. (2002) '"This is my EUtopia . . .": Narrative as power', *Journal of Common Market Studies*, 44(4): 767–92.

North, D. (1990) *Institutions, Institutional Change, and Economic Performance*, New York: Cambridge University Press.

Novosseloff, A. (2004) *EU-UN Partnership in Crisis Management: Development and Prospects*, New York: International Peace Academy.

Nowak, A. (2006) 'Introduction', in Nowak, A. (ed.) *Civilian Crisis Management: the European Way*, Chaillot Paper, No. 90, Institute for Security Studies (EU-ISS), Paris, online, available at: http://www.iss.europa.eu/uploads/media/cp090.pdf (accessed 18 August 2010).

Nuttall, S. (1992) *European Political Cooperation*, Oxford: Clarendon Press.

—— (2001) 'Consistency and the CFSP: A Categorization and its Consequences', *EFPU Working Paper*, London School of Economics.

Nye, J.S. (2009) *Understanding International Conflicts. An Introduction to Theory and History*, 7th ed, New York: Pearson Longman.

Oakes, M. (2000) *European Defence From Pörtschach to Helsinki*, International Affairs and Defence Section House of Commons Library, Research Paper 00/20 (February).

—— (2001) *European Security and Defence Policy: Nice and Beyond*, International Affairs and Defence Section House of Commons Library, Research Paper 01/50.

Obama, B. (2009) Obama's Speech to the United Nations General Assembly, 23 September 2009, online, available at: http://www.un.org/ga/64/generaldebate/US.shtml (accessed 18 August 2010).

Olsen, G.R. (2005) 'The European Union: "European Interests", Bureaucratic Interests and International Options', in Engel, U. and Olsen, G.R. (eds) *Africa and the North: Between Globalization and Marginalization*, Oxon and New York: Routledge, 124–41.

OSCE (2003) *Annual Report*, online, available at: http://www.osce.org (accessed 17 August 2009).

Orsini, D. (2006) 'Future of ESDP: Lessons from Bosnia', *European Security Review*, 29 June: 9–12.

Pace, M. (2008) 'The EU as a Force for Good in Border Conflict Cases?', in Diez, T., Albert, M. and Stetter, M. (eds) *The EU and Border Conflicts. The Power of Integration and Conflicts*, Cambridge: Cambridge University Press, 203–19.

Packenham, R. (1973) *Liberal America and the Third World*, Princeton, NJ: Princeton University Press.

Packett II, V. L. et al. (2005) 'Bosnia and Herzegovina: Coalition Doctrine and LOT Houses', *Military Review*, March–April 2005.

Page, S. (2001) 'Regionalism and/or Globalisation', in *Regionalism and Regional Integration in Africa: A Debate of Current Aspects and Issues*, Nordiska Afrikainstitutet, Discussion Paper 11, Uppsala, 5–26.

Paris, R. (2003) 'Peacekeeping and the Constraints of Global Culture', *European Journal of International Relations*, 9(3): 441–73.

Patten, C. (2000) 'Projecting Stability', *The World Today*, 56(7), July, 17–19.

Penksa, S. E. (2006) *Policing Bosnia and Herzegovina 2003–05. Issues of Mandates and Management in ESDP Missions*, Centre for European Policy Studies (CEPS), Brussels.

Peral, L. (2009) 'EUPOL Afghanistan: The EU Police Mission in Afghanistan', in Grevi, G., Helly, D. and Keohane, D. (eds), *European Security and Defence Policy: The First Ten Years (1999–2009)*, Paris, EU Institute for Security Studies, 325–37.

Peters, B. G. (1992) 'Bureaucratic Politics and the Institutions of the European Community', in Sbragia, A. M. (ed.) *Europolitics. Institutions and Policymaking in the 'New' European Community*, Washington, DC: The Brookings Institution.

—— (1999) *Institutional Theory in Political Science. The 'New Institutionalism'*, London; New York: Pinter.

—— (2005) *Institutional Theory in Political Science. The 'New Institutionalism'*, London; New York: Continuum, 2nd ed.

Petersberg Declaration (1992) *On Relations between WEU and the other European Member States of the European Union or the Atlantic Alliance*, Western European Union Council of Ministers, Bonn, online, available at: http://www.weu.int/documents/920619peten. pdf (accessed 25 August 2009).

Peterson, J. and Shackleton, M. (2002) *The Institutions of the European Union*, Oxford: Oxford University Press.

Piening, C. (1997) *Global Europe: The European Union in World Affairs*, Boulder: Lynne Rienner.

Pierson, P. (1996) 'The Path to European Integration. A Historical Institutionalist Analysis', *Comparative Political Studies*, 29(2): 123–63.

—— (2004) *Politics in Time. History Institutions and Social Analysis*, Princeton: Princeton University Press.

Pollack, M. A. (1996) 'The New Institutionalism and EC Governance: The Promise and Limits of Institutional Analysis', *Governance: An International Journal of Policy and Administration*, 9(4): 429–58.

—— (1997) 'Delegation, Agency and Agenda Setting in the European Community', *International Organization*, 51: 99–135.

—— (2003) *The Engines of European Integration. Delegation, Agency, and Agenda Setting in the EU*, Oxford: Oxford University Press.

—— (2004) 'The New Institutionalisms and European Integration', in Wiener, A. and Diez, T. (eds) *European Integration Theory*, Oxford: Oxford University Press, 137–56.

Pond, E. (1999) 'Kosovo: Catalyst for Europe', *The Washington Quarterly*, 22(4): 77–92.

Popescu, N. (2009) 'The EU's Conflict Prevention Failure in Georgia', *Central Asia-Caucasus Analyst*, online, available at: http://www.cacianalyst.org (accessed 18 November 2009).

Portela, C. and Raube, K. (2009) '*(In-)Coherence in EU Foreign Policy: Exploring Sources and Remedies*', paper presented at the European Studies Association Bi-annual Convention, Los Angeles, April 2009.

Presidency of the EU (2008) *Presidency Conclusions*, Extraordinary European Council, 12594/08, 1 September.

Pressman, J. L. and Wildavsky, A. (1973) *Implementation: How Great Expectations in Washington Are Dashed in Oakland or Why It's Amazing that Federal Programs Work At All*, Berkeley: University of California Press.

Quille, G. (2003) 'What Does the EU Agreement on Operational Planning Mean for NATO?', *NATO Notes*, 5(8), December. Brussels: ISIS Europe.

Radaelli, C. (1997) 'Policy Transfer in the European Union: Institutional Isomorphism as a Source of Legitimacy', *Jean Monnet Working Papers in Comparative and International Politics*, 10.97.

Ramsbotham, O., Woodhouse, T. and Miall, H. (2005) *Contemporary Conflict Resolution*, Cambridge: Polity Press, 2nd ed.

Regelsberger, E. (2004) *Die Gemeinsame Außen-und Sicherheitspolitik der EU (GASP). Konstitutionelle Angebote im Praxistest 1993–2003*, Baden-Baden: Nomos.

Reno, W. (1998) *Warlord Politics and African States*, Boulder and London: Lynne Rienner.

Rettman, A. (2009) 'France Stymies Call to Expand EU Mission in Georgia', EU Observer, 28 July, online, available at: http://euobserver.com (accessed 18 November 2009).

Reynolds, C. (2005) 'Understanding the Development of the ESDP: Perspectives and

Insights from Historical Institutionalism and Theories of Learning', *European Foreign Policy Observatory Working Papers*, Barcelona, June 2005.

—— (2007) 'Governing Security in the European Union: Institutions as Dynamics and Obstacles', in de Bievre, D. and Neuhold, C. (eds) *Dynamics and Obstacles of European Governance*, Chelthenham: Edward Elgar, 51–76.

Rice, C. (2006) *Transformational Diplomacy*, online, available at: http://www.state.gov/r/pa/prs/ps/2006/59339.htm (accessed 1 September 2006).

—— (2008) 'Welcome to My World, Barack', *New York Times Magazine*, 13 November.

Richards, P. (2005) 'To Fight or To Farm? Agrarian Dimensions of the Mano River Conflicts (Liberia and Sierra Leone)', *African Affairs*, 104(417): 571–90.

Robert, A.-C. (2002) 'L'étrange politique étrangère de l'Union Européenne', *Le Monde Diplomatique*, December, 24–25.

Rostow, W. (1985) *Eisenhower, Kennedy and Foreign Aid*, Austin, TX: University of Texas Press.

Rummel, R. (1996) '*The European Union's Politico-Diplomatic Contribution to the Prevention of Ethno-National Conflict*', in Chayes, A. and Chayes, A., *Preventing Conflict in the Post-Communist World*, Washington DC: The Brookings Institution, 197–236.

Rummel, R. and Wiedemann, J. (1998) 'Identifying Institutional Paradoxes of CFSP', in Zielonka, J. (ed.) *Paradoxes of European Foreign Policy*, The Hague: Kluwer Law International.

Rutten, M. (ed.) (2001) 'From St. Malo to Nice. European Defence: Core Documents', *Chaillot Papers*, 47, Paris: WEU Institute for Security Studies.

Sawyer, E. (2008) 'Remove or Reform? A Case for (Restructuring) Chiefdom Governance in Governance in Post-Conflict Sierra Leone', *African Affairs*, 107(428): 387–403.

Schimmelfennig, F. (2004) 'Liberal Intergovernmentalism', in Wiener, A. and Diez, T. (eds) *European Integration Theory*, Oxford: Oxford University Press.

Schmidt, V. A., Tsebelis, G., Risse, T. and Scharph, F.W. (1999) 'Approaches to the Study of the European Union', *ECSA Review Forum*, (Spring).

Schoenbaum, T. (1988) *Waging Peace and War: Dean Rusk in the Truman, Kennedy and Johnson Years*, New York and London: Simon and Schuster.

Schroeder, U. (2007) 'Governance of EU Crisis Management', in Emerson, M. and Gross, E. (eds) *Evaluating the EU's Crisis Missions in the Balkans*, Brussels, Center for European Policy Studies, 17–45.

Seitz, T. and Anderson, S. (2008) 'A Tale of Two Cities On The Hill: Nation-Building, Exceptionalism and Universalism in US and EU Foreign Policies', Paper presented at the *49th Annual Meeting of the International Studies Association*, San Francisco, 26–30th March 2008.

Semneby, P. (2006) Interview with Hrair Tamrazian and Kenan Aliyev for Radio Free Europe/Radio Liberty, 9 June 2006, online, available at: http://www.rferl.org/content/article/1069032.html (accessed on 15 December 2009).

Single European Act (SEA) (1986) *Official Journal of the European Communities*, No L 169/1.

Sjostedt, G. (1977) *The External Role of the European Community*, Hampshire: Saxon House.

Sjursen, H. (2004) 'Security and Defence', in Carlsnaes, W., Sjursen, H. and White, B. (eds) *Contemporary European Foreign Policy*, London/Thousand Oaks/New Delhi: SAGE.

Skocpol, T. (1979) *States and Social Revolution*, New York: Cambridge University Press.

Smith, K. (2000) 'The End of Civilian Power EU: A Welcome Demise or a Cause for Concern?', *The International Spectator*, 35(2): 11–28.

—— (2003) *European Union Foreign Policy in a Changing World*, Cambridge: Polity Press.

Smith, M. (1996) 'The European Union and a Changing Europe: Establishing the Boundaries of Order', *Journal of Common Market Studies*, 34(1): 5–28.

—— (2006) 'The Commission and External Relations', in Spence, D. (ed.) *The European Commission*, 3rd ed, London: John Harper.

Smith, M. E. (2004a) 'Toward a Theory of EU Foreign Policy-Making: Multi-Level Governance, Domestic Politics, and National Adaptation to Europe's Common Foreign and Security Policy', *Journal of European Public Policy*, 11(4): 740–58.

—— (2004b) *Europe's Foreign and Security Policy: the Institutionalization of Cooperation*, Cambridge: Cambridge University Press.

Solana, J. (2003) 'Europe and America: Partners of Choice', speech to the *Annual Dinner of Foreign Policy Association*, New York, 7 May.

—— (2008) 'Address at the European Union Monitoring Mission (EUMM) Headquarters in Georgia', Tbilisi, 30 September.

Spence, D. (2006) 'The Commission and the Common Foreign and Security Policy', in Spence, D. and Edwards, G. (eds) *The European Commission*, London: John Harper Publishing.

Stewart, E. J. (2003) 'Conflict Prevention: Consensus or Confusion?', *Peace, Conflict and Development*, 3(3), June, online available at: http://www.peacestudiesjournal.org.uk/dl/ConflictPrevention.PDF (accessed on 26 August 2010).

—— (2006) *The European Union and Conflict Prevention. Policy Evolution and Outcome*, Münster: Lit Verlag.

—— (2008a) 'Capabilities and Coherence? The Evolution of European Union Conflict Prevention Policy', *European Foreign Affairs Review*, 13(2): 229–53.

—— (2008b) 'Restoring EU-OSCE Cooperation for Pan-European Conflict Prevention', *Contemporary Security Policy*, 29(2): 1–19.

Streinz, R. (2003) *Europarecht*, Heidelberg: C. F. Müller.

Strömvik, M. (2005) *To Act as a Union. Explaining the Development of the EU's Collective Foreign Policy*, Lund: Lund University, Department of Political Science.

Tardy, T. (2005) 'EU-UN Cooperation in Peacekeeping: A Promising Relationship in a Constrained Environment', in Ortega, M. (ed.) *The EU and the UN: Partners in Effective Multilateralism*, Chaillot Paper no. 78, June 2005, Paris: EU Institute for Security Studies, 48–68.

Telò, M. (1998) 'Le développement de l'Union Politique Européenne', in Durand, M -F. and de Vasconcelo, A. (eds) *La PESC: Ouvrir l'Europe au Monde*, Paris: Presses de Sciences Po, 93–134.

The Guardian (2008) '*Georgia: Divided EU Prepares to Review Stand on Russia at Emergency Summit*', 1 September.

Thelen, K. and Steinmo, S. (1992) 'Historical Institutionalism in Comparative Politics', in Thelen, K., Steinmo, S. and Longstreth, F. (eds) *Structuring Politics. Historical Institutionalism in Comparative Analysis*, Cambridge: Cambridge University Press, 1–33.

Thier, A. (2004). Reestablishing the Judicial System in Afghanistan, *CDDRL Working Papers*, no. 19, Stanford University, 1 September.

Tocci, N. (2007) *The EU and Conflict Resolution: Promoting Peace in the Backyard*, London: Routledge.

Toje, A. (2008) 'The EU, NATO and European Defence – A Slow Train Coming', *EU Occasional Paper*, No. 74, Paris: EU Institute for Security Studies.

Tonra, B. (2003) 'Constructing the Common Foreign and Security Policy: The Utility of a Cognitive Approach', *Journal of Common Market Studies*, 41(4): 731–56.

Tonra, B. and Christiansen, T. (eds) (2004) *Rethinking European Union Foreign Policy*, Manchester: Manchester University Press.

Treacher, A. (2004) 'From Civilian Power to Military Actor: The EU's Resistible Transformation', *European Foreign Affairs Review*, 9(1): 49–66.

Treaty of Amsterdam (1997) Luxembourg: Office for Official Publications of the European Communities.

Treaty on the European Union (TEU) (1992) Luxembourg: Office for Official Publications of the European Communities.

Tsebelis, G. (1994) 'The Power of the European Parliament as a Conditional Agenda Setter', *American Political Science Review*, 88(1): 128–42.

US Department of State (1950) 'NSC 68: United States Objectives and Programs for National Security', 14 April 1950. Foreign Relations of the United States, Vol. 1, 234–92.

Valasek, T. (2008) 'What Does the War in Georgia Mean for EU Foreign Policy?', *Briefing Note*, Centre for European Reform, London, August 2008.

Vanhoonacker, S. (2008) 'The European Security and Defence Policy and Coherence Challenges in the Council', in Blockmans, S. (ed.) *EU Crisis Management*, The Hague: Asser Press, 145–56.

Vanhoonacker, S. and Dijkstra, H. (2007) 'Beyond Note-Taking: CFSP Challenges for the Council Secretariat', *CFSP Forum*, 5(6): 1–5.

Van Tongeren, P., Van de Veen, H. and Verhoeven, J. (2002) *Searching for Peace in Europe and Eurasia. An Overview of Conflict Prevention and Peacebuilding Activities*, Boulder, CO and London: Lynne Rienner Publishers.

Vogel, T. (2009) 'The EU's Heavy Burden in Georgia', *European Voice*, 30 July.

Wagner, W. (2003) 'Why the EU's Common Foreign and Security Policy Will Remain Intergovernmental: A Rationalist Institutional Choice Analysis of European Crisis Management Policy', *Journal of European Public Policy*, 10(4): 576–95.

Wallace, H. (2005) 'An Institutional Anatomy and Five Policy Modes', in Wallace, H., Wallace, W. and Pollack, M. A. (eds) *Policy-Making in the European Union.* Oxford: Oxford University Press.

Waltz, K. (1979) *Theory of International Politics*, Reading: Addison Wesley.

Ward, A. (ed.) (2004) 'NATO's Istanbul Summit', *IISS Strategic Comments* 10(5): 1–2. London: International Institute for Strategic Studies.

Webber, M., Croft, S., Howorth, J., Terriff, T. and Krahmann, E. (2004) 'The Governance of European Security', *Review of International Studies*, 30(1): 3–26.

Wendt, A. (1999) *Social Theory of International Politics*, Cambridge: Cambridge University Press.

WEU (2000) *WEU Today*, WEU Secretariat-General, Brussels, January 2000.

—— (2004) European security policy fifty years after the signing of the modified Brussels Treaty – reply to the annual report of the Council, Assembly of the Western European Union (Fiftieth Session), (A/1878), Paris, 29 November 2004.

White House Office (1955), Report of the NSC 1290-d Working Group, 16 February 1955, OCB Central File, box 16, OCB (1)(2), Eisenhower Library.

Whitman, R. (1998) *From Civilian Power to Superpower? The International Identity of the European Union*, London: Macmillan.

—— (1999) 'Amsterdam's Unfinished Business: The Blair Government's Initiative and the Future of the Western European Union', *Occasional Paper* 7, Paris: WEU Institute for Security Studies.

Whitman, R. and Juncos, A. E. (2009) 'The Lisbon Treaty and the Foreign, Security and Defence Policy: Reforms, Implementation and the Consequences of (non) Ratification', *European Foreign Affairs Review*, 14(1), 25–46.

Williams, A. (2007) 'The Bringing of Peace and Plenty of Occult Imperialism', *Global Society*, 21(4): 539–51.

Woodward, S. L. (2005) 'Construire l'Etat: légitimité internationale contre légitimité nationale?', *Critique internationale*, 28: 139.

Youngs, R. (2004) 'Normative Dynamics and Strategic Interests in the EU's External Identity', *Journal of Common Market Studies*, 42(2): 415–35.

—— (2006) 'The EU and Conflict in West Africa', *European Foreign Affairs Review*, 11: 333–52.

—— (2007) 'Fusing Security and Development: Just Another Euro-platitude?', *CEPS Working Document*, Brussels: Centre for European Policy Studies.

Zartman, I. W. (1995) *Collapsed States: The Disintegration and Restoration of Legitimate Authority*, Boulder and London: Lynne Rienner.

Index